THE TRIAL OF FAITH OF
SAINT THÉRÈSE OF LISIEUX

For His Holiness,
Pope John Paul II,
who on October 19, 1997
declared Saint Thérèse of Lisieux
a Doctor of the Church

The Trial of Faith of
Saint Thérèse of Lisieux

Frederick L. Miller

ALBA·HOUSE   NEW·YORK

SOCIETY OF ST. PAUL, 2187 VICTORY BLVD., STATEN ISLAND, NEW YORK 10314

ST PAULS

Library of Congress Cataloging-in-Publication Data

Miller, Frederick L.
    The trial of faith of St. Thérèse of Lisieux / Frederick L. Miller.
      p.   cm.
    Includes bibliographical references.
    ISBN 0-8189-0799-1
    1. Thérèse, de Lisieux, Saint, 1873-1897. 2. Christian saints —
    France — Biography.   I. Title.
    BX4700.T5M55   1998
    282'.092 — dc21   97-23190
    [B]   CIP

Produced and designed in the United States of America by the
Fathers and Brothers of the Society of St. Paul,
2187 Victory Boulevard, Staten Island, New York 10314,
as part of their communications apostolate.

ISBN: 0-8189-0799-1

Printing Information:

Current Printing - first digit   1   2   3   4   5   6   7   8   9   10

Year of Current Printing - first year shown

1998   1999   2000   2001   2002   2003   2004   2005

TABLE OF CONTENTS

INTRODUCTION

On September 30, 1897, Marie-Françoise-Thérèse Martin died of tuberculosis at the age of twenty-four as a professed member of the Discalced Carmelite Monastery of Lisieux in France. Since Sister Thérèse of the Child Jesus and of the Holy Face had spent more than a third of her life in the Carmel, no one would have expected her death to elicit any notice. Only a handful of relatives, friends and some local clergymen accompanied her body to the Carmelite plot of the municipal cemetery.[1]

Sister Thérèse's religious life had been lived in such unassuming simplicity that few of her sisters in religion thought her extraordinary in any sense. One of the nuns who had lived with her for seven years testified: "There was nothing to say about her. She was very kind and very retiring. There was nothing conspicuous about her. I would never have suspected her sanctity."[2]

Her companions in Carmel testified that Thérèse had been a faithful religious and had suffered her long illness patiently and with resignation. There was little else to be said, or so it seemed on October 4, 1897, the morning of her funeral.

Within a few years of her death, largely as a result of her writings, the attention of the Church was drawn to the young Carmelite of Lisieux. Under the hand of Divine Providence, her three blood sisters, also nuns of the Lisieux Carmel, had encouraged Thérèse to write accounts of her spiritual journey. These re-

---

[1] Guy Gaucher, OCD, *The Story of a Life*, trans. Sr. Anne Marie Brennan, OCD (San Francisco: Harper and Row Publishers, 1987), p. 206.

[2] *Carmelite Studies: Experiencing Saint Thérèse Today*, ed. John Sullivan, OCD (Washington, DC: ICS Publications, 1990), pp.117-118. (Henceforth cited as *Carmelite Studies*.)

flections, biographical in content, are collected in one book which is entitled *Story of a Soul*.

During the last months of her life, Thérèse came to realize that God had ordained a posthumous mission for her. She perceived that through the publication of the *Story of a Soul*, many people would come to know, love, and serve God. She entrusted the work of editing and revising the manuscripts for publication to her sister Pauline, known in religion as Mother Agnes of Jesus.

On August 1, 1897, less than two months before her death, Thérèse expressed her conviction that the manuscripts be published as expeditiously as possible. She sensed that the world, at the brink of the twentieth century, needed to hear the story of her experience of God's mercy. She also felt that Satan would seek to destroy or at least impede her work. She told Mother Agnes:

> After my death, you mustn't speak to anyone about my manuscript before it is published; you must speak about it only to Mother Prioress. If you act otherwise, the devil will make use of more than one trap to hinder the work of God, a very important work![3]

Shortly after Thérèse's death, Mother Agnes of Jesus obtained permission from the prioress, Mother Marie de Gonzague, to publish the manuscript. On September 30, 1898, the first anniversary of her death, Thérèse's *Story of a Soul* was ready for distribution.

The simple message of the spiritual journal bolted through the Church like a flash of lightning. The young and the old, religious and laity, bishops and seminarians, the intellectual and the unlettered, experienced deep consolation in Thérèse's writing. Many discovered a satisfying remedy for the complexity of the twentieth century and a simple way to put the love of God into practice.

---

[3] St. Thérèse of Lisieux, *Her Last Conversations*, trans. John Clarke, OCD (Washington, DC: ICS Publications, 1977), p. 126. (Henceforth cited as *L.C.*)

The message of Thérèse's sanctity spread rapidly throughout the world. Mother Agnes of Jesus reported that between July 1909 and July 1910, the Lisieux Carmel received nearly 10,000 letters requesting information about Thérèse. Many others wrote, telling of favors received from God through her intercession. By July 1909, over 100,000 copies of the *Story of a Soul* had been sold.[4] In a decade, Thérèse of Lisieux had become the spiritual guide of Catholics everywhere. Also, through contact with her *Story of a Soul*, scores of people embraced or returned to the Catholic Faith. The hierarchy quickly took notice.

Thérèse soon made her influence felt on the shores of North America. In 1902 four Discalced Carmelite nuns came to Philadelphia from Boston carrying one of the very first French editions of *Story of a Soul*. They also brought with them a keen appreciation of the spiritual doctrine of their recently deceased sister in the Carmel of Lisieux. Upon settling in their new foundation in Philadelphia, and in spite of the adversities of ill health and those innate to becoming established in a new location, the nuns began to spread devotion to Sister Thérèse in earnest. Through their instrumentality devotion was fostered on a large scale among the local clergy and benefactors of the monastery and beyond to all parts of the country and the world.[5] The Carmel of Philadelphia became

---

[4] *St. Thérèse of Lisieux by Those Who Knew Her: Testimonies from the Process of Beatification*, ed. and trans. Christopher O'Mahony, OCD (Dublin: Veritas Publications, 1975), p. 71. (Henceforth cited as *P.*)

[5] In the early 1900's a popular devotion to St. Thérèse grew strong among the Catholic faithful of Philadelphia also through the efforts of the chaplain of the Carmel, the Rev. John J. Moore, a noted spiritual director. He preached regularly in the Monastery chapel about the life, virtues and power of intercession of the French Carmelite. Thus, the demand in Philadelphia for more knowledge of her increased dramatically during the first decades of the twentieth century, years before her actual canonization.

Dennis Cardinal Dougherty, Archbishop of Philadelphia from 1918-1951, was introduced to the spirituality of St. Thérèse when, as a missionary bishop in the Philippines, he visited the Carmel of Philadelphia in 1912. Having received remarkable favors for his diocese through her intercession, he gladly signed the petition for her beatification. He became an avid promoter of her cause, leading pilgrimages to Lisieux. Later as Archbishop of Philadelphia, he worked with the nuns of the Carmel in spreading devotion to St. Thérèse.

the "depot" for the distribution of literature, relics and pictures of Thérèse.

On September 6, 1910, Thérèse's body was exhumed. Unlike the somber day of her funeral in 1897, her remains were taken to a new resting place in the Carmelite chapel accompanied by more than 50,000 devotees.

In 1914, merely seventeen years after her demise, the cause of Thérèse's canonization was opened. On April 29, 1923, Pope Pius XI signed the decree of beatification. On May 17, 1925, only twenty-eight years after her death, the same Pontiff declared Thérèse of Lisieux a saint. Since her canonization, she has been designated the patroness of the Church's missionary activity along with St. Francis Xavier, as well as the heavenly guardian of the Church's efforts for the conversion of Russia.[6]

During her final illness, Thérèse had commissioned her sister, Mother Agnes of Jesus, to prepare her autobiographical manuscripts for publication:

> Dear Mother, everything that you judge proper to add or take away in the manuscript of my life is as if I had done it myself. You must remember this for later on and in this matter, you should have no scruples.[7]

Mother Agnes, a "born corrector," was in fact an able and talented editor and writer. However, the result of her strong personality and heavy pen was a drastically altered text, that, many hold, obscured the true personality and charism of Thérèse. The renowned Carmelite scholar, Otilio Rodriguez, in reference to Mother Agnes' editing of the *Story of a Soul* notes:

---

[6] See Lucian Lamza, "Saint Thérèse of the Child Jesus And The Conversion of Russia," *Soul* (September-October 1990), pp. 10-11.

[7] From the *Procès de L'Ordinaire*, Vol. I, Fol 1660, quoted in Otilio Rodriguez, OCD, "The New Face of St. Thérèse," *Spiritual Life* (Vol. 19, No. 3, Fall 1963), p. 149. See also, Jean-Francois Six, *Light of the Night*, trans. John Bowden (London: SCM Press, Ltd., 1996), pp. 1-19.

Her changes in the manuscripts were not simply a matter of correcting minor grammatical errors. She went so far as to change the author's thoughts and ideas about herself, her parents and relatives, and her doctrine. These changes distorted the original texts to such an extent that they presented an unrealistic view of Thérèse's personality. The quantity of material that Mother Agnes deleted is astonishing. About one third of the original manuscript was suppressed, entire pages being omitted.[8]

For decades, theologians of the spiritual life had clamored for access to Thérèse's original, unedited writings. There was a more or less general feeling that the true Thérèse had somehow been hidden beneath Mother Agnes of Jesus' edition of her writings.

And so, long before the 1973 centenary of Thérèse's birth, scholars, notably Father François de Sainte Marie, O.C.D., began working towards a new critical edition, not only of the *Story of a Soul* but of all Thérèse's writings. In 1988, this project, carried out by a team of nuns of the Carmel of Lisieux, as well as French Carmelites and Dominican priests and sisters, reached completion with the publication of Thérèse's prayers. Her complete works include: *Derniers Entretiens* (1971), *Histoire d'une Ame* (1972), *Correspondance Générale*, Vol. I (1972), *Correspondance Générale*, Vol. II (1973), *Poésies* (1979), *Récréations Pieuses* (1985), and *Prières* (1988).

John Clarke, O.C.D., has translated several of these critical editions of Thérèse's writings into English. They have each been published, with the exception of the prayers[9] and religious dramas, by the Institute of Carmelite Studies Publications in Washington, D.C.: *Story of a Soul* (1975), *St. Thérèse of Lisieux: Her Last Conversations* (1977), *General Correspondence*, Vol. I (1982), *Gen-*

---

[8] Otilio Rodriguez, OCD, *op. cit.*, p. 149.

[9] It should be noted that two of her prayers most pertinent to our topic — her Profession Prayer as well as the "Act of Oblation to Merciful Love," are found in an Appendix to the 1975 ICS edition of *Story of a Soul*; see pp. 275-278.

eral Correspondence, Vol. II (1988), and *Poetry* (translated by Donald Kinney, O.C.D., 1996).[10]

It is impossible to underestimate the value of these documents in studying Thérèse's spiritual doctrine. As Otilio Rodriguez has noted: "It is only by approaching St. Thérèse herself and her authentic writings that we can contemplate the wonders that God has done for her and is ready to work in each of us."[11]

The publication of these primary sources has led students of the spiritual life to find in Thérèse's writings many riches hitherto unsuspected. John Paul II has observed that one finds an uncanny contemporaneity in most of Thérèse's themes.[12] It may be said that she anticipated many of the concerns of the Fathers of the Second Vatican Council. Consider, for instance, her sharp focus on Scripture as the foundation of the spiritual life; the Eucharist as the source and summit of daily prayer; the vital importance of every Christian participating unreservedly in Christ's redemptive work; Mary's faith as the guiding principle of Marian doctrine and devotion; the vocation of women in the Church. Relentlessly, Thérèse cut through accretions to seize the authentic tradition of the Church whether it be in theology,[13] liturgical practice,[14] or religious life.[15]

---

[10] A past editor of the Institute of Carmelite Studies, Rev. John Sullivan, OCD, notes that Thérèse's message continues to have special significance today as is evidenced in the demand for her writings. He states: "Strikingly Thérèse continues to maintain her appeal to thinkers and readers today; Thérèse still attracts many devotees. Our sales figures rank her *Story of a Soul* as the best Carmelite book we have published bar none." See *Carmelite Studies, op. cit.,* p. vii.

[11] Otilio Rodriguez, OCD, *op. cit.,* p. 148.

[12] Pope John Paul II, "Fervent Communion with Christ's Sufferings," *L'Osservatore Romano,* (June 23, 1980) pp. 13-14. English ed. (Henceforth cited as Pope John Paul II.)

[13] Thérèse consistently rejected the current trend to sensationalize and sentimentalize the life of Christ or Mary. Leaving behind the imaginative meditations of others, she chose instinctively to adhere solely to the content of the Gospel. See *L.C.,* pp. 161-162.

[14] Thérèse, for instance, understood that the Liturgy of the Hours extends the praise of the Eucharist throughout the day and allows those who participate in the prayer to enter, as a priestly people, into Jesus' adoration of his Father. See *L.C.,* p. 137.

[15] Thérèse, upon entry into Carmel, understood that her relationships with her blood sisters must always remain on the supernatural level. See *L.C.,* p. 130.

In his homily at Lisieux on June 2, 1980, Pope John Paul II has pinpointed one of Thérèse's contributions to the Church in our century:

> Of Thérèse of Lisieux, it can be said with conviction that the Holy Spirit of God permitted her heart to reveal directly to the men of our time, the fundamental mystery, the reality of the Gospel; the fact of having really received "the spirit of Sonship," when we cry, "Abba, Father." The "little way" is the way of "holy childhood." In this way there is something unique; the genius of St. Thérèse of Lisieux. At the same time there is the confirmation and renewal of the most fundamental and most universal truth. What truth of the Gospel message is, in fact, more fundamental and more universal than this one: God is Our Father and we are his children?[16]

Many believers have experienced prodigious growth in the spiritual life by following Thérèse's "Little Way" of spiritual childhood. She is widely reputed to help Christians cultivate a healing and transforming relationship with God as loving Father, with Jesus as intimate Friend, Brother, Savior and Spouse, and with Mary as Mother in the Holy Spirit. Her writings also provide clear direction in the sanctification of daily duty as well as the means to supernaturalize all physical, psychological, and spiritual suffering. In short, Thérèse's mission, accomplished largely through her *Story of a Soul,* is to help ordinary Christians to become perfect in their love of God and neighbor through the ordinary means of prayer, fidelity to duty, and sacrifice.

However, Thérèse exercises an appeal beyond the confines of the Church. Studying her writings one discovers a disconcerting and fascinating fact — a fact that relates her directly to many of our contemporaries. For the final eighteen months of her life, as she was literally being suffocated by pulmonary tuberculosis, Thérèse experienced a harrowing "trial of faith." Although never

---

[16] Pope John Paul II, *op. cit.,* p. 13.

faltering in her profession of faith, Thérèse had to struggle to believe in the existence of life beyond the grave. In her reasoning and at deep levels of her affectivity, she felt one with the atheist, apostate and materialist. During these months her faith seemed to be merely the will to believe. Her struggle to assent to the existence of heaven caused her more agony than her physical disease. By her own admission, her trial was a veritable martyrdom.

A number of students of the spiritual life have sought to explain Thérèse's "trial of faith" as the preparation of her soul for union with her Divine Bridegroom. In the categories of the ascetico-mystical theology of St. John of the Cross, these theologians have explained Thérèse's "trial of faith" as passive purification in preparation for the transforming union also known as the mystical marriage. Some spiritual writers who accept this interpretation, hold Thérèse up as a model for those who struggle to live faithfully in the ascetical way. Her crisis of faith, they claim, is one among several indications that she followed the ordinary way of the masses who never attain mystical union with God in this life. Others, including Hans Urs von Balthasar, go even further and assert that Thérèse never experienced any degree of mystical prayer and, therefore, has made no contribution to the sphere of mystical theology.[17]

However, a careful reading of Thérèse's writings indicates that she had indeed attained the mystical marriage before April 1896, when she entered the "dark tunnel" of her "trial of faith."

At first sight these two spiritual states: a "trial of faith" and the mystical marriage, appear to be incompatible. St. John of the Cross, Thérèse's master in the spiritual life, teaches that:

> The soul in union enjoys all peace, tastes all sweetness and delights in all delights insofar as this earthly state allows...
> so little of this is describable that we would never succeed

---

[17] See Hans Urs von Balthasar, *Thérèse of Lisieux: The Story of a Mission*, trans. Donald Nicholl (New York: Sheed & Ward, 1954), pp. 251-272. (Henceforth cited as Balthasar.)

in fully explaining what takes place in the soul that has reached this happy state.... This sometimes takes such an inward hold on her that nothing painful can reach her... the delight of this union absorbs the soul within herself and gives her such refreshment that it makes her insensible to the disturbances and troubles mentioned.[18]

St. John of the Cross' description of the mystical marriage and Thérèse's description of her "trial of faith"[19] appear to be, at least on the surface of things, incompatible. It is exactly such comparisons that have led students of spirituality to explain Thérèse's trial of faith as passive purgation in preparation for union with Christ, and by so doing, to deny her the grace of mystical marriage.

In this study, analyzing Thérèse's writings in the context of the spiritual doctrine of St. Teresa of Jesus and St. John of the Cross, I shall attempt to prove that Thérèse had indeed attained the mystical marriage before the inception of the "trial of faith." I shall also seek to demonstrate that this trial, far from indicating a need for purification in Thérèse, manifests an intensity of union with Christ acknowledged intuitively by the Church but not fully recognized in the field of spiritual theology until the publication of the critical editions of Thérèse's writings.

To accomplish these ends, I shall utilize largely, although not exclusively, the primary sources. In particular, in Thérèse's *Story of a Soul* and *Her Last Conversations*, I shall seek evidence that she had experienced the mystical marriage before entering upon the "trial of faith." Also, I shall seek in Thérèse's writings indications that the trial did not in any way challenge her personal conviction of having attained mystical union with Christ.[20]

Furthermore, by examining Thérèse's experience in the light

---

[18] St. John of the Cross, *Collected Works: The Spiritual Canticle*, trans. Kieran Kavanaugh, OCD, and Otilio Rodriguez, OCD (Washington, DC: ICS Publications, 1991), p. 558.

[19] We shall carefully analyze Thérèse's many descriptions of her "trial of faith" later in this study.

of the doctrine of St. Teresa of Jesus' *Interior Castle* and St. John of the Cross' *Spiritual Canticle*, I shall seek to demonstrate that her "trial of faith," rather than preparing her for mystical union, was, in the categories of the Doctors of the Carmelite reform, a stupefying manifestation of her oneness with Christ in His redemptive work.

In Chapter I of this study, I shall examine some of the events in Thérèse's life that indicate her spiritual development. I shall then seek to demonstrate that in spite of ordinary human problems, Thérèse had attained a high degree of unity with God at a tender age. Freely cooperating with "preservative grace" analogous to the grace received in its fullness by the Mother of God, Thérèse had been prepared early in life to offer herself in union with Christ in expiation for sins against the Faith.

Consequently, the first chapter of this study will investigate the antecedents of Thérèse's "trial of faith." In this light we shall see that the trial, rather than an interruption of Thérèse's spiritual growth was, in fact, the consummation of her lifelong gift of self to Christ.

In Chapter II, a study of Thérèse's writings will focus on her description of the "trial of faith." In Chapter III, I shall peruse the various "sources" through which Thérèse came to understand and explain her own spiritual development up to and including the "trial of faith."

Finally, in Chapter IV and Chapter V, I shall analyze Thérèse's "trial of faith" as the logical manifestation of an intense degree of mystical union with Christ. I shall seek confirmation of this interpretation in the writings of St. John of the Cross and St. Teresa of Jesus.

Through this research I shall attempt to demonstrate that Thérèse's "trial of faith" should no longer be interpreted as pas-

---

[20] We shall see that during the entire period of her "trial of faith" Thérèse was convinced that she would experience the "death of love." In the teaching of St. John of the Cross, the "death of love" is a grace reserved only for those who have experienced the mystical marriage.

sive purification. Rather, it should be understood and presented as a manifestation of the high reaches of the unitive way which specifies a unique and hitherto largely unappreciated facet of Thérèse's mission; namely, to expiate sins against the Faith and to impart and strengthen the gift of faith in the members of the Church on earth.

It is also my hope that, through this study of Thérèse's spiritual development, certain aspects of the doctrines of redemption, grace and ecclesiology, often overlooked and at times even denied at the level of popular spirituality, will be highlighted; in particular, sharing in Christ's redemptive work as an essential development of sanctifying grace in the life of every Christian. I hope to make a contribution to the field of spirituality by demonstrating that the heights of mystical union with Christ need not and evidently must not be understood apart from the love of God expected of every Christian by virtue of Baptism. In this context, Thérèse, the saint of the "little," and might we not also add, "universal" way, illustrates by her life and teaching the centerpiece of the Second Vatican Council: the Universal Call to Holiness of all the Faithful.[21]

---

[21] Vatican II, *Dogmatic Constitution on the Church (Lumen gentium)*, Ch. V.

Abbreviations

SIGNIFICANT EVENTS IN THÉRÈSE'S LIFE

August 28, 1877:	Death of her mother, Marie Zélie Guérin Martin.
October 2, 1882:	Pauline, Thérèse's surrogate mother, enters Carmel.
May 13, 1883:	The "Smile of the Virgin" and Thérèse's cure.
May 8, 1884:	Thérèse's First Holy Communion.
May 22, 1884:	Her Second Holy Communion.
June 14, 1884:	Her Confirmation.
December 25, 1886:	The Christmas "grace of conversion."
May 29, 1887:	Thérèse receives her father's permission to enter Carmel.
July, 1887:	She grasps her apostolic mission while contemplating a picture of Jesus crucified.
September 1, 1887:	Thérèse learns of Pranzini's execution and "conversion."
November 20, 1887:	Thérèse asks Pope Leo XIII's permission to enter Carmel at the age of fifteen.
January 1, 1888:	She learns that Bishop Hugonin had granted her permission to enter Carmel.
April 9, 1888:	Thérèse enters Carmel.
June 23, 1888:	M. Martin's mental problems become evident.
January 10, 1889:	Reception of the habit.
September 8, 1890:	Thérèse's first profession.
April-July, 1891:	She prays and offers sacrifice for the apostate Carmelite priest, Hyacinthe Loyson.
July 29, 1894:	Mr. Martin dies.
June 9, 1895:	Thérèse is inspired to offer herself as a victim to the merciful love of God.
June 11, 1895:	With Celine, she offers herself as a victim to the merciful love of God, and, shortly afterwards, receives a "wound of love."
April 3, 1896:	First hemoptysis in her cell.
April 5, 1896 (or shortly thereafter):	Sudden entrance into the "trial of faith."
April 5, 1896 - September 30, 1897:	Thérèse undergoes intense physical and spiritual suffering.
September 30, 1897:	After an agony of two days, Thérèse dies.

THE TRIAL OF FAITH OF
SAINT THÉRÈSE OF LISIEUX

Chapter I

THE LIFE OF THÉRÈSE

Marie-Françoise-Thérèse, the last child of Louis Martin and Marie Zélie Guérin, was born on January 2, 1873 in the Norman town of Alençon.

Two days after her birth, Thérèse became a Christian at the baptismal font of the Church of Notre Dame de Alençon. Louis and Zélie Martin had nine children in all. Near the end of the nineteenth century, nearly half the infants born did not survive. The Martin family was no exception to this sad rule. Thérèse joined only four sisters in the Martin household: Marie-Louise, Marie-Pauline, Marie-Leonie and Marie-Céline. Two sisters, Marie-Hélène (d. 1870) and Marie-Melanie-Thérèse (d. 1870) and two brothers, Marie-Joseph (d. 1867) and Marie-Jean Baptiste (d. 1868) were deceased at the time of Thérèse's birth.

Church and State during Thérèse's life

The French society into which Thérèse was born, was still suffering the ideological after-shock of the French Revolution. Two sets of ideas divided the population into two armed political camps. The Royalists (or Monarchists) favored the "old ways" of government and morality as well as a strong union of State and Church. The Republicans, on the other hand, children of the French Revolution, represented atheism, Freemasonry, and liberalism. They were, by and large, antagonistic to the Church.

The Church in France was also still internally unsettled as a result of the persecution she had experienced during and after the French Revolution. The already stale question of Gallicanism vs. Ultramontanism often surfaced to further disturb the peace of the Church. Thérèse and Céline would discover, at a very tender age, that many members of the clergy were in need of personal reformation. Jansenism continued to plague the Church in France with its dreary views of God's justice and man's dereliction. Modernism was also beginning to disturb the faithful.

Although Thérèse was to discover disturbing manifestations of Jansenistic spirituality in the Lisieux Carmel, she found no trace of it in her family life. Her parents, so healthy in their religious observance, had been carefully formed by several anti-Jansenistic Jesuits. Also, through Zélie Martin, the balanced spirituality of St. Francis de Sales exercised a strong influence in the Martin home. Jean Guitton, in his work *The Spiritual Genius of St. Thérèse* notes:

> If one compares the Martin Family with a number of other families belonging to the end of the same middle-class century, it is surprising never to find the slightest whiff of Jansenism, not even clinging like a perfume or in a dormant state.[1]

There was no question regarding the political or religious positions of Thérèse's family. On both the Martin and Guérin sides were found faithful and devout Catholics whose loyalties were unquestionably on the side of the Royalists and the Ultramontanists.

Before her entry into Carmel, Thérèse had a keen interest in world and ecclesiastical events. She was in touch with current ideological and political issues through her uncle, Isidore Guérin, and his skills in journalism. Thérèse also had an avid interest in science

---

[1] Jean Guitton, *The Spiritual Genius of St. Thérèse*, trans. by a Religious of the Retreat of the Sacred Heart (Westminster: The Newman Press, 1958), p. 17. For an excellent survey of the conditions of Church and State during the lifetime of St. Thérèse, see the essay of Leopold Glueckert entitled "The World of Thérèse: France, Church and State in the Late Nineteenth Century" in *Carmelite Studies: Experiencing St. Thérèse Today*, ed. John Sullivan, OCD (Washington, DC: ICS Publications, 1990), pp. 10-27.

and its discoveries. Through these various sources, Thérèse came to be aware of the rising tide of liberalism, Freemasonry and atheism in the modern world. She also came to be aware of a frightening polarization that was beginning to surface in the Catholic Church.

Thérèse was no stranger to any of these issues. Her clearest perception, based in part on her own experience, was, as we shall see more amply further on, that there was a problem in the Catholic priesthood of her day. She first discerned the problem as she, her father and Céline journeyed to Rome in November of 1887 in the company of seventy-five French priests. Discreetly, not discussing particular problems, Thérèse pointed out to Céline the need to pray and make sacrifice for priests. "I lived in the company of many *saintly priests* for a month and I learned that, though their dignity raises them above the angels, they are nevertheless weak and fragile men."[2]

During the canonical examination preceding her profession as a Carmelite, Thérèse clearly declared: "I have come to Carmel to save souls and to pray for priests."[3]

Later in her life as a religious, Thérèse was to make the painful discovery that there were, among her contemporaries, priests who had lost the Catholic faith. She was deeply disturbed by the case of Father Hyacinthe Loyson, a Carmelite priest, who had left the priesthood, married, and formed a schismatic church based upon liberal, anti-dogmatic principles. Thérèse's "Oblation to the Merciful Love of God," which was directly related to the "trial of faith," was occasioned in no small part by Loyson's defection from the Catholic priesthood.

Thérèse was by no means abstracted from the problems of her day. Rather, the ideological and political clashes which impacted at various levels in civil and ecclesiastical society, became, in a sense, the motive, the cause célèbre of her life.

---

[2] Thérèse of Lisieux, *Story of a Soul*, trans. John Clarke, OCD (Washington, DC: ICS Publications, 1975), p. 122. (Henceforth cited as *S.*)

[3] *S.*, p. 149.

Thérèse's Childhood

In the *Story of a Soul* Thérèse delineates three separate periods in her life up to her entry into Carmel: (1) From the dawning of reason (c. 1875) until her mother's death (August 28, 1877);[4] (2) from her mother's death until her "conversion" (December 25, 1886);[5] (3) from her "conversion" until her entrance into Carmel (April 9, 1888).[6]

Early in the *Story of a Soul*, Thérèse reveals that she had attained the use of reason as a very young child: "God granted me the favor of opening my intelligence at an early age and of imprinting childhood recollections so deeply on my memory that it seems the things I am about to recount happened only yesterday."[7] Thérèse offers at least two instances of her precocity: at the age of two, having heard that her sister Pauline would become a religious, Thérèse decided: "I will be a religious, too."[8] Naturally, this is easily attributable to the child's innate tendency to imitate an older sibling. Thérèse admitted that Pauline had been her model and ideal in life. However, Thérèse, as a mature religious, continued to believe that she had decided to give her life to God on her own at that tender age.

While acknowledging a keen natural intelligence in Thérèse, as well as an extraordinary bestowal of grace, we must not fail to consider the influence of her family and home life on her human and spiritual development.

Clearly, Louis and Zélie Martin were extraordinary human beings and outstanding Christians. They also had a definite plan for raising their children in Christian virtue. We might say that they not only understood "Christian anthropology" but also knew how to be the "formators" of their offspring in the life of faith.

---

[4] *S.*, p. 16.
[5] *S.*, p. 34.
[6] *S.*, p. 98.
[7] *S.*, pp. 16-17.
[8] *S.*, p. 20.

It is refreshing to read Thérèse's account of the Christian life practiced in her home. Every member of the family was deeply committed to the Catholic faith. Whenever possible, they attended daily Mass together. Often in the afternoon, Louis Martin would take his children for a walk about town. Together they would visit the Blessed Sacrament in one of the several churches of Lisieux. Prayer and conversation about God and Christian virtue were daily family occurrences. The great liturgical feasts were the high points of every passing year. In fact, each evening, as part of a period of family prayer, Louis Martin would read a section from Dom Prosper Guéranger's *The Liturgical Year (L'Année Liturgique)* to his children.[9]

Through the informal instruction and formation Thérèse received from her parents and sisters at home, she formed a vivid concept of the mystery of heaven. Thérèse relates in the *Story of a Soul* that when she began to read, the very first word she was able to decipher without help from anyone was "heaven."[10] Concomitantly, there grew in her an awareness that heaven is truly our homeland and earth, a place of exile.[11] Thérèse's longing for heaven grew in intensity with the death of her mother in 1877. These longings were further strengthened by her reading of Fr. Charles Arminjon's *The End of the Present World and the Mysteries of the Future Life (Fin du Monde Present et Mystères de La Vie Future)*.[12]

To the end of her life, Thérèse was convinced that the instruction and solid human and spiritual formation she had received at home had prepared her to lovingly respond to God's grace in Carmel.

The second "period" of Thérèse's life before her entry into Carmel began with the death of her mother. On the day of the

---

[9] Prosper Guéranger (d. 1875), founder of the Benedictine Congregation of Solesmes, was largely responsible for the modern liturgical revival which in a sense, came to term with the promulgation of the *Constitution on the Sacred Liturgy* (*Sacrosanctum Concilium*) of the Second Vatican Council.

[10] *S.*, p. 36.

[11] *S.*, p. 37.

[12] *S.*, p. 102.

funeral, Thérèse chose Pauline to be her mother.[13] Several months after the passing of Zélie Martin, the family moved to a new home in Lisieux, called "Les Buissonnets." Louis Martin wanted his children to have the benefit of familiarity with his wife's brother, Isidore Guérin, his wife, Céline Guérin, and their two daughters, Jeanne and Marie.

However, in spite of the comfort of the extended family circle, her mother's death caused a deep disturbance in Thérèse's affective life.[14] In spite of the suffering the trauma of her mother's death caused her, Thérèse, nonetheless, cooperating with divine grace, continued to grow steadily in prayer and the attainment of Christian virtue. She explains that during this difficult time, she learned how to meditate[15] and developed a love and concern for the poor.[16]

During these years of personal and spiritual growth, Thérèse came to dwell more and more on the "melancholy" of this world and to pine for the kingdom of heaven.[17] In October of 1881, at the age of eight and a half, Thérèse entered a school conducted by Benedictine nuns near the Abbey of Notre-Dame-du-Pré in Lisieux. Thérèse relates her feelings without any ambiguity: "The five years spent in school were the saddest in my life."[18]

Although she had no taste for grammar or mathematics, Thérèse was a gifted student. Her difficulties did not originate in her studies. Rather, she found it burdensome to be away from home and family and relate with the other students.

Thérèse's personal problems were seriously aggravated when Pauline announced her intention to leave home for Carmel. The pending second separation caused her again to taste the fragility

---

[13] Zélie Martin died of cancer of the breast on August 28, 1877 after a long ordeal. Thérèse was then four and a half years old. She recounts the details of her mother's illness and death in *S.*, pp. 33-34.

[14] *S.*, p. 34-35.

[15] *S.*, p. 37.

[16] *S.*, p. 38.

[17] *S.*, p. 42.

[18] *S.*, p. 53.

of human existence. Overhearing Pauline discussing her plans to enter Carmel, Thérèse experienced another human support pulled out from beneath her.[19]

Pauline, consoling her nine-year-old sister, explained the life of Carmel to her. Thérèse tells us in the *Story of a Soul* that as the result of this conversation, she perceived a clear call to also enter Carmel:

> When thinking over all you had said, I felt that Carmel was the *desert* where God wanted me to go also and hide myself. I felt this with so much force that there wasn't the least doubt in my heart; it was not the dream of a child led astray but the *certitude* of a divine call; I wanted to go to Carmel not for Pauline's sake, but for *Jesus alone.* I was thinking *very much* about things which words could not express but which left a great peace in my soul.[20]

Thérèse's Illness

After Pauline's entrance into Carmel, Thérèse, emotionally upset, became physically ill. It is interesting to note that Thérèse herself attributes her mysterious illness to two sources: the mental and emotional strain she endured in losing Pauline which, in a sense, aggravated the yet unhealed wound inflicted by the death of her mother; and the anger of the devil over the harm that her family would cause him.[21] For the next two months, Thérèse, with one remarkable remission on the day Pauline received her habit in Carmel, suffered a severe and mysterious illness which defied exact prognosis.[22]

---

[19] *S.*, p. 58.

[20] *S., ibid.*

[21] *S.*, p. 60.

[22] Thérèse was attended by a Dr. Notta during this illness. His conclusions were that the illness was very serious. See *S.*, p. 61. In any event, Dr. Notta treated the

Marcelline Husé, who served as a maid in the Martin household, gave testimony regarding the symptoms of the illness:

> Thérèse suffered a nervous trembling, followed by seizures of fright and hallucination which recurred several times a day. In the intervening periods, the sick child was in a very weak state and could not be left alone.[23]

Jeanne Guérin gives the following account of her cousin's illness:

> At the worst time, there were also several attacks when the motor nerves were affected and she was able to wheel her whole body around which she would have been absolutely incapable of doing when well.[24]

Perhaps the most graphic description of Thérèse's illness is given by her Sister, Marie:

> Thérèse had terrifying dreams that depressed all who heard her cries of distress. Some nails fixed in the wall of the room suddenly became as thick, charred fingers to her and she cried out: "I'm afraid, I'm afraid." Her eyes, usually so calm and so kindly had a terror stricken expression that is impossible to describe. Another time, when my father came to sit by her, he happened to have his hat in his hand. Thérèse looked at him without saying a single word, as

---

illness as a nervous disease. It has been suggested that Thérèse suffered from Chorea, a disease of the nervous system similar to St. Vitus' Dance. However, certain symptoms tend to disprove this possibility. Jeanne (Guérin) Néele recalled Dr. Notta's diagnosis; she said: "The doctor treating her called the disease St. Vitus' Dance. Nevertheless, it seems to me that he was somewhat hesitant about this diagnosis and suggested that something else might be present — but what?" We must recall that in Thérèse's day mental/emotional problems were looked upon as a cause of dishonor for an entire family. See Ida Görres, *The Hidden Face* (New York: Pantheon Books, 1959), pp. 416-421 for an excellent explanation of the illness.

[23] Guy Gaucher, *op. cit.*, p. 46.

[24] Guy Gaucher, *ibid*.

she spoke very little during her illness. Then, suddenly, as always, her expression changed. Staring at the hat, she wailed: "Oh, the great black beast!" Her cries had something supernatural about them: one had to have heard them to have any idea of them. One day the doctor was present during one of these attacks and he said to my father: "Science is powerless before these phenomena; there is nothing to be done."[25]

Thérèse also attributed her strange illness, as noted before, to the anger of the devil:[26]

> The sickness became so grave that, according to human calculations, I wasn't to recover from it. I can't describe this strange sickness, but I'm now convinced it was the work of the devil.[27]

And again:

> I believe the devil had received an *external* power over me, but was not allowed to approach my soul nor my mind except to inspire me with very great *fears* of certain things.[28]

The Virgin's Smile

On May 13, 1883, in the midst of intense suffering, Marie, Léonie, and Céline, at a loss over how to help Thérèse in her tortured, hallucinogenic state, turned in desperation to the Blessed Virgin Mary and sought a miracle. The three sisters were convinced that their youngest sister was at death's door. Thérèse notes:

---

[25] *P.*, pp. 86-87.
[26] *S.*, p. 60.
[27] *S.*, p. 62.
[28] *S.*, p. 63.

"Marie obtained what she wanted." The Saint then describes the miracle of the "Smile of the Virgin":

> Finding no help on earth, poor little Thérèse had also turned toward the Mother of heaven and prayed with all her heart that she take pity on her. All of a sudden the Blessed Virgin appeared *beautiful* to me, so *beautiful* that never had I seen anything so attractive; her face was suffused with an ineffable benevolence and tenderness, but what penetrated to the very depths of my soul was the "*ravishing smile of the Blessed Virgin.*" At that instant, all my pain disappeared and two large tears glistened on my eyelashes and flowed down my cheeks silently, but they were tears of unmixed joy.[29]

There have been various interpretations of Thérèse's miraculous cure. Some have said that Thérèse experienced a direct apparition of the Blessed Virgin. Others assert that the statue near her bed became animated and in fact smiled at her. The pertinent text in Chapter III of the *Story of a Soul* does not read "*la statue s'anima*" (The statue was animated); rather, "*Tout a coup, la Ste. Vierge me parut belle.*"[30] This has been correctly translated in the Clarke edition as "all of a sudden, the Blessed Virgin appeared beautiful to me."[31]

Later in Chapter IV, Thérèse, describing her First Communion, related that she had recited the "Act of Consecration to the Holy Virgin" in the name of each of the first communicants. This act of piety caused her to recall the miracle that had occurred one year before. She makes it quite clear that the Blessed Virgin was visibly present to her: "It seems to me that the Blessed Virgin must have looked upon her little flower and smiled at her, for wasn't it

---

[29] S., pp. 65-66.

[30] Sainte Thérèse De L'Enfant-Jesus, *Histoire d'une Ame; Manuscrits Autobiographiques* (Paris: Editions du Cerf-Desclée De Brouwer, 1972), p. 79. (Henceforth cited as *Histoire d'une Ame.*)

[31] S., p. 65.

she who cured her with a visible smile?"[32] The French text reads: "*par un visible sourire.*"[33]

Reflecting upon the occurrence, Thérèse was certain of three things: She had experienced the sweet maternal presence of Mary in a direct, personal manner; she had received, through the Blessed Virgin's presence, powerful graces; she was miraculously cured of her strange and undiagnosed malady.[34]

In the face of the many hypotheses regarding Thérèse's illness, the one proposed by Ida F. Görres in her well-known work entitled *The Hidden Face*, seems most plausible.[35] Thérèse's collapse was caused primarily, though not exclusively, by accumulated and excessive psychic tension stemming from the loss of her mother.

Görres asserts that Pauline, thinking she was training Thérèse in virtue, had unwittingly taught her to suppress her emotional difficulties. In other words, Thérèse had never been allowed to deal with her mother's death on the level of her affectivity. Rather, she had simply become absorbed in her family life. Immediately after her mother's death, she chose Pauline as surrogate mother and began to relate to her as such. Consequently, the trauma of her mother's death was never dealt with directly and, in large portion, had been repressed.

Early symptoms of the affective problem include: a marked tendency to hypersensitivity; a lack of security outside of the family circle and, in a sense, even in the home of her Aunt and Uncle Guérin; multiple problems in developing relationships with others; and repressed, irrational fears. Thérèse herself admits her difficulties unabashedly in the first three chapters of the *Story of a Soul*.

---

[32] *S.*, p. 78.

[33] *Histoire d'une Ame*, p. 92.

[34] For a survey of the Blessed Virgin's place in the life of St. Thérèse, see "Thérèse and the Mother of God," by Eamon Carroll, O. Carm., *Carmelite Studies: Experiencing Saint Thérèse Today*, ed. John Clarke, OCD (Washington, DC: ICS Publications, 1990), p. 82.

[35] Ida F. Görres, *op. cit.*, pp. 64-80.

Görres held that the mental and physical maladies of Thérèse were preeminently real. However, they were rooted firmly in her inability to cope with life without the support of Pauline. Görres also accepts Thérèse's conviction that the devil was involved in her illness. The author, however, does not believe that the evil spirit was the direct cause of the sickness. Rather, taking advantage of Thérèse's vulnerability, the devil invited her to despair. Görres notes:

> The diabolical invitation could have led to stifling inhibitions, erroneous interpretations of the self, lifelong hypochondria about one's "weak sides" — all attitudes which may later on hinder radical, heroic commitment. And we may well assume — many events from the lives of the saints seem to confirm this — that the demons discern a lofty vocation in a person much sooner than do human beings and bring to bear their power against him.[36]

While keeping in mind that she was the object of a special bestowal of grace, Thérèse, like all children of Adam and Eve, experienced a number of human problems, some of which had their roots in her early childhood. God's grace seeks to heal our wounds, but ordinarily not without human cooperation.

Görres describes the dark, elemental, and subconscious matrix of Thérèse's illness. All of her symptoms said: "I want Pauline, I must go to Pauline; I don't want her to be away; I can live only with her; I will fall sick, go mad, die without Pauline; none of you can help me, I don't want any of the rest of you to help me."[37]

Of course, Thérèse was not conscious of her internal hysteria, which included, to some degree, willfulness and possessiveness. Neither was she pretending to be sick or deliberately making herself ill. However, in the midst of the trial, a grace was offered to

---

[36] Ida F. Görres, *op. cit.*, p. 78.
[37] Ida F. Görres, *op. cit.*, p. 79.

her through Our Lady of Victories through which she recognized her temptation. Görres brilliantly describes Thérèse's trial:

> Thérèse was confronted with alternatives, and the second of these alternatives was the perilous one. She could accept the offered comfort, the new support and protection. That is, she could abandon her wild despair over what she had lost, could really carry out the unendurable renunciation within the core of her ego, could release the hand of Pauline and reach across the irrevocable gulf for the hand of the Blessed Virgin. Or — and this was the other possibility — she could cling to her despair, could hold tight to her neurosis, could maintain her protest, stubbornly persist at all costs in the sinister attempt at blackmail which this disease represented.[38]

Thérèse understood the significance of this incident and explains it with disarming simplicity. As the Holy Virgin cast her smile upon her, Thérèse chose Jesus' mother to be her own and was restored to health. It is very important not to underestimate the formative influence of this event on the spirituality Thérèse would later articulate.

Thérèse's "Little Way" is the way of confidence and love. One practices this way, she tells us, primarily by acknowledging one's nothingness and radical weakness and by humbly accepting the all-powerful grace of God offered in Christ. On May 13, 1883, Pentecost Sunday, Thérèse, through Mary's mediation, experienced in a dramatic way the workings of Christ's saving grace. In her nothingness and weakness, the Lord saved her, not because of her virtues or religious practices, but simply on account of His love.

In an article entitled "The Timeliness of Lisieux," Hans Urs von Balthasar explains the "matter" and "form" of heroic sanctity. The "form" is a specific mission given by God: the "matter" is the natural disposition of the individual placed freely at the ser-

---

[38] Ida F. Görres, *ibid.*

vice of the specific divine mission. Von Balthasar notes: "Simon, Son of John, thus lends himself as matter to the form of Peter."[39] Through the "Smile of the Virgin," Thérèse, broken and helpless, received her divine vocation: to reveal the merciful love of God through her own nothingness. The rock foundation of Thérèse's "Little Way of Spiritual Childhood" was set firmly in place that Pentecost Sunday.

Three Formative Graces

We turn now to three graces Thérèse received over the short span of five weeks: her First Holy Communion (May 8, 1884); her second Communion and her "vocation" to suffer (Ascension Thursday, May 22, 1884); and her Confirmation (June 14, 1884).

Thérèse's account of her First Holy Communion is among the most beautiful and revealing texts of the *Story of a Soul*:

> Ah, how sweet was that first kiss of Jesus! It was a kiss of *love*; I *felt* that I *was loved*, and I said: "I love You and I give myself to You forever!" There were no demands made, no struggles, no sacrifices; for a long time now Jesus and poor little Thérèse *looked at* and understood each other. That day it was no longer simply a *look*, it was a fusion; they were no longer two, Thérèse had vanished as a drop of water is lost in the immensity of the ocean. Jesus alone remained; He was the master, the King. Had not Thérèse asked Him to take away her *liberty*, for her *liberty* frightened her? She felt so feeble and fragile that she wanted to be united to the divine strength! Her joy was too great, too deep for her to contain, and tears of consolation soon flowed, to the great consternation of her companions. They asked one another "why was she crying, was there something bothering her?" — "no, it was because

---

[39] Hans Urs von Balthasar, "The Timeliness of Lisieux," *Carmelite Studies*, ed. John Sullivan, OCD (Washington, DC: ICS Publications, 1980), p. 103.

her mother was not there or her sister whom she loved so much, her sister the Carmelite."

They did not understand that all the joy of heaven having entered my heart, this exiled heart was unable to bear it without shedding tears. Oh! no, the absence of mama didn't cause me any sorrow on the day of my First Communion. Wasn't heaven itself in my soul, and hadn't mama taken her place there a long time ago? Thus, in receiving Jesus' visit, I received also mama's. She blessed me and rejoiced at my happiness. I was not crying because of Pauline's absence. I would have been happy to see her by my side, but for a long time I had accepted my sacrifice of her. On that day, joy alone filled my heart and I united myself to her, who gave herself irrevocably to Him who gave Himself so lovingly to me![40]

Thérèse reveals that by the time of her first Holy Communion, she had already attained a high degree of union with Christ. Some have attempted to conclude from this text that Thérèse had already attained mystical union with Christ by the age of eleven. It is difficult to deny an indication of deep union in this text. Thérèse notes, for instance, that up until her First Communion, she and Jesus had only looked at each other in love. Now there was a fusion of persons; as a result of the encounter, only one Person remained, Jesus. Thérèse had surrendered herself and her liberty totally to Him. Her human weakness, which she experienced in a profound way, was taken up into the divine strength. Furthermore, she reveals that in union with Christ, she had found all else besides, including her dear mother.

In her second Holy Communion, which took place on Ascension Thursday, May 22, 1884, Thérèse had another experience of profound union with Christ. The encounter with Him brought her again the gift of tears and an ineffable sweetness. She found

---

[40] *S.*, pp. 77-78.

great joy in repeating Galatians 2:20: "It is no longer I that live, it is Jesus Who lives in me."[41]

Thérèse's sister, Marie, was given to making pious prophecies as was the custom in those days. As she prepared Thérèse for her second Communion, Marie made one such prophecy. Her younger sister, she said, would not travel the road of suffering, she would rather be carried and supported by God as a little child. Thérèse recalled this "prophecy" as she described one of the greatest graces of her life, a grace she received on the day of her second Communion: "The day after my Communion, the words of Marie came to my mind. I felt born within my heart a *great desire* to suffer and at the same time the interior assurance that Jesus reserved a great number of crosses for me. I felt myself flooded with consolations so *great* that I looked upon them as one of the *greatest* graces in my life."[42]

Thérèse also described the effect of the reception of this grace: "Suffering became my attraction; it had charms about it which ravished me without my understanding them very well. Up until this time, I had suffered without *loving* suffering, but since this day I felt a real love for it. I also felt the desire of loving only God, of finding my joy only in Him."[43]

Thérèse also reveals that a quotation from *The Imitation of Christ* became her Communion prayer: "O Jesus, unspeakable sweetness, change all the consolation of this earth into bitterness for me."[44] It seems clear that the Holy Spirit had infused this prayer into Thérèse's soul. Her description leads directly to this conclusion: "This prayer fell from my lips without effort, without constraint; it seemed I repeated it not with my will but like a child who repeats the words a person he loves has inspired in him."[45]

---

[41] *S.,* p. 79.

[42] *S., ibid.*

[43] *S., ibid.*

[44] Thomas à Kempis, *The Imitation of Christ*, ed. Clare L. Fitzpatrick (New York: Catholic Book Publishing Co., 1985), pp. 170-171.

[45] *S.,* pp. 79-80.

André Combes, in his work entitled *St. Thérèse and Suffering*, delineates four distinct elements in this foundational grace: (1) Thérèse's heart was inflamed with an ardent desire to suffer; (2) she felt a deep conviction that God had decreed a number of crosses for her; (3) she experienced great consolation in this knowledge — perhaps the greatest consolation of her spiritual life. (The French text reads: "*Je me sentis inondée de consolations se grandes que je les regarde comme une des graces les plus grandes de ma vie.*"[46]); (4) the prayer she had made on the occasion of her First Holy Communion was answered: her weakness was taken up into Jesus' strength. The fragile child, afraid of suffering and reticent to a fault, was transformed in a supernatural encounter with the Lord of the Redemption.[47]

Father Combes notes:

> In truth, this thanksgiving can be compared to a watershed in Thérèse's spiritual life. It was a crucial date, a decisive event of mystical character.... Strength to meet suffering comes no longer from her own inner resources, nor from external helps but from His presence in her soul. Most amazing of all, it is at the very moment when she becomes sure of the coming of the Cross, that this young child, so sensitive to pain, far from being frightened, opens her heart to receive most abundant consolations.[48]

This grace was supernatural on three distinct counts: First, the grace is Eucharistic. Thérèse is transformed in her reception of Holy Communion. No longer does she fear or shrink from suffering, but rather she experiences a burning desire to share in the Cross of Jesus. Second, the grace was neither sought nor prepared

---

[46] *Histoire d'une Ame*, p. 94.

[47] See André Combes, *St. Thérèse and Suffering: The Spirituality of St. Thérèse in Its Essence*, trans. by Msgr. Philip E. Hallett (New York: P.J. Kennedy and Sons, 1951), pp. 39-59.

[48] André Combes, *op. cit.*, p. 42.

for by the cultivation of any preexisting natural dispositions, but rather was the result of an immediate, unexpected and gratuitous act of God. Third, the grace brought an abundance of light, desire and consolation.[49]

Recalling the "Smile of the Virgin," we begin to recognize a pattern in Thérèse's spiritual life. God offers her grace. Thérèse's response is simply to freely receive the gift. In her surrender to the grace, a profound transformation occurs at the core of her personality. We must note again the prayer that God seems to have infused into Thérèse's soul on the occasion and as the result of this grace: "O Jesus, unspeakable sweetness, change all the consolations of this earth into bitterness for me."

It is impossible to understand Thérèse's spiritual development, especially as it relates to the "trial of faith," apart from this solemn petition in which she had asked God to expunge from her life all natural and supernatural consolation. Through this prayer, Thérèse expressed a desire for union with Christ specifically in the mystery of His dereliction on the Cross. The consolation she chose was to have absolutely no consolation for the sake of Jesus. The "trial of faith" which she was to suffer during the last year and a half of her life can be understood as the answer, *par excellence*, to this prayer. In fact, every element of the "trial of faith" is present *in potentia* in Thérèse at the moment of her reception of this grace.

On June 14, 1884, three weeks after her encounter with Christ the Redeemer in the Eucharist, Thérèse received the Sacrament of Confirmation from Monsignor Flavien-Abel-Antoine Hugonin, the Bishop of the Diocese of Bayeaux. In her description of the reception of this Sacrament, Thérèse speaks not only of the "temporal mission" of the Holy Spirit to all of the baptized, but also of the confirmation of her personal mission to suffer: 'That day I received the strength to *suffer*, for soon afterwards the martyrdom of my soul was about to commence."[50]

---

[49] André Combes, *op. cit.*, pp. 42-43.
[50] *S.*, p. 80.

Thérèse believed that the coming of the Holy Spirit had sealed her own "vocation" of suffering. At this point she as yet did not understand the "why" or the "how" of suffering. She did, however, in some inchoate way, understand that her suffering would be so comprehensive that it might rightly be called a martyrdom or a holocaust.

In the 1880's there were indications that Catholics might suffer open persecution at the hands of the Third Republic. Thérèse understood, as noted above, the ideological tensions of her time. She also understood the possibility of an open persecution of the Church, not unlike the persecution endured during the French Revolution. However, Thérèse came to understand that her "martyrdom" would be a spiritual crucifixion. As we shall see, when she endured the "trial of faith," Thérèse discerned that sins against the Faith were being expiated through her intense physical, mental and spiritual suffering. She came to recognize in this a profound union with the crucified Christ.

At this juncture in our study one point must be boldly underscored. By the age of eleven, Thérèse of Lisieux understood — in an inchoate way — that she was one with Christ and would become even more perfectly united to Him through suffering. Herein we realize precisely why Thérèse came to love suffering passionately. She began to understand that she would find Jesus in the midst of her suffering. After all, this had been her experience in her first trial: Thérèse suffered, the Virgin looked lovingly upon her and she experienced the healing power of Christ.

The Christmas Grace of 1886

Over the next year and a half, Thérèse's suffering basically took two forms: scrupulosity and hypersensitivity. Explaining her scrupulosity, she says:

> I was assailed by the terrible sickness of scruples. For me to express what I suffered for *a year and a half* would be

impossible. All my most simple thoughts and actions became the cause of trouble for me, and I only had relief when I told Marie. This cost me dearly, for I believed I was obliged to tell her the absurd thoughts I had even about her. As soon as I laid down my burden, I experienced peace for an instant; but this peace passed away like a lightning-flash and soon my martyrdom began over again.[51]

Thérèse continued to be shy and awkward in her relationships outside of the family circle. Reflecting on her behavior, she observed: "I was really unbearable because of my extreme touchiness."[52]

In the *Story of a Soul*, Thérèse relates that on Christmas Eve, 1886, she received from God the grace of her "complete conversion."[53] The mature Thérèse frequently looked back to her thirteenth Christmas as one of the most significant moments in her spiritual development.

Thérèse obviously does not use the word "conversion" in its primary sense; that is, the turning away from grievous sin to surrender to the living God. Since the dawn of her use of reason, Thérèse had lived by faith. She had sought to obey God's commandments and, in fact, had always lived in intimate friendship with Him. Her personal awareness of the mystery of sanctifying grace, even as a child, was astonishing. Later, as a novice in Carmel, her spiritual father, the Jesuit, Fr. Almire Pichon, will assure her that she had never committed a grievous sin.[54] Consequently, there was no question of conversion from mortal sin to a life of faith and grace.

However, from the occasion of her mother's death up to this point in her life, Thérèse had experienced a certain paralysis in her

---

[51] *S.*, p. 84.
[52] *S.*, p. 97.
[53] *S.*, pp. 98-99.
[54] *S.*, p. 149.

affective life — a weakness and powerlessness that influenced her at various levels of her human and spiritual development. As noted earlier, her mother's death had caused Thérèse to be painfully shy, awkward in her relationship with those outside of her family circle, dependent upon her surrogate mothers and overwhelmingly sensitive and changeable. In this she experienced, as we have already observed, a temptation to cling in fear to her wounded emotional state and to refuse to walk the path of selfless love of others.

In the "Smile of the Virgin," Thérèse had indeed experienced liberation from self and personal inner healing through the grace of God. However, she admits that, in spite of the healing grace, she had remained a child who, in her own words "was unbearable because of [her] touchiness."[55] After the "miracle," which included the restoration of physical health and a certain degree of psychic strengthening, Thérèse continued to experience powerlessness at a newly discovered level of her personality. She wanted to change and, indeed, expended great effort on the project. However, the power was not in her. Thérèse came to understand that deeper healing was needed — a healing which was exclusively in the power of God. The Christmas grace of 1886 unleashed that power.

On the surface, the primary effect of the Christmas grace seems rather insignificant: Thérèse overcame her sensitivity in order to bring joy to her father's heart on Christmas Eve. For Thérèse, this "victory" was the direct result of God's grace and one of the most significant and formative events in her life. Ida Görres perceptively observes: "Here we see yet another instance of that essential trait of our Saint, the ability to receive and comprehend the divine in the banalities of everyday life."[56]

Let us examine the episode: Thérèse had attended Midnight Mass with M. Martin and Céline and had received Holy Communion. As was the custom in France in those days, gifts were ex-

---

[55] *S.*, p. 97.
[56] Ida F. Görres, *op. cit.*, p. 106.

changed on New Year's day. Small children, however, would leave their shoes near the household mantle. Father Christmas would come on Christmas Eve and fill the "magic shoes" with small gifts. The Martin household had observed this custom.

Note, however, that in 1886, Thérèse was thirteen years old and should have long before outgrown this custom. However, Céline had wanted to continue this practice, which had afforded the Martin girls such joy in their childhood days. Thérèse hints in her text that she had placed her shoes near the mantle in order to lighten her father's heart who had "always loved to see my happiness and listen to my cries of delight as I drew each surprise from the *magic shoes*."[57] Louis Martin was tired after Midnight Mass and with unusual sharpness, expressed irritation over Thérèse's childishness. He said: "Well, fortunately this will be the last year!"[58]

Ordinarily, such a reaction would have caused Thérèse to break down in tears — perhaps for hours. However, she had received a special grace from the "*strong and powerful* God"[59] — a grace that worked a miracle in her. Thérèse describes the miracle:

> I was going upstairs to remove my hat and Céline, knowing how sensitive I was and seeing the tears already glistening in my eyes, wanted to cry too, for she loved me very much and understood my grief. She said: "Oh, Thérèse, don't go downstairs, it would cause you too much grief to look at your slippers right now!" But Thérèse was no longer the same; Jesus had changed her heart! Forcing back my tears, I descended the stairs rapidly; controlling the poundings of my heart, I took my slippers and placed them in front of papa, and withdrew all the objects joyfully. I had the happy appearance of a Queen. Having regained his own cheerfulness, Papa was laughing: Céline believed it was all a *dream*! Fortunately,

---

[57] S., p. 98.
[58] S., p. 98.
[59] S., p. 98.

it was a sweet reality. Thérèse had discovered once again the strength of soul which she had lost at the age of four and a half and she was to preserve it forever.[60]

Thérèse never lost her conviction that this Christmas grace was of paramount importance in her spiritual life and mission: "It was December 25, 1886, that I received the grace of leaving my childhood; in a word, the grace of my complete conversion."[61]

What exactly was the grace of conversion that Thérèse received that Christmas night? André Combes, in his work entitled *St. Thérèse and Suffering*, observes that Thérèse had received four distinct graces which would give direction to every aspect of her spiritual life. Thérèse had asked for and struggled to obtain only one grace: the strength of will to face all trials. She observes: "The work I had been unable to do in ten years was done by Jesus in one instant, contenting Himself with my *good will* which was never lacking."[62]

Combes underscores the absolute sovereignty of Christ in the bestowal of this grace. The self-mastery which had been impossible for Thérèse to attain was given to her in a moment by God. In this fact, we recognize a close affinity existing between this grace and the prior grace of the "Smile of the Virgin." Experiencing her own powerlessness, Thérèse encountered for a second time, again in a dramatic manner, the omnipotence of Christ. Combes observes: "It is Christ who takes the initiative in the whole affair. His role is not merely unique; it is sovereign. Thérèse's conviction is that Jesus, in an instant, accomplished what all her efforts during the long years had been quite incapable of accomplishing."[63]

The primary grace received by Thérèse on Christmas Eve, 1886 was a regained possession of her soul and of all its faculties.

---

[60] *S.*, p. 98.
[61] *S.*, p. 98.
[62] *S.*, p. 98.
[63] André Combes, *op. cit.*, p. 54.

In her second Holy Communion, Thérèse had prayed for suffering. Until she received this Christmas grace, suffering continued to cause her to fall apart, at least interiorly.

In the grace of that Christmas night, Thérèse regained perfect control of herself. She began to welcome and love suffering for the sake of others. Simply stated, Thérèse received the ability to die to herself by not giving vent to her wounded affectivity. Christ's grace was the exclusive source of this self-control. Its motive was solely charity.

To some, Thérèse's first "victory" over herself might seem superficial and banal. For her, it had a profound significance. In this grace, Thérèse had encountered the person of Christ, Who empowered her to act in a supernatural manner. Here we are at the root and core of Thérèse's mystical life: in dying to self, Thérèse encounters Christ as living and loving others through her.

Father Combes indicates three other graces related to this primary grace: the virtue of constant self-forgetfulness; fraternal charity in winning souls for Christ; and a desire to work for the conversion of sinners.[64]

Thérèse writes: "I experienced a great desire to work for the conversion of sinners, a desire I hadn't felt so intensely before. I felt *charity* enter my soul and the need to forget myself and please others; since then I have been happy!"[65]

Several facts lead us to accept unreservedly Thérèse's "Christmas grace" as authentically supernatural in nature. Apart from control of her affectivity, Thérèse had not actively sought an increase of charity and apostolic zeal from God. These gifts were given in an instant by the direct, sovereign intervention of the grace of Christ. Furthermore, this grace created a permanent and significant transformation in Thérèse's interior life.

In his work *St. Thérèse and Suffering*, Combes notes that Thérèse's altruistic self-mastery was, in fact, not the grace, but to

---

[64] André Combes, *op. cit.*, pp. 56-57.
[65] S., p. 99.

be precise, the direct effect of the grace. He writes: "The scene at Les Buissonnets did not constitute the grace of Christmas, but rather, brought it into action."[66]

This gifted author points out that Thérèse had not only attended the Christmas Midnight Mass but also "had the happiness of receiving the strong and omnipotent God."[67] Combes observes:

> Surely, these epithets, "strong and omnipotent" are most significant. Why should Thérèse apply them to Our Lord in the Eucharist unless she wishes to emphasize that it was at the moment of His union with her that she received the privilege of sharing in quite a new way, in His strength and omnipotence. She is convinced that Jesus placed His weapons in her hand and it is in this communication of strength that she sees her Christmas grace. May we not suppose that it was precisely at the moment of Holy Communion, or during her Thanksgiving, that there took place that transformation by which Thérèse was "converted" finally and forever?[68]

Combes cogently argues that the grace of Thérèse's conversion was given in her reception of Holy Communion that Christmas Eve. The self-mastery demonstrated at Les Buissonnets later that night was simply the first manifestation of the transformation accomplished in her by grace.

It is worthwhile to recall here the "fusion" with Jesus that Thérèse experienced in her First Holy Communion and the desire for suffering which was the direct effect of her second Holy Communion. In this Christmas Communion another fusion was accomplished: Thérèse and Jesus became one in the desire to suffer for the salvation of souls.

---

[66] André Combes, *op. cit.*, p. 58.
[67] *S.*, p. 98.
[68] André Combes, *op. cit.*, p. 59.

Thérèse and the Mystery of Salvation

Two related incidents which followed upon this grace underscore the validity of our interpretation. Thérèse tells us that one Sunday, as she looked at a picture of Christ on the Cross, she was deeply moved by the Blood flowing from Jesus' hands. In her contemplation she realized a burning desire to directly cooperate with Christ in the application of the grace of redemption to souls — especially the souls of great sinners:

> I felt a great pang of sorrow when thinking this blood was falling to the ground without anyone hastening to gather it up. I was resolved to remain in spirit at the foot of the Cross and to receive the divine dew. I understood I was then to pour it out upon souls. The cry of Jesus on the Cross sounded continually in my heart: "*I thirst*" (John 19:28). These words ignited within me an unknown and very living fire. I wanted to give my beloved to drink and I felt myself consumed with the *thirst for souls*. As yet it was not the souls of priests that attracted me, but those of *great sinners*; I *burned* with the desire to snatch them from the eternal flames.[69]

Thérèse was soon to be given a "sign" of her apostolic fecundity in saving souls in union with Jesus crucified. Through prayer and penance, she was to give birth to her first child.

During the night of March 19, 1887, two women and a young girl were savagely murdered in Paris. The gruesome details of the crime were the talk of all of France. News of the murder reached the Martin household through the publication *La Croix*. Several days later police arrested a suspect in Marseilles: A 30-year-old man named Henri Pranzini. Charges mounted against him. The trial which opened in July became international news. Pranzini consistently protested his own innocence. On July 13, he was condemned to death.[70]

---

[69] S., p. 99.
[70] Guy Gaucher, *op. cit.*, pp. 66-68.

Upon hearing of the murder, Thérèse immediately adopted Pranzini's cause. Her goal was to save him from the fires of hell. She notes:

> Feeling that of myself I could do nothing, I offered to God all the infinite merits of Our Lord, the treasures of the Church and finally I begged Céline to have a Mass offered for my intentions.[71]

Thérèse was confident that through her prayers and acts of penance, united to the merits of Christ, God would grant Pranzini the grace of conversion. However, for her consolation, she asked God to give her a sign that this grace had indeed been welcomed by the condemned criminal.

August 31, 1887 was the date set for Pranzini's execution. The following morning, Thérèse, disregarding her father's desire that his daughters not read the newspapers, devoured the account of the criminal's last moments. In the shadow of the guillotine, Pranzini continued to plead his innocence. He even refused to confess his sins to the prison chaplain, Fr. Faure. However, at the last moment the murderer took the priest's crucifix and kissed the wounds of Christ twice.[72]

Describing the spiritual joy that Pranzini's conversion caused her, Thérèse writes:

> I had obtained the "sign" I requested and this sign was a perfect replica of the grace Jesus had given me when He attracted me to pray for sinners. Wasn't it before the *wounds of Jesus*, when seeing His divine *blood* flowing, that thirst for souls had entered my heart? I wished to give them this *immaculate blood* to drink, this blood which was to purify them from their stains, and the lips of my "*first child*" were pressed to the sacred wounds.[73]

---

[71] *S.*, p. 99.

[72] Thérèse wrote that Pranzini had kissed the wounds of the crucified three times. The *La Croix* article says twice. See Gaucher, *op. cit.*, p. 68.

[73] *S.*, p. 100.

In these two episodes — the first, an instance of contemplative illumination and the second, an instance of fecund contemplative love — the fourteen-year-old Thérèse came to understand both the Christian's power to share in the redemptive work of Christ as well as her own vocation to spiritual motherhood in Carmel:

> After this unique grace, my desire to save souls grew each day and I seem to hear Jesus say to me what he said to the Samaritan woman: *"Give me to drink"* (John 4:7). It was a true interchange of love: to souls I was giving the *blood of Jesus*, to Jesus I was offering these same souls refreshed by the *divine dew*. I slaked His thirst and the more I gave Him to *drink*, the more the thirst of my poor little soul increased, and it was this ardent thirst He was giving me as the most delightful drink of His love.[74]

Thérèse soon conceived the plan to enter Carmel on the first anniversary of the grace of her "conversion." In fact, it was her plan to enter the enclosure after Midnight Mass; at the very hour that she had been converted to the life of charity the year before.[75]

We pause at this point to isolate the dominant motif in Thérèse's spiritual life. This motif is clearly audible during her fourteenth year and will be further clarified and amplified during her remaining years, and in particular, in her "trial of faith." In her experience of her powerlessness, Thérèse encounters Christ in suffering; and, through her cooperation with grace, that suffering is transformed into an act of love for the salvation of others. For Thérèse, suffering becomes pure joy for two reasons: in her suffering she becomes one with the all-powerful Jesus and in union

---

[74] *S.*, pp. 100-101.

[75] "After all, I was going to be fourteen and a half and six months separated us from the beautiful *night of Christmas*, the day I was determined to enter, at the very hour I received my grace the year before." *S.*, p. 107.

with Him, reaches out to embrace those in need of God's merciful love.[76]

During the process which preceded Thérèse's beatification, Céline presented testimony regarding Thérèse's "conversion" and the resulting thirst she experienced for the salvation of souls:

> The change was permanent; never ever afterwards was she dominated by the dictates of her sensitiveness. Nor was the transformation limited to her self-possession; she blossomed forth and took an interest in practical expressions of zeal and charity. She longed for the salvation of souls and dedicated herself generously and fervently to the conversion of sinners.[77]

Also at this time, Thérèse and Céline became very close in the spiritual life. They spent hours together in prayer and spiritual conversation. Thérèse recognized later in life that God had given her great gifts of prayer at the age of fourteen. She notes:

> It appears we were receiving graces like those granted to the great saints. As *The Imitation of Christ* says, God communicates Himself at times in the midst of great splendor or "*gently veiled under shadows and figures*" (III, 43, 4). It was in this way He deigned to manifest Himself to our souls but how *light* and *transparent* the veil was which hid Jesus from our gaze! Doubt was impossible, faith and hope were unnecessary, and *Love* made us find on earth the one whom we were seeking. The practice of virtue became sweet and natural to us. At the end, it is true, my face betrayed the struggle, but little by little this vanished and renunciation was easy, even the first call of grace.[78]

---

[76] Cf. André Combes, *op. cit.*, pp. 39-59, for an excellent exposition of Thérèse's supernatural attraction for suffering.

[77] *P.*, pp. 115-116

[78] *S.*, p. 104. In this context, Fr. Combes' evaluation of Thérèse's spiritual growth is pertinent: "Even before she was twelve, the state of her soul was too complex to be classified under our everyday categories." André Combes, *op. cit.*, p. 46.

On the Road to Carmel

On May 29, 1887, in her fourteenth year, Thérèse confided her desire to enter Carmel to her father. Louis Martin accepted her decision and promised to help her obtain the necessary dispensations from the ecclesiastical authorities. Besides having the blessing of her father, Thérèse also had the support of the Superior of Carmel, Mother Marie de Gonzague. The monastic chapter had also decided to accept Thérèse, if the Bishop would give his permission.

For nearly an entire year, Thérèse faced one disappointment after another. The first to oppose her was her uncle, Isidore Guérin. Thérèse related his reaction to her plans: "He showed me great tenderness but did not grant me his permission to leave. He forbade me to speak about my vocation to him until I was seventeen. It was contrary to human prudence, he said, to have a child of fifteen enter Carmel.... He even said that for him to decide to allow me to leave would require a *miracle*."[79]

Isidore Guérin must have had his miracle, because within four days of his conversation with Thérèse, he gave his consent. No doubt, the letter of encouragement he had received from his niece, Sister Agnes of Jesus,[80] helped to change his mind.[81]

The clerical superior of the Carmel, Father Delatroëtte, however, was determined to prevent Thérèse's entrance. It would seem that he was often at odds with the temperamental superior of Carmel, Mother Marie de Gonzague, who was frequently given to extravagances. Perhaps the prudent priest saw Thérèse's acceptance by the Carmelites, at the age of fifteen, as another instance of the caprice of Mother Superior. He received Thérèse coldly and suggested that she live the life of Carmel at home for several years.

---

[79] S., p. 109.
[80] Thérèse's own sister, Pauline.
[81] Guy Gaucher, *op. cit.*, p. 71.

He added, however, that the final decision was in the hands of the Diocesan Bishop.[82]

Consequently, Louis Martin made an appointment with the Bishop. On October 31, 1887, Thérèse was interviewed by Bishop Hugonin. Although the meeting was cordial, the Bishop suggested that Thérèse remain at home for a few more years. Louis Martin intervened and offered his parental consent. The Bishop then decided to postpone his decision until he had an opportunity to speak with Fr. Delatroëtte. Louis Martin told the Bishop of his plans to participate in a pilgrimage to Rome with Thérèse and Céline to honor Leo XIII's jubilee. The Bishop said that he would mail his decision to Thérèse in Rome. Thérèse had already decided to seek a dispensation to enter Carmel directly from the Holy Father.

On November 20, 1887, the Martin family attended a papal audience. At the conclusion of the audience, each of the pilgrims was invited to greet the Holy Father personally. Thérèse, full of trepidation, approached Pope Leo XIII. Placing her hands on his knees, she asked for a favor: "Holy Father, in honor of your jubilee, permit me to enter Carmel at the age of fifteen." The Holy Father did not understand the request. He turned to one of the chaplains who happened to be Monsignor Révérony, the Vicar General of Thérèse's diocese. Amazed and embarrassed by her audacity, the priest said to the Pope: "This is *a child* who wants to enter Carmel at the age of fifteen, but the superiors are considering the matter at the moment." Leo XIII turned back to Thérèse and said: "Well, my child, do what the superiors tell you." Thérèse, still hoping to receive the dispensation from the Pope, persisted: "O, Holy Father, if you say 'yes', everyone will agree!!" Leo XIII answered her: "Go... go... *You will enter if God wills it!*" At that moment, Monsignor Révérony and two of the guards picked Thérèse up and returned her to her father.[83]

---

[82] Guy Gaucher, *op. cit.*, pp. 71-73.
[83] *S.*, pp. 134-135.

The heartbroken Thérèse described her feelings in the *Story of a Soul*: "In the bottom of my heart I felt a great peace since I had done everything in my power to answer what God was asking of me. This *peace*, however, was in the *depths* only; bitterness *filled* my soul, for Jesus was silent."[84] The Bishop's letter never reached Thérèse in Rome. She began her homeward journey knowing that she would not be able to enter Carmel at Christmas.

Why, it has been asked, was Thérèse so anxious to enter Carmel at the age of fifteen? An urgency is readily detectable in her persistence. One might also note a certain uncharacteristic brashness in her tactics. It would be wrong to see Thérèse's desire as the whim of a spoiled child. Rather, it is clear from her own testimony that she was determined to enter Carmel simply because she knew that Christ willed it. Consecrated already to a life of redemptive love through her Christmas grace, Thérèse was sure that Jesus was calling her to Carmel to share in His work. The intense interior suffering she experienced from Christmas 1886 until her entry into Carmel on April 9, 1888, was due to what she perceived as the frustration of the divine plan in her regard. It has been suggested that during this period Thérèse experienced a profound purification of both her intellect and will.

Imagining herself as a plaything, a ball of the Child Jesus, Thérèse felt herself at times put aside; at other times, pierced. Combes notes: "Although united, their wills still remained exterior, one to the other. The metaphor Thérèse employs suggests a complete distinction, a duality. On one side Jesus; on the other side this little ball. What He wills, she does not know. The toy is pierced and makes no resistance, but it does not understand the design of its owner."[85]

It must also be noted that during their pilgrimage to Italy, Thérèse and Céline had made a startling and disconcerting discovery: priests are weak and fragile men! Thérèse's parents and

---

[84] *S.*, pp. 135-136.
[85] André Combes, *op. cit.*, p. 77.

sisters had taught her to have a profound respect for the office of the priest.[86] Although a number of priests visited Les Buissonnets, rarely, if ever, were they invited to stay for dinner. Until the time of her pilgrimage, Thérèse had only dealt with priests in a formal, ministerial setting.

On the pilgrimage to Rome, which lasted longer than a month, Thérèse lived in the company of over 75 French priests. She conversed with them on the train, dined with them and stayed in the same hotels. She had the opportunity of seeing them at close range and of experiencing their weaknesses and foibles. It seems that a good amount of gossip during the pilgrimage was stimulated as a result of Céline's friendship with a young priest, Fr. Leconte.[87]

Thérèse's discovery helped her to understand her Carmelite vocation. She writes:

> I understood *my vocation* in *Italy*. I lived in the company of many *saintly priests* for a month and I learned that though their dignity raises them above the angels, they are nevertheless weak and fragile men. How beautiful is the vocation, O Mother, which has as its aim, the *preservation* of the *salt* destined for souls! This is Carmel's vocation since the sole purpose of our prayers and sacrifices is to be the *apostle* of the *apostles*. We are to pray for them while they are preaching to souls through their words and especially their example.[88]

Thérèse takes up this theme again in many letters to Céline. In one dated July 14, 1889, she writes: "O Céline, let us live for souls, let us be apostles, let us save especially the souls of priests; these souls should be more transparent than crystal... Alas, how

---

[86] *S.*, p. 40
[87] Guy Gaucher, *op. cit.*, pp. 76-77.
[88] *S.*, p. 122.

many bad priests, priests who are not holy enough... let us pray, let us suffer for them."[89] Again: "Céline, I feel that Jesus is asking *both of us* to *quench* His thirst by giving Him souls, the souls of *priests* especially."[90] Also: "Let us convert souls; this year we must form many priests who love Jesus and who *handle* Him with the same *tenderness* with which Mary *handled* Him in the cradle."[91]

On New Year's day of 1888, the day before her fifteenth birthday, Thérèse learned that Bishop Hugonin had granted permission for her to enter the Carmel. She also discovered that Mother Marie de Gonzague had decided that her entrance should be postponed until after Easter. This decision caused Thérèse to experience new anguish:

> I saw all my *bonds broken* as far as the world was concerned, but this time it was the holy Ark itself which refused entrance to the poor little dove. I really wanted to believe I must have appeared unreasonable in not accepting my three months' exile joyfully, but I also believe that without it appearing so, this trial was *very great* and made me *grow* very much in abandonment and the other virtues.[92]

Life In Carmel

Thérèse finally entered Carmel on April 9, 1888. She was to remain within the monastic enclosure for nine years and several months. The chronology of her life after her entry is easily outlined. Less than four months after her departure from home, Louis Martin suffered mental problems and physical paralysis; on January 10, 1889, after an exceptionally long delay, Thérèse received

---

[89] *Thérèse of Lisieux: General Correspondence*, Vol. I, trans. John Clarke, OCD (Washington, DC: ICS Publications, 1982), p. 578. (Henceforth cited as *G.C. I.*)

[90] *G.C. I*, pp. 587-588.

[91] *G.C. I*, p. 602.

[92] *S.*, p. 143.

the Carmelite habit and the name Thérèse of the Child Jesus; on September 8, 1890, in the midst of great aridity, Thérèse pronounced her vows as a Carmelite; in December of 1891, the Carmel was ravaged by an epidemic of influenza. Perhaps at that time, as a result of her strenuous work and exposure to the disease, Thérèse contracted tuberculosis, which would be the cause of her own death[93]; on February 20, 1893, Thérèse's sister, Pauline, Mother Agnes of Jesus, was elected prioress. She immediately named Thérèse "assistant mistress of novices."

During this time, Thérèse began to develop her ability for verse, painting and drama. On July 29, 1894, Louis Martin died. On September 14 of that same year, Céline entered Carmel. On June 9, 1895, Trinity Sunday, Thérèse was inspired during Mass to offer herself as a victim to the merciful love of God. On June 11, 1895, Thérèse and Céline formally made this offering. In the wake of her self-offering, Thérèse received the "mystical wound of love" and began to understand the scope of her vocation. On April 2 and 3, 1896, Thérèse experienced her first hemoptysis, and shortly thereafter, entered into her "trial of faith." After eighteen months of excruciating physical and spiritual agony, Thérèse expired on September 30, 1897.[94]

Following the rule established by St. Teresa of Jesus for the reformed Carmels, Thérèse's daily routine was without significant variation. She spent at least six or seven hours a day in formal prayer, which included Mass, the Divine Office, two hours of mental prayer and various devotional practices. The nuns took their meatless meals at ten in the morning and six o'clock in the evening. Each meal was followed by an hour of recreation in community. Five hours of manual labor rounded out the daily horarium. During this work period, the Sisters made hosts and religious articles, engaged in general housework, laundry and sewing.

---

[93] Ida F. Görres, *op. cit.*, p. 161.
[94] For a clear and concise chronology, see *S.*, pp. 279-285 and Ida F. Görres, *op. cit.*, pp. 161-162.

The nuns of Lisieux, faithful to St. Teresa's prescriptions, lived an austerely penitential life. Meat was taken only in the case of severe illness. The ordinary daily fare was sparse and, in the Lisieux Carmel, sometimes even unwholesome. The Sisters slept on thin mattresses of straw in tiny unheated cells. In fact, the only source of heat in the monastery was in the recreation room. The Sisters took the discipline at least once a week and practiced other personal forms of penance.[95]

The Lisieux Carmelite community, founded in 1833, was housed in a small and poor compound made up of a chapel, refectory, internal cloisters, including the nun's cells and a garden. Thérèse found twenty-six nuns in the Carmel. Their average age was forty-seven.

Most of the nuns had come from the country and had received little or no formal education. Reading between the lines of Thérèse's commentaries on community life, one has the distinct impression that a great amount of simple human formation had been left undone. Guy Gaucher describes the makeup of the Carmel: "In this community, rather poorly endowed with natural talents, the Prioress, the Martin sisters and two or three other nuns stood out. At a time when women finished their studies at fifteen, these few privileged ones seemed very "learned" to the group from the country, where extremely hard manual labor began at an early age."[96]

Mother Geneviève, venerated as a saint by Thérèse,[97] was one of the foundresses of the Lisieux community. The obituary notice that circulated among the various Carmelite monasteries discreetly alludes to the fact that Mother Geneviève had governed the Lisieux Carmel with "too great leniency."[98] Perhaps the tenderhearted Mother Geneviève had sought in her role as superior, to mitigate

---

[95] See Guy Gaucher, *op. cit.*, pp. 87-91.
[96] Guy Gaucher, *op. cit.*, p. 90.
[97] *S.*, p. 169.
[98] Ida F. Görres, *op. cit.*, pp. 195-197.

the rigors of Jansenism which had deeply influenced the attitudes and praxis of the Lisieux community.[99]

In any event, the community at the time of Thérèse's entry continued to experience the after-shock of the French Revolution. The nuns feared a new persecution of the Church and religious Orders at the hands of the Freemasons and other enemies of the Church. As a result of all of these forces, Mother Marie de Gonzague and Mother Agnes of Jesus, the two superiors under whom Thérèse lived out her religious life, experienced many difficulties in keeping the internal affairs of the community even moderately balanced.

A Life Offered to God for Priests

In the light of these factors, Thérèse's first reaction to Carmel is astonishing. She had anticipated many problems and expected profound suffering. She offered everything from the first day of her religious life for priests: "Yes, suffering opened wide its arms to me and I threw myself into them with love. I had declared at the feet of Jesus-Victim in the examination preceding my profession, what I came to Carmel for: 'I came to save souls and especially to pray for priests.'"[100]

One priest in particular became the focus of Thérèse's prayers and sacrifices during her years in Carmel: the notorious ex-Carmelite, Hyacinthe Loyson. Ordained a priest of the Society of St. Sulpice in 1851, Loyson left that community in 1859 to become a Dominican. Five months later he transferred to the Discalced Carmelites. Hyacinthe Loyson became famous as a preacher and was much in demand throughout France, especially in the Cathedral of Notre Dame de Paris and also in Rome. In 1869, capitalizing upon the internal agitation caused in the Church

---

[99] Ida F. Görres, *op. cit.*, pp. 234, 254 and 405.
[100] S., p. 149.

concerning the definition of Papal infallibility, he left the Church, contracted a civil marriage with an American widow in 1872, and returned to Paris in 1879 to establish a schismatic national church in France, known as *L'Église Catholique Gallicane.* Loyson traveled extensively throughout France in his efforts to establish a new national church. He also wrote exhaustively on this topic. In 1891, he made a tour of Normandy, the province where the town of Lisieux is located. His lectures were reported and heavily criticized in the religious press, even coming to the notice of Thérèse and Céline.

Those who joined Loyson were required to reject the definition of the doctrine of Papal infallibility. Several rallying points, such as the call for a married clergy and the election of bishops by priests and laity, as well as a demand for the vernacular in the liturgy, caused disturbance among the loyal French Catholic people.[101] Loyson himself was not greatly interested in the modernist heresy whose influence was just beginning to be felt in Catholic circles; rather, he propagated an undogmatic form of mysticism and rationalism which, in a sense, prepared the way for the hearty reception of Modernism properly so-called.

Thérèse set herself to pray and offer sacrifice for his return to communion with the Church. Up until her death, she kept Loyson's conversion uppermost in her daily life of prayer and penance. On August 19, 1897, she would offer up her last Holy Communion for him. She sought to engage Céline in a project that would absorb her energies for the remaining years of her life: "And if Jesus were not to desire it (Loyson's conversion), would He have placed in the heart of His poor little spouses a desire that He could not realize? No, it is certain that He desires more than we do to bring back this poor stray sheep to the fold... Let us not grow tired of prayer; confidence works miracles."[102]

---

[101] Guy Gaucher, *op. cit.*, pp. 115-116.

[102] *Thérèse of Lisieux: General Correspondence,* Vol. II, trans. John Clarke, OCD (Washington, DC, ICS Publications, 1988), pp. 728-729. (Henceforth cited as *G.C. II.*)

Thérèse offered her life in Carmel for all of the priests of the Catholic Church. She had a keen understanding of the relationship of the ministerial priesthood to Christ, the great high Priest and her Spouse, and to all of those redeemed in His precious Blood. On entering Carmel, she had committed herself to be an "apostle of apostles." Even after Thérèse had been given two priest brothers[103] to sanctify through her life of penance, her primary focus remained on Loyson, the priest who in her mind had turned his back on Jesus' redemptive work. In her eyes, Loyson's conversion was urgent not only because the work he had been ordained to do was being left undone, but also for the sake of all those whom Loyson was leading away from Christ into his own willful apostasy from the Church.

Two related reasons compel us to note the place Loyson took in Thérèse's life:

First of all, her spiritual relationship with the apostate priest reveals that she had understood in a profound manner an essential component of her religious institute; that is, the formation and sanctification of priests through a hidden life of contemplation and sacrifice; second, her "Oblation to the Merciful Love of God" and the subsequent "trial of faith" seemed to be directly related to the expiation of the apostasy that she came face to face with in the person of Loyson. With this "end" of her consecrated life in mind, we may well consider some of the specific sufferings Thérèse endured in Carmel.

A Life of Suffering for Others

At the canonical hearing which preceded Thérèse's beatification, Céline enumerated some of her sister's early trials in Carmel:

---

[103] On October 17, 1895, Mother Agnes chose Thérèse to be the spiritual sister to Father Maurice Bellière, a seminarian and future missionary to Africa. On May 30, 1896, Mother Marie de Gonzague assigned a second spiritual brother to Thérèse: Father Adolphe Roulland of the Foreign Mission Society in Paris.

Thérèse had suffered:

"1. An almost uninterrupted dryness in prayer.

  2. The indiscretion of some nuns, who took advantage of her heroic patience: seeing her so meek and uncomplaining they gave her leftovers to eat when they should have been building her up; several times she had nothing on her plate but some herring heads and other rubbish re-heated several times in a row;

  3. The unsatisfactory governing of the community by Mother Marie de Gonzague, whose unstable and eccentric temperament inflicted a lot of suffering on the nuns. Everything depended on her latest fancy; anything good never lasted for long and it was only by dint of diplomacy and tact that stability could be achieved even for a few weeks."[104]

Thérèse's first five years in Carmel were, in a sense, her "hidden years." She devoted only twelve pages of the *Story of a Soul* to this period. Besides the unforgettable description of her reception of the habit and religious profession and the agony inflicted on her and her blood sisters by the illness of her father, Thérèse wrote little of the state of her soul during these years. It was precisely this lack of information which prompted Pauline to seek permission for Thérèse to write the final section of the *Story of a Soul*.

Why had she said so little concerning her religious life? Perhaps she had been reluctant to disclose the full extent of the workings of divine grace in her soul. Or perhaps she had been motivated by prudence; for to say too much would have revealed the sad disarray of the community. In any case, Thérèse did admit that these first years in Carmel had been filled with intense suffering:

> Jesus made me understand that it was through suffering that He wanted to give me souls, and my attraction for suffering grew in proportion to its increase. This was my

---

[104] *P.*, p. 119.

way for five years; exteriorly nothing revealed my suffering which was all the more painful since I alone was aware of it. Ah! What a surprise we shall have at the end of the world when we shall read the story of souls! There will be those who will be surprised when they see the way through which my soul was guided![105]

Here and elsewhere in Thérèse's writings, she indicates a suffering far deeper than that inflicted by her personal circumstances. This becomes painfully obvious as she endured the "trial of faith." Thérèse, by her own admission, always told the truth and sought to live in it.[106]

Thérèse was not prone to exaggerations in any form. She was given, rather, to understatement. These facts lead us to question whether Thérèse, from her early adolescence until her death, might not have experienced an infused share in Christ's suffering for the sake of souls. She frequently states that people will be astonished at the sufferings she had endured when everything is revealed on the Last Day. We shall return to this point later in our study.

During this period of the terrible mental and physical sufferings of her father, Thérèse discovered in Isaiah 53 (the Song o the Suffering Servant of Yahweh), the theological source of her devotion to the Holy Face of Jesus. She notes: "The little flower transplanted to Mount Carmel was to expand under the shadow of the Cross. The tears and blood of Jesus were to be her dew and her Sun was His adorable Face veiled with tears."[107]

During this period of Thérèse's life, her understanding of abandonment to divine providence was perfected. She came to realize in an ever deeper way that every trial accepted as God's will offered her the opportunity of showing her love for Him. Consequently, she was able to say: "How merciful is the way God has

---

[105] *S.*, p. 149.

[106] See Hans Urs von Balthasar, *St. Thérèse of Lisieux: The Story of a Mission*, pp. 3-12, for a discussion of Thérèse's relentless quest for truth in all of the circumstances of her life.

[107] *S.*, pp. 151-152.

guided me. *Never* has He given me the desire for anything which He has not given me, and even His bitter chalice seemed delightful to me."[108]

Thérèse was consistent in her exposition of God's working in her life: every suffering offered her an opportunity to encounter Jesus in the fullness of His strength and to offer herself with Him for the salvation of sinners, especially for priests.

Victim of God's Merciful Love

On June 9, 1895, Trinity Sunday, during the seventh year of her religious life, Thérèse was inspired to offer herself as a victim to the merciful love of God. This Oblatin, which she made with Céline on June 11, 1895, held a paramount place in Thérèse's spiritual life. She understood this act as the culmination of her spiritual life and the existential perfection of her religious vocation.

It is important to look carefully at the various components of Thérèse's "Act of Oblation to the Merciful Love of God." It provides invaluable insight into Thérèse's spiritual life.[109] At the beginning of the Act, Thérèse states her intention:

> O my God! Most Blessed Trinity, I desire to *love* You and make You *loved*, to work for the glory of holy Church by saving souls on earth and liberating those suffering in purgatory. I desire to accomplish Your will perfectly and to reach the degree of glory You have prepared for me in Your Kingdom. In a word I desire to be a saint, but I feel my helplessness and I beg You, O my God, to be Yourself my *Sanctity.*[110]

---

[108] *S.,* p. 152.

[109] The complete text of Thérèse's "Act of Oblation" which we are quoting, is found in the Appendix of *S.,* pp. 276-277. For a theological study of the Oblation, see Fr. Camillus, OCD, "The Act of Oblation to Merciful Love," *Spiritual Life,* Vol. XII, No. 2, Summer 1966.

[110] *S.,* p. 276.

Thérèse affirms in the prayer that her intention in making and living this Oblatin is not to gain merit for herself, but rather to give God pleasure through her love for Him and for souls: "After earth's Exile, I hope to go and enjoy You in the Fatherland, but I do not wish to lay up treasures for heaven. I want to work for Your *Love alone* with the purpose of pleasing You, consoling Your Sacred Heart and saving souls who will love You eternally."[111]

Thérèse also asks God to allow her every act to be an expression of perfectly selfless love: "In order to live in one single act of perfect love, I OFFER MYSELF AS A VICTIM OF HOLOCAUST TO YOUR MERCIFUL LOVE, asking You to consume me incessantly, allowing the waves of *infinite tenderness* shut up within You to overflow into my soul, so that thus I may become a *martyr* of Your *love*, O my God."[112]

In the light of the doctrine of St. John of the Cross, Thérèse asked to "die of love." St. John of the Cross taught that only those who attain to the transforming union in this life actually die of love.[113] It is impossible to believe that Thérèse was not aware of this.[114] In asking to "die of love" Thérèse reveals that she has attained this high degree of union with God or at least expected, through grace, to enter the state of spiritual marriage through her Oblation: "May this martyrdom, after having prepared me to appear before you, finally cause me to die and may my soul take its flight without any delay into the eternal embrace of *Your Merciful Love*."[115]

---

[111] *S.*, p. 277.

[112] *S., ibid.*

[113] See St. John of the Cross, *The Living Flame of Love*, in *The Collected Works of St. John of the Cross*, trans. Kieran Kavanaugh, OCD, and Otilio Rodriguez, OCD (Washington, DC: ICS Publications, 1991), pp. 652-657. (Henceforth cited as *Living Flame of Love*.)

[114] See *S.*, p. 179: "...how many lights have I not drawn from the Works of our holy Father, St. John of the Cross! At the ages of seventeen and eighteen I had no other spiritual nourishment..."

[115] *S.*, p. 277.

"My Vocation Will Be Love"

After her Oblation to Merciful Love, Thérèse lived those experiences which are related in the latter chapters of the *Story of a Soul.* Love became her one consistent theme. It would seem that she had found perfect inner tranquility in her abandonment to the will of God. One meets in these chapters a woman mature beyond her twenty-three years. The degree of perfection she had achieved is evident.

During this period of her life, Thérèse continued to work with the novices. Although she was not officially the novice mistress, she had the task of training the novices in the Carmelite way of life and directing their spiritual formation. In this difficult position, Thérèse did not trust her own talents and insights. Rather, she abandoned herself into the hands of God. She acknowledged that the work and the results were not her own. In the following passage from the *Story of a Soul,* one witnesses Thérèse's docility to the operation of the Holy Spirit and the degree of spiritual union with Christ she had already attained:

> When I was given the office of entering into the sanctuary of souls, I saw immediately that the task was beyond my strength. I threw myself into the arms of God as a little child and, hiding my face in His hair, I said: "Lord, I am too little to nourish Your children; if You wish to give through me what is suitable for each, fill my little hand and without leaving Your arms or turning my head, I shall give your treasures to the soul who will come and ask for nourishment."[116]

After offering herself to the merciful love of God, Thérèse's desire to work for the salvation of souls was intensified. In fact, she seems to have been set on fire with apostolic zeal. Together with her longing to save sinners, she experienced even more than

---

[116] S., pp. 237-238.

before the desire to pray and suffer for the sanctification of priests and seminarians. As these longings intensified, Thérèse was forced to grapple with them intellectually and integrate them into her contemplative vocation. Thérèse knew that her zeal for the work of the Church was inspired by God. She observes in her writing that God frequently made His will known to her through her desires. In other words, Thérèse was convinced that her desires were revelatory of God's Will. Here we discover another indication of the profound degree of union Thérèse had attained even before her "Oblation to Merciful Love."

While always seeking to animate the Church's pastoral ministry, Thérèse never doubted the value of her contemplative vocation in Carmel. She knew that she was exactly where God desired her to be. Her query was: How does a contemplative nun fulfill the holy desires within her heart as she lives within the monastic enclosure? Thérèse gave voice to her infinite desires to save souls in manuscript "B" of the *Story of a Soul*, written in September, 1896.

> To be your *Spouse*, to be a *Carmelite*, and by my union with you to be the *Mother* of souls, should not this suffice me? And yet it is not so. No doubt these three privileges sum up my true *vocation: Carmelite, Spouse Mother* And yet I feel within me other *vocations*. I feel the *vocation* of THE WARRIOR, THE PRIEST THE APOSTLE, THE DOCTOR, THE MARTYR. Finally, I feel the need and the desire of carrying out the most heroic deeds for *you, O Jesus*. I feel within my soul the courage of the *crusader*, the *papal guard*, and I would want to die on the field of battle in defense of the Church.[117]

In the midst of this struggle to find her exact place in the life of the Church, Thérèse received a great influx of light. Through St. Paul's hymn to charity in 1 Corithians 13, she came to the

---

[117] *S.*, p. 192.

conclusion that the practice of her "Little Way of Spiritual Child-hood," was her specific contribution to the mission of the Church in the world. Here she reflected the mystical theology of St. John of the Cross, who had taught that a simple act of pure contempla-tive love of God, made by a Christian in the transforming union, is more valuable and fruitful than "active" work for souls. The Mystical Doctor notes in his *Spiritual Canticle*:

> It should be noted that until the soul reaches this state of union of love, she should practice love in both the active and contemplative life. Yet once she arrives, she should not become involved in other works and exterior exercises that might be of the slightest hindrance to the attentive-ness of love toward God, even though the work be of great service to God. For a little of this pure love is more pre-cious to God and the soul and more beneficial to the Church, even though it seems one is doing nothing, than all these other works put together.[118]

Thérèse personally affirmed this truth in *Story of a Soul*. She acknowledges that through her contemplative love of God, she will be able to save souls and animate the Church's priests in their sav-ing works. Here again Thérèse tells us, by implication, that she is enjoying a high degree of mystical union with God:

> I finally had rest. Considering the mystical body of the Church, I had not recognized myself in any of the mem-bers described by St. Paul or rather I desired to see myself in them *all*. *Charity* gave me the key to my *vocation*. I understood that if the Church had a body composed of different members, the most necessary and most noble of all could not be lacking and so I understood that the Church *had a heart and that this heart* was BURNING

---

[118] St. John of the Cross, *The Spiritual Canticle*, in *The Collected Works of St. John of the Cross*, trans. Kieran Kavanaugh, OCD, and Otilio Rodriguez, OCD (Washing-ton, DC: ICS Publications, 1991), p. 587. (Henceforth cited as *Spiritual Canticle*.)

WITH LOVE. *I understood it was love alone* that made the Church's members act, that if *love* ever became extinct, apostles would not preach the Gospel and martyrs would not shed their blood. I understood that LOVE COMPRISED ALL VOCATIONS, THAT LOVE WAS EVERYTHING, THAT IT EMBRACED ALL TIMES AND PLACES.... IN A WORD THAT IT WAS ETERNAL.

Then, in the excess of my delirious joy, I cried out, O Jesus, my love, my *vocation* at last I have found it, MY VOCATION IT IS LOVE!

Yes, I have found my place in the Church and it is You, O my God who have given me this place; in the heart of the Church, my mother, I shall be *Love*. Thus, I shall be everything and thus my dream will be realized.[119]

In reading these glowing words, it is important to remember that earlier this year, after Thérèse had observed all of the austerities of Lent, she suffered her first hemoptysis in the early hours of Good Friday. Seeing the blood on her pillow in the morning, Thérèse observed: "I was interiorly persuaded that Jesus, on the anniversary of His death, wanted to have me hear His first call. *It was like a sweet and distant murmur which announced the Bridegroom's arrival.*"[120]

Thérèse accepted her impending death with deep resignation and without fear. Her dominant sentiment was joy in the prospect of soon beholding her Beloved face to face in heaven. However, Thérèse's initial response of elation was soon marred. Engulfed in profound inner darkness, the twenty-four-year-old woman began to doubt the reality of eternal life. The prayer she had made ten years before was finally answered definitively: "O Jesus, unspeakable sweetness, change all the consolations of this earth into bitterness for me."[121] The point that must be stressed is

---

[119] *S.*, p. 194.
[120] *S.*, p. 211.
[121] *S.*, p. 79.

this: Thérèse discovered her vocation "to be love at the heart of the Church" in the midst of her harrowing "trial of faith."

The Trial of Faith

Shortly after her first hemoptysis and the initial joy she had experienced over the prospect of being with Christ in heaven, Thérèse entered the dark tunnel of her "trial of faith." She began to doubt the existence of heaven, which had always been the main source of her joy and hope. She described her trial graphically in manuscript "C" of the *Story of a Soul*:

> Then suddenly the fog which surrounds me becomes more dense; it penetrates my soul and envelopes it in such a way that it is impossible to discover within it the sweet image of my Fatherland; everything has disappeared! When I want to rest my heart, fatigued by the darkness which surrounds it by the memory of the luminous country after which I aspire, my torment redoubles; it seems to me that the darkness, borrowing the voice of sinners, says mockingly to me: "You are dreaming about the light, about a fatherland embalmed in the sweetest perfumes; you are dreaming about the *eternal possession* of the Creator of all these marvels; you believe that one day you will walk out of this fog which surrounds you! Advance, advance; rejoice in death which will give you not what you hope for but a night still more profound, the night of nothingness."[122]

As the tuberculosis slowly suffocated Thérèse, these doubts tortured her spiritually. It should be recalled that Thérèse's trial lasted throughout the entire course of her terminal illness. During these months, her blood sisters in Carmel carefully recorded

---

[122] S., p. 213.

her every word. These texts are published under the heading, *Her Last Conversations.*

Reading through these texts, one is hard pressed to distinguish between Thérèse's descriptions of physical and spiritual suffering. It would seem that her final trial was a complicated and harrowing combination of physical and spiritual anguish. During the final stages of her pulmonary tuberculosis, Thérèse received little medical attention. She endured her physical agony patiently and with profound resignation. In the midst of this suffering, she found little spiritual consolation. On the day of her death, Thérèse exclaimed: "Never would I have believed it was possible to suffer so much. Never, never! I cannot explain this except by the ardent desires I have had to save souls."[123]

In order to understand the nature of Thérèse's "trial of faith," a few observations are in order. First of all, elements of the trial eluded Thérèse herself. As a result, she could neither fully comprehend the trial's significance nor adequately explain it to others. In spite of the constant distress it caused her, she continued to experience a deep inner peace. She realized that she could still give God pleasure in the humble acceptance of this darkness. She remarked to Mother Agnes: "If I didn't have this spiritual trial, that is impossible to understand, I really believe I would die of joy at the thought of leaving this earth."[124] It would seem that Thérèse was at a loss, at least initially, to integrate the trial into the pattern of spiritual development that the Carmelite masters had taught her. One thing is certain: Thérèse did not interpret the trial in terms of passive purgation.

In the midst of her trial, Thérèse doubted neither the existence of God nor Christ's love for her. Also, throughout the trial, she maintained a vivid sense of Mary's presence and personal love for her. The focus of the trial was the existence of life *for her* beyond the grave. On July 3, 1897, Mother Agnes of Jesus asked

---

[123] *L.C.*, p. 205.
[124] *L.C.*, p. 48.

her: "How is it that you want to die with your trial against faith that doesn't come to an end?" Thérèse answered: "Ah! But I really believe in the 'Thief' (cf. Mt. 24:43). It is upon heaven that everything bears. How strange and incomprehensible it is."[125]

Throughout her trial, Thérèse clung tenaciously to the faith in which she had been so carefully instructed as a child. Echoing the sentiments of her spiritual mother, St. Teresa of Jesus, Thérèse remarked:

> Ah! May Jesus pardon me if I have caused Him any pain, but He knows very well that while I don't have *the joy of faith*, I am trying to carry out its works at least. I believe I have made more acts of faith in this past year than all through my whole life. At each new occasion of combat, when my enemy provokes me, I conduct myself bravely. Knowing it is cowardly to enter into a duel, I turn my back on my adversary without deigning to look him in the face; but I run toward my Jesus. I tell Him I am ready to shed my blood to the last drop to profess my faith in the existence of *heaven*.[126]

The Articles of Faith stated in a simple catechetical format became Thérèse's anchor. Following the advice given her by the Praemonstratensian Father, Godefroy Madelaine, Thérèse carried the Creed on her person and placed her hand on it whenever tempted to doubt the Faith. She even went further. She wrote out the Creed in her own blood and carried it in the book of the Gospels which never left her person. To the day of her death, Thérèse was able to distinguish her own emotions and doubts from the Faith she continued to firmly profess in her intellect and will. Her solid faith was the source of the lucidity and tranquility that reigned in the depths of her soul.

In the midst of her "trial of faith," Thérèse's light continued to be the very Faith she doubted. Here we discover an appar-

---

[125] *L.C.*, p. 72.
[126] *S.*, pp. 213-214.

ent paradox. Thérèse, doubting the existence of heaven, abandoned herself to the Faith professed by the Church and therein found strength and peace. Four days before her death, Mother Agnes of Jesus asked her if she had any intuition concerning the exact day of her death. Thérèse responded: "Ah! Mother, intuitions! If you only knew what poverty I'm in! I know nothing except what you know; I understand nothing except through what I see and feel. But my soul, in spite of this darkness, is in an astonishing peace."[127]

Throughout her trial, Thérèse saw herself mysteriously identified with those among her contemporaries who had lost the Catholic faith. It would seem that Thérèse, while never wavering in her profession of the Faith, was permitted to experience the darkness of unbelief that afflicts the modern world. She came to understand interiorly that her trial gave her an opportunity to offer herself for the salvation of all faithless souls. We must recall again that Thérèse had solemnly committed herself to work for priests and in particular, for Hyacinthe Loyson, the priest who had lost his faith. In the *Story of a Soul*, Thérèse identifies herself with apostates and others who had sinned against the Faith:

Your child, however, O Lord, has understood Your divine light and she begs pardon for her brothers. She is resigned to eat the bread of sorrow as long as You desire it; she does not wish to rise up from this table filled with bitterness at which poor sinners are eating until the day set by You. Can she not say in her name and in the name of her brothers, *"Have pity on us O Lord for we are poor sinners"* (Lk 18-13). O Lord, send us away justified. May all those who were not enlightened by the bright flame of faith one day see it shine. O Jesus! If it is needful that the table soiled by them be purified by a soul who loves You, then I desire to eat this bread of trial at this table until it pleases You to bring me into Your bright kingdom. The only grace I ask of You is that I never offend You![128]

---

[127] *L.C.*, p. 199.
[128] *S.*, p. 212.

During the last difficult months of her life, Thérèse realized that after her death, her writings would do great good for souls. She placed the *Story of a Soul* in the hands of Mother Agnes, urging her not to talk openly about the work lest Satan find some way of destroying it. She recognized that many people would find consolation and direction in the story of her relationship with God. She considered the *Story of a Soul* "the work of God, a very important work."[129]

As death approached, Thérèse also revealed to her sisters that her mission was just about to begin. The selfless love that God had formed in her was about to overflow for the good of the Church. *Her Last Conversations* are full of references to the good she would do for souls after her death. For instance, on July 17, 1897, she said:

> I feel that I am about to enter into my rest. But I feel especially that my mission is about to begin, my mission of making God loved as I love Him, of giving my little way to souls. If God answers my desires, my heaven will be spent on earth until the end of the world. Yes, I want to spend my heaven in doing good on earth... I can't make heaven a feast of rejoicing; I can't rest as long as there are souls to be saved. But when the angel will have said: "Time is no more!" then I will take my rest! I'll be able to rejoice because the number of the elect will be complete and because all will have entered into joy and repose. My heart beats with joy at this thought.[130]

Thérèse interpreted her "trial of faith" as directly related to her Oblation of herself to the merciful love of God. On the day of her death, in terrible agony she cried out:

> O Mother, I assure you the chalice is filled to the brim! O Mother, present me quickly to the Blessed Virgin; I'm a

---

[129] *L.C.*, p. 126.
[130] *L.C.*, p. 102.

baby who can't stand anymore! Prepare me for death! I am not sorry for delivering myself up to love. Oh! no, I'm not sorry. On the contrary! Never would I have believed it was possible to suffer so much! I can't explain it except by the ardent desire I have had to save souls.[131]

With great reserve, Thérèse recognized in her sufferings both physical and spiritual, a reflection of Our Lord's suffering on the Cross. Like Him, she was dying of love: "Our Lord died on the Cross in agony and yet this is the most beautiful death of love. To die of love is not to die in transports. I tell you frankly, it seems to me that this is what I am experiencing."[132]

A few hours before her death, Thérèse's sisters did not fail to recognize this mysterious and profound identification with Christ in His Passion. Céline writes:

On the day of her death, in the afternoon, Mother Agnes of Jesus and I were with her and our dear little sister called us over to help her. She was suffering extremely in all her members and, placing one arm on Mother Agnes' shoulder and the other on mine, she remained thus, her arms in the form of a cross. At that very moment, three o'clock sounded and the thought of Jesus on the Cross came to our mind; was not our poor little martyr a living image of Him?[133]

Thérèse's "trial of faith" ended just a few moments before her death. Lifting herself up in order to see the crucifix, she said: "Oh! I love Him! My God... I love You."[134] She fell back and seemed, for a few moments before her death, to enter into an ecstatic state. Pauline, witnessing the death of her sister, offered the following description:

---

[131] *L.C.*, p. 205.
[132] *L.C.*, p. 73.
[133] *L.C.*, p. 229.
[134] *L.C.*, p. 206.

Her face had regained the lily-white complexion it always had in full health; her eyes were fixed above, brilliant with peace and joy. She made certain beautiful movements with her head as though someone had divinely wounded her with an arrow of love, then had withdrawn the arrow to wound her again. This ecstasy lasted about the space of a Credo and then she gave her last breath.[135]

---

[135] *L.C.*, pp. 206-207.

Chapter II

THÉRÈSE'S WRITINGS

In this chapter, within the context of an overview of Thérèse's writings,[1] I shall summarize Thérèse's own testimony regarding the "trial of faith." This will be done in the form of a general consideration of each of Thérèse's writings with a view to a particular investigation of the role the "trial of faith" plays in that work.

The *Story of a Soul* is Thérèse's principal work and the main source of our knowledge of her. It must be granted that it is impossible to understand Thérèse or any other person apart from the events and details of his or her life. Thérèse would herself be the first to defend the crucial significance of each event as a revelation of the Father's loving Providnce in her life.

The *Story of a Soul* is not an autobiography in a formal sense although many continue to label it as such. The saint's work is more properly a *confessio* in the genre of St. Augustine's monumental *Confessions*, St. Teresa of Jesus' *Life* and the Venerable John Henry Newman's *Apologia Pro Vita Sua*. In the *Story of a Soul* Thérèse

---

[1] As noted in the Introduction, the centenary of Thérèse's birth (1973) was the occasion of the production of critical editions of all of her writings. *Derniers Entretiens* (*Her Last Conversations*, 1971); *Histoire d'une Ame* (*Story of a Soul*, 1972); *Correspondance Générale* (*General Correspondence*) Vol. I (1972); Vol. II (1973); *Poésies* (*Poems*, 1975); *Récréations Pieuses* (*Plays*, 1985) and *Prières* (*Prayers*, 1988).

The late Discalced Carmelite Friar, John Clarke, brought most of these critical editions of Thérèse's writings into English. They have each been published, with the exceptions of the religious drama and prayers, by the Institute of Carmelite Studies in Washington, DC. These works are quoted throughout this text.

allows the reader to enter the sanctuary of her soul so that she might share her experience of God. In writing with the sole intent of doxology, Thérèse seeks to draw the reader into her confession of God's merciful love.

One aspect of Thérèse's genius[2] is her ability to explain the intimate working of God's grace in her soul by utilizing the simplest imagery and language. Holding herself up as a model, Thérèse brilliantly manifests the beauty of the conjunction of human freedom and divine grace as each reality is revealed in her life.

In his work *Thérèse of Lisieux: The Story of a Mission*, Hans Urs von Balthasar observes that Thérèse developed the habit of keen self-observation, as well as a marked tendency to hold her own behavior up to others as a model for imitation.[3]

These tendencies in Thérèse are themselves responses to grace. Thérèse's mission is, at least in part, to possess a profound understanding of the working of grace in her soul and consequently to be an exemplar of holiness for others. She had lived the evangelical life in such a perfectly self-reflective manner in order to become a pattern of her specific "Way" t union with God for others. Her gift is, in part, to penetrate and utilize her own response to grace as a pattern of holiness to be shared. Need it be said that Thérèse modeled her "Little Way" in obedience to God's Will without the slightest trace of pride or vainglory?

Because of her transparent exemplarity, it is tempting to make assertions regarding the stages of Thérèse's spiritual development. For instance, one might see in the Christmas grace of 1886, Thérèse's transition from the purgative to the illuminative way, or in the mystical event which followed upon her "Oblation to Merciful Love," a transition from the illuminative to the unitive way. I suspect that it is more than hazardous to engage in such precise pinpointing in reference to her spiritual development. In spite of her transparency, Thérèse, in a certain sense, shatters the

---

[2] See Jean Guitton, *op. cit.*, pp. 13-16.
[3] Hans Urs von Balthasar, *op. cit.*, p. 18.

mold of preconceived categories of spiritual development. She consistently uses the terms and phraseology of classical asceticism and mysticism in a singularly unique and creative way, as we shall see.

It has unfortunately become commonplace to say that Thérèse of Lisieux experienced few mystical graces during her life. Through careful analysis of her writings, however, marvelous graces of mystical union are easily discernible. Thérèse, for instance, admitted that from her third year of life she was never conscious of having denied God any request. The accounts of her First Communion and Confirmation are filled with allusions to mystical union with Jesus. One also readily recalls her admission of practicing a deep level of mental prayer at a very tender age. Throughout her entire religious life, and in particular during her "trial of faith," Thérèse frequently indicated that she was the recipient of the grace of mystical marriage. In several ways she revealed that in spite of her trial, she was experiencing the mystical marriage with Christ and, following the doctrine of St. John of the Cross, she expected to die of love.

It is also worth noting that many have attempted to see in the sufferings of Thérèse, which were indeed intense and varied, instances of spiritual purgation. As we have already observed, Thérèse embraced suffering as her special calling from God and, by her own admission, she was passionately in love with suffering for the sake of Christ and His Church. Thérèse reveals that in her short life she had never committed one serious offense against Almighty God. Hence, her soul needed very little purgation. Thérèse consistently explains her suffering as a privileged means of attaining union with Christ. In her "system" of spirituality, suffering attains a new and ingenious signification: a signification which is derived directly from Sacred Scripture.

Suffice it to say that at this point in our study it is necessary, when analyzing Thérèse's spiritual development, to permit the Saint to lead the way and not to impose upon her "story" preconceived categories of spiritual growth. As Father André Combes notes:

If we are dealing with the history of a soul, we must not proceed by deductions, we must look at the facts. If a historian is prudent, he will check his imagination and refrain from constructing his narrations according to probabilities. If this is so, as regards to men in general, how much more will it be when he is dealing with the saints in whom God Himself works supernaturally and for ends known to Himself alone.[4]

Having assimilated and internalized the spiritual doctrine of St. Teresa of Jesus and St. John of the Cross as a young religious, Thérèse interpreted her own spiritual experience within the framework of the thought of the Spanish mystics. She does this with great discretion, seemingly attempting to hide her formidable and comprehensive understanding of their teaching.

As we progress, we shall see that Thérèse is a Discalced Carmelite to the very marrow of her bones. Besides having a precocious grasp of the subtleties of the thought of the Reformers of Carmel, she ingeniously renders this knowledge accessible to "little souls" who would blanch with fright at the prospect of studying the volumes of St. Teresa and St. John. Thérèse communicates her wisdom primarily by living the spirituality of Carmel in a faithful and remarkably creative way. The *Story of a Soul* is the medium which puts the reader in touch with both Thérèse, the exemplar of the "Little Way of Spiritual Childhood," and, ultimately, with the Father in heaven Who is rich in mercy. It might be said, in fact, that the aim of all of Thérèse's writings is to reveal her intimate relationship with the heavenly Father for the edification and instruction of others.

Here we find the entry point into her life that Thérèse herself had devised. We shall allow her to reveal to us the operations of God's grace in her soul. We will also allow her to interpret this operation within the categories of her spiritual mother and father,

---

[4] André Combes, *The Spirituality of St. Thérèse*, p. 68.

St. Teresa of Jesus and St. John of the Cross. We shall seek in our survey of all of Thérèse's writings, everything that relates directly to her "trial of faith," the theme of this book.

The Story of a Soul

The working of Divine Providence alone explains the existence of the *Story of a Soul*. The work has frequently been referred to as Thérèse's autobiography, as if it were one uninterrupted account of her personal history. However, closer scrutiny of the book's genesis proves otherwise.

In reality, the *Story of a Soul* is made up of three distinct manuscripts written over the course of the last two and a half years of Thérèse's life. Manuscript "A," the longest of the three, written during the course of 1895, was addressed to Mother Agnes of Jesus, who at the time of its composition, was superior of the Lisieux Carmel. It is a composition of her childhood memories, written at her sister's request, that tells of the manifestation of God's merciful love in her life.[5]

Manuscript "B," written in September, 1896, is actually a letter written to her oldest sister and godmother, Sister Marie of the Sacred Heart, who had asked her to write an explanation of her "little doctrine" of spiritual childhood. Before the retreat that would be Thérèse's last, Marie, who had previously read Manuscript "A," obtained Mother Marie de Gonzague's permission, and formally requested this from her sister.[6]

After Mother Agnes of Jesus' term of office expired in March of 1896, she finally had the leisure to read Thérèse's manuscript. Immediately recognizing its great worth, she felt that it was incomplete. Thérèse, following her orders exactly, had written extensively about her childhood and early youth. She wrote little,

---

[5] *P.*, p. 33.
[6] *G.C. II*, pp. 991-996; see also *P.*, p. 83.

though, about her observance of religious life. Mother Agnes of Jesus, knowing the riches that would be uncovered in a commentary on Carmelite life, devised a way for Thérèse to continue her composition. On June 2, 1897, realizing that her sister would soon succumb to her terminal illness, Mother Agnes diplomatically approached the re-elected Prioress, Mother Marie de Gonzague, with the request that Thérèse continue to write; this time, about her religious life.[7] It was thus that manuscript "C" was composed — on her deathbed, over the course of one month. She was frequently interrupted in her work by many Sisters who visited her in the infirmary, and her intense physical pain and fatigue made the task nearly impossible. She continued with heroic determination until, in the first days of July, 1897, she literally terminated the manuscript in the middle of a sentence. Appropriately, her last written words were: "I go to Him with confidence and love."[8]

It is safe to assert that the *Story of a Soul* contains the entire spiritual doctrine of Thérèse of Lisieux. Her other writings unquestionably illumine and amplify her teaching, but add nothing substantial to it. As Thérèse approached death, she understood that her mission would be accomplished through the publication of these three autobiographical manuscripts.[9] She mentions no other writing as being directly related to her mission to souls.

The *Story of a Soul* reveals neither a new doctrine nor a new way of spiritual life. The Reverend Jordan Aumann, O.P., observes in an article entitled "Spiritual Childhood": "The doctrinal message of St. Thérèse was not to propagate a new and original message but to recall to the minds and hearts of men the fatherhood of God and His mercifl love and exhort them to become as little children in order to enter His kingdom."[10]

---

[7] *P.*, pp. 33-34.

[8] *S.*, p. 259.

[9] *L.C.*, p. 126.

[10] Jordan Aumann, OP, "Spiritual Childhood," *Cross and Crown* (December 1957, Vol. IX, No. 4), pp. 386-387.

Thérèse's teaching, known commonly as the "Little Way of Spiritual Childhood"[11] rests firmly upon the doctrines of the Incarnation and Redemption: God, the Son, became Man not only to reveal the Father's tender love for His children, but also, through the mystery of grace, to draw all men and women into His filial relationship with the Father in heaven.

According to Thérèse, one practices "Spiritual Childhood" by: (1) the acknowledgment of one's absolute nothingness; (2) total abandonment to Christ in faith and love; (3) the experience of Christ's movement *Ad Patrem* (to the Father) in His Passion, Death and Resurrection, which is the only source of the Christian's ontological transformation in the image of Christ. As already noted, every experience of human suffering led Thérèse instinctively to cast herself into the arms of Christ in order to experience His power and love. Suffering became Thérèse's joy because through it she experienced both Christ's power and His loving self-surrender to the Father.

From her childhood, the thought of union with Christ in heaven was the principal source of her consolation.[12] The conferences of Fr. Charles Arminjon on the "Last Things," published in book format under the title *The End of the Present World and the Mysteries of the Future Life* were, as we shall see in greater detail in the following chapter, a formative influence in Thérèse's faith development. These conferences had provided her with a vivid concept of the Beatific Vision based upon the data of Divine Revelation; a concept which was the source of joy in the midst of her many sufferings.

However, in the wake of her first hemoptysis, after an initial elation over the prospect of soon being one with Christ in heaven,[13] Thérèse entered the dark tunnel of her "trial of faith." She could

---

[11] Actually, Thérèse herself never used the phrase "Little Way of Spiritual Childhood" to describe her spiritual doctrine.

[12] S., p. 17.

[13] S., p. 211.

no longer draw any comfort whatsoever from the thought of heaven and was even tempted to deny its existence. The desire she had expressed to God on the day of her second reception of the Eucharist was granted perfectly: her chief source of consolation, the hope of heaven, was turned into a source of bitterness for her.

Manuscripts "B" and "C" of the *Story of a Soul*, written during Thérèse's "trial of faith," allow us to reconstruct the various stages. First of all, there was the hemoptysis in which Thérèse "heard" the summons to join Christ in heaven. This took place early in the morning of April 3, Good Friday, 1896. Another hemorrhage occurred that same evening.

On Easter Sunday or at least early in the Paschal season of 1896, Thérèse came to understand that there are people who really do not believe in the existence of God, the immortal human soul, or life beyond the grave:

> At this time I was enjoying such a living faith, such a clear *faith* that the thought of heaven made up all my happiness and I was unable to believe there were really impious people who had no faith. I believed they were actually speaking against their own inner convictions when they denied the existence of heaven, that beautiful heaven where God Himself wanted to be their eternal reward. During those very joyful days of the Easter season, Jesus made me feel that there were really souls who have no faith and who, through the abuse of grace, lost this precious treasure, the source of the only real and pure joys.[14]

Apostasy and atheism became realities in Thérèse's life. She came to accept that the faith of individuals may be lost through neglect and sin. Realizing that there are people who truly deny the existence of God and heaven, Thérèse herself lost the ability to draw any personal consolation from the hope of union with Christ in heaven: "Jesus permitted my soul to be invaded by the thickest darkness and that the thought of heaven, up until then so

---

[14] S., *ibid.*

sweet to me, be no longer anything but the cause of struggle and torment."[15] She had entered the dark tunnel of her "trial of faith."

At the very beginning of manuscript "B," Thérèse observes that in the midst of the darkest storm of faith, Jesus allowed the light of His grace to shine upon her. This grace took the form of a vivid and deeply consoling dream. Three Carmelites visited Thérèse in her dream early in the morning of May 10, 1896. She immediately understood that they were from heaven and that one was Venerable Anne of Jesus, the foundress of Carmel in France. Anne of Jesus told Thérèse that she would soon be in heaven. Embracing her warmly, she also said that God was very content with all that Thérèse was doing for Him.

Reflecting upon this dream, Thérèse observed:

> O Jesus, the storm was no longer raging, heaven was calm and serene. I *believed*; I *felt* there was a *heaven* and that *heaven* was peopled with souls who actually love me, who consider me their child.[16]

Thérèse was soon to realize that the trial had simply abated. Holding tenaciously to the consolation of this dream, she continued to be tormented by both the inability to conceive of heavenly union with God and by a strong temptation to deny the existence of eternal life.

Near the end of manuscript "B," Thérèse uses a beautiful image to describe the state of her soul in the midst of her shattering "trial of faith." She compares herself to a weak little bird unable to fly. God is the sun, hidden and invisible behind dark storm clouds. The little bird longs to fly up towards the sun and to be consumed in it. However, all she can do is lift her wings, since to fly is not within her power.

In this image Thérèse again exults in and magnifies her powerlessness. She is certain that when God so desires, Jesus the

---

[15] S., *ibid.*
[16] S., p. 191.

eternal Eagle will take her upon His wings and plunge her for all eternity into the burning abyss of His love to which she has offered herself as a victim.[17] Graphically synthesizing Thérèse's "Little Way," this image reveals that she had been prepared to live through her "trial of faith" in a meritorious manner precisely through the faithful practice of Spiritual Childhood.

In the meantime, the "little bird" would simply not be troubled:

> With bold surrender, it wishes to remain gazing upon its Divine Sun. Nothing will frighten it, neither wind nor rain, and if the dark clouds come and hide the Star of Love, the little bird will not change its place because it knows that beyond the clouds its bright Sun still shines on and that its brightness is not eclipsed for a single instant.[18]

Shortly after the dream of Venerable Anne of Jesus, as Thérèse suffered the "trial of faith," she received what she called "the greatest graces God wished to bestow upon me."[19] Consumed by infinite desires to do all things possible and to suffer every imaginable martyrdom for the sake of Christ and the salvation of souls, Thérèse was led to understand her precise vocation in the Church: "Yes, I have found my place in the Church and it is You, O my God, who have given me this place; in the heart of the Church, my Mother, I shall be *Love*. Thus I shall be everything and my dream will be realized."[20]

At this time in her life, Thérèse began to realize that as a result of the love created in her by God's grace, she would continue doing a great deal of good for souls even after her death. Commenting on Thérèse's desire to spend her eternity doing good on earth, Jean Guitton has noted:

---

[17] *S.*, p. 200.
[18] *S.*, p. 198.
[19] *S.*, p. 192.
[20] *S.*, p. 194.

Thérèse Martin intends to continue her activity in glory and to work effectively. She has no desire to be rewarded for her virtues and even less to enter into the rest we ask for our dead. She would not say *requiem aeternum*, but on the contrary, if we may say so she would chant: *actionem aeternum dona nobis Domine.*[21]

In manuscript "B" one comes face to face with what appears to be, on the surface, a blatant contradiction. Thérèse, on the one hand, admits that she is in absolute darkness and must struggle to will to believe in heaven. On the other hand, she knows with certainty that God exists beyond the dark clouds of her trial. She not only experiences profound peace deep within herself but also feels burning desires to save the entire world through her contemplative love. Furthermore, she is absolutely certain that in spite of this trial, or perhaps partly as a result of it, her mission was just beginning and would continue until the end of the world.

We must return to manuscript "C" in order to conclude our survey of Thérèse's revelations of the "trial of faith" in the *Story of a Soul.* The major bulk of the material on the trial is found in this final document.

Writing manuscript "C" sixteen months after this experience, Thérèse made it clear that her trial had become a permanent disposition of her soul: "This trial was not to last a few days or a few weeks, it was not to be extinguished until the hour set by God Himself and this hour has not yet come."[22]

As in manuscript "B," Thérèse creates an image through which she hopes to manifest the state of her soul: it is the image of a dark, foreign land covered with impenetrable fog. She lives in that land of shadows and has only heard from others that the sun does indeed shine and illuminate the beauty of nature. For her all is darkness and shadows.

Thérèse formed this image slightly less than two months

---

[21] Jean Guitton, *op. cit.*, p. 29.
[22] S., pp. 211-212.

before her death. The pulmonary tuberculosis was a constant source of physical agony and affected, no doubt, her psychological and emotional balance. Significantly, the "trial of faith" seems to have become more intense as Thérèse came closer to her death. Hence, this image is harsher than that of the little bird found in manuscript "B." No longer do dark clouds or a veil stand between Thérèse and her God; rather: "It is a wall which reaches right up to the heavens and covers the starry firmament."[23]

This inner darkness spoke to Thérèse and suggested that her desire for the possession of God in heaven would never be satisfied and that death would bring "a night still more profound, the night of nothingness."[24] In the face of these thoughts, which in her mind bordered on blasphemy, Thérèse continued to make acts of faith in the existence of heaven: "I believe I have made more acts of faith in this past year than all through my whole life.... I tell Jesus I am ready to shed my blood to the last drop to profess my faith in the existence of *heaven*."[25]

Thérèse indicates that she accepted the trial of faith in order to expiate sins committed against the faith. She was content to "sit at the table filled with bitterness" to plead for her brothers who were without faith. It seems that Thérèse hints in a very discreet way that through her trial she is to aid priests who had lost the Faith. Might the allusion to "table" in the following text refer to the altar?: "O Jesus, if it is needful that the table soiled by them be purified by a soul who loves You, then I desire to eat this bread of trial at this table until it pleases You to bring me into Your bright Kingdom. The only grace I ask of You is that I never offend You!"[26]

Thérèse also indicates in manuscript "C" of the *Story of a Soul* that through the "trial of faith," she, innocent of any violation against the Faith, was suffering vicariously in place of unbelievers.

---

[23] *S.*, p. 214.

[24] *S.*, p. 213.

[25] *S.*, pp. 213-214.

[26] *S.*, p. 212.

The mystical nature of this suffering becomes even clearer in *Her Last Conversations*.

Finally, in manuscript "C," as in manuscript "B," Thérèse reveals that in spite of her trial, her primary focus remains the practice of supernatural charity. In fact, in her characteristic manner, she accepted the trial as a splendid means of adoring God's Will and transformed it into an eloquent act of love for those who live in the darkness of unbelief. As noted earlier, in the midst of her harrowing trial, Thérèse became certain that her mission was about to begin — a mission to lead others to living faith in Jesus Christ.

Her Last Conversations

The book published in France under the title *J'Entre dans la Vie, Derniers Entretiens*[27] and in the United States as *Her Last Conversations*, contains words which come from the lips of Thérèse, but not from her pen. This volume contains the last conversations Thérèse held with her three blood sisters in Carmel, Mother Agnes of Jesus, Sr. Marie of the Sacred Heart, and Sr. Geneviève of St. Teresa; her cousin, Sr. Marie of the Eucharist, and several other nuns.[28]

The bulk of the recorded material, however, comes from the pen of Mother Agnes of Jesus. She was in a privileged position; she had always been Thérèse's spiritual confidante. In fact, Thérèse was more candid regarding the "trial of faith" in her conversations with her than with any other of her blood sisters. Thérèse was always reserved when speaking of the trial with anyone else. She feared, no doubt, that she might become a source of temptation and scandal. Her "little mother," she knew, would understand her

---

[27] Thérèse de L'Enfant-Jesus et de la Sainte-Face, *J'Entre dans la Vie, Derniers Entretiens* (Paris: Cerf-Desclée de Brouwer, 1973).

[28] Besides her blood sisters and cousin, Marie Guérin, *Her Last Conversations* are addressed to Sr. Marie of the Trinity, Sr. Marie of the Angels, Sr. Aimée of Jesus and Sr. Thérèse of St. Augustine.

and not be shaken by her trial. Thérèse did share the trial with others but in a much more discreet manner.

After Thérèse had been confined to the infirmary, Mother Agnes of Jesus had obtained permission to visit Thérèse every day. She was asked to relieve the infirmarians daily so that they might join the community for Vespers. *Her Last Conversations* provides invaluable information regarding both Thérèse's spiritual development as well as the "trial of faith."

Although Thérèse had presented Mother Agnes with manuscript "A" of the *Story of a Soul* on January 20, 1896, she did not find time to read it until after the community elections in late March of the same year. The manuscript, in a sense, caused Mother Agnes to realize both the maturity and sanctity of her youngest sister and to recognize the value of her spiritual insights.

Both Mother Agnes and Sr. Marie of the Sacred Heart felt that manuscript "A" was incomplete. Consequently, Mother Agnes asked permission for Thérèse to flesh out in writing her life as a religious. Sr. Marie of the Sacred Heart asked her sister to commit her "little way of spiritual childhood" to letter form. Sr. Geneviève, as a novice, had kept careful records of everything that Thérèse had taught her.[29] It is not surprising then, that Thérèse's sisters would want to record, as carefully as possible, her spiritual insights and intuitions during the last months of her life.

Her Last Conversations provides us with invaluable information on Thérèse's last days. Apart from these recorded words of Thérèse, most often short and to the point, it would be extremely difficult to penetrate the significance of her "trial of faith."

It is possible to separate the content of *Her Last Conversations* into three general categories: (1) Thérèse's mystical graces; (2) the "trial of faith" as Thérèse's mystical identification with Christ in the mystery of the redemption; (3) Thérèse's posthumous mission.

---

[29] See Sr. Geneviève of the Holy Face and St. Teresa (Céline Martin), *A Memoir of My Sister, St. Thérèse*; authorized translation by the Carmelite Nuns of New York of *Conseils et Souvenirs* (New York: P.J. Kennedy & Sons, 1959).

Thérèse spoke of various other matters on her deathbed, such as her intense physical suffering, her "Little Way," her theory of religious life, charity, etc. However, I shall focus solely on the subjects listed above, since they are directly related to our subject and do, in fact, occupy a major place among her last recorded words.

We shall see later that Thérèse had acquired a thorough, penetrating grasp of the ascetical and mystical theology of St. Teresa of Jesus and St. John of the Cross before her twentieth birthday. Utilizing the categories and vocabulary of the Carmelite reformers in a precise manner, she reveals her profound mystical life in *Her Last Conversations*.

For instance, Thérèse states that by her fourteenth year she had already experienced "transports of love."[30] She also relates an encounter with the Blessed Virgin during her Novitiate which might well have initiated or at least heralded her unitive life:

> It was as though a veil had been cast over all the things of this earth for me.... I was entirely hidden under the Blessed Virgin's veil. At this time, I was placed in charge of the refectory and I recall doing things as though not doing them; it was as if someone had lent me a body. I remained that way for one whole week.[31]

On July 7, 1897, the day before she was brought to the infirmary, she explained to Mother Agnes of Jesus the "wound of love" she received after having offered herself as an oblation to the merciful love of God:

> Well, I was beginning the Way of the Cross; suddenly I was seized with such a violent love for God that I can't explain it except by saying it felt as though I were totally plunged into fire. Oh! what fire and what sweetness at one and the same time! I was on fire with love and I felt that

---

[30] *L.C.*, p. 77.
[31] *L.C.*, p. 88.

one minute more, one second more, and I wouldn't be able to sustain this ardor without dying. I understood, then, what the saints were saying about these states which they experienced so often. As for me, I experienced it only once and for one single instant, falling back immediately into my habitual state of dryness. At the age of fourteen, I also experienced transports of love. Ah! how I love God! But it was not at all as it was after my oblation to love; it wasn't a real flame that was burning me.[32]

Thérèse's mystical life is also clearly revealed in the perfect union of her will with God's Will, especially during the last months of her life. She said on one occasion:

I no longer understand anything about my sickness. Here I am getting better! However, I abandon myself to Him and I am happy just the same. What would become of me if I did not nourish the hope of dying soon? What disappointments! But I don't have a single one, because I am totally content with what God does; I desire only His Will.[33]

On September 4, 1897, Mother Agnes asked Thérèse if she would prefer to die or to live. Over and over again the nuns asked this inane question among a number of others. Always her answer was the same: "O Little Mother, I don't love one thing more than another; I could not say like our Holy Mother St. Teresa: 'I die because I do not die.' What God prefers and chooses for me, that is what pleases me more."[34]

Throughout her last months, Thérèse had re-read St. John of the Cross' mystical doctrine in the *Spiritual Canticle* and *Living Flame of Love*.[35] No doubt she needed help to comprehend

---

the fire of love that had consumed her since her momentous "Oblation to the Merciful Love of God."

Thérèse understood and did not hesitate to explain to her sisters that as the direct result of her self-oblation to God for the conversion of sinners, she was literally being consumed in the fire of divine love and would, in fact, die, not of the pulmonary tuberculosis which racked her body, but rather of the love which filled her soul.

Thérèse had learned in St. John of the Cross' *Living Flame of Love* that those who attain the perfection of love in the mystical marriage do not die of natural causes, even though they may be very ill or advanced in age. Rather, they die of the love of God and the ardent desire to be joined to Him eternally. The souls of the perfect, he notes, "are not wrested from them unless by some impetus and encounter of love, far more sublime than previous ones; of greater power, and more valiant, since it tears through this veil and carries off the jewel, which is the soul."[36]

Expressing her certainty that she would die of love, Thérèse notes: "It is incredible how all my hopes have been fulfilled. When I used to read St. John of the Cross, I begged God to work out in me what he wrote, that is, the same thing as though I were to live to be very old; to consume me rapidly in love, and I have been answered."[37]

Thérèse relates her death of love directly to her "trial of faith." The raptures of love are experienced at the core of her soul, yet at various other levels she is tormented by doubts of faith and thoughts which in her mind border on blasphemy. She explains that this mysterious state of soul is for the edification of those who suffer without any consolation.[38]

---

during the course of her illness. She had marked off the passages which dealt directly with the phenomenon of the "death of love" in the *Living Flame of Love*, stanza 1, No. 33 & 34, pp. 655-656.

[36] *Living Flame of Love*, p. 654.

[37] *L.C.*, p. 177.

[38] *L.C.*, p. 148.

In a stroke of genius and with profound common sense, Thérèse stripped all sentimentality, romance, and glamour from the pious conceptualization of the "death of love." Christ, experiencing personally the guilt of every human sin in His dereliction on the Cross, was for her the paradigm of "dying of love." She notes: "Do not be troubled, little sisters, if I suffer very much and if you see in me, as I've already said, no sign of happiness at the moment of my death. Our Lord really died as a victim of love, and you see what his agony was!"[39] And again: "Our Lord died on the Cross in agony and yet this is the most beautiful death of love. This is the only one that was seen; no one saw that of the Blessed Virgin. To die of love is not to die in transports. I tell you frankly, it seems to me that this is what I am experiencing."[40]

In *Her Last Conversations*, Thérèse speaks frequently of the "trial of faith." We find what is perhaps the most harrowing description of her trial in an August conversation with Mother Agnes of Jesus. One evening in the infirmary she said:

> If you only knew what frightful thoughts obsess me! Pray very much for me in order that I do not listen to the devil who wants to persuade me about so many lies. It is the reasoning of the worst materialists which is imposed upon my mind: later, unceasingly making new advances, science will explain everything naturally; we shall have the absolute reason for everything that exists and that still remains a problem because there remain very many things to be discovered, etc., etc.
>
> I want to do good after my death, but I will not be able to do so! It will be as it was for Mother Geneviève: we expected to see her work miracles and complete silence fell over her tomb....
>
> O, little Mother, must one have thoughts like this when one loves God so much!

---

[39] *L.C.*, p. 56.
[40] *L.C.*, p. 73.

Finally, I offered up these very great pains to obtain the light of faith for poor unbelievers, for all those who separate themselves from the Church's belief.[41]

Thérèse states that the reasoning of atheism and materialism is "imposed upon her mind." Might this not suggest a mystical grace; i.e., not only a divinely-willed vicarious sharing in the lot of unbelievers in order to expiate their sins, but even perhaps an infused share in the dereliction suffered by Christ on the Cross as a result of sins against the Faith? Thérèse herself clearly says that she offered up the "trial of faith" in order to achieve the reconciliation of those who had broken faith with the Lord.[42]

In a number of other conversations, Thérèse states that her trial is the direct result of her "Oblation to the Merciful Love of God" and will aid those who live in the darkness of unbelief: "I have offered up my trial against faith especially for a member united to our family, who has lost the faith."[43] On the day of her death, Thérèse said: "Never would I have believed it was possible to suffer so much! Never! Never! I cannot explain this except by the ardent desires I have had to save souls."[44]

Thérèse, on several occasions, told her sisters that her "trial of faith" did not disturb the peace that habitually filled her soul:

> My heart is filled with God's will and when someone pours something on it, this doesn't penetrate its interior; it is a nothing which glides off easily, just like oil which can't mix with water. I remain always at profound peace in the depths of my heart; nothing can disturb the peace.[45]

---

[41] *L.C.*, pp. 257-258.

[42] *L.C.*, p. 258.

[43] *L.C.*, p. 181. This was M. René Tostain, who was married to Mme. Guérin's niece, Marguerite-Marie Maudelonde. A very upright man, he was a declared atheist.

[44] *L.C.*, p. 205.

[45] *L.C.*, pp. 97-98.

Thérèse's disposition of soul and even physical appearance in her agony drew those who visited her to the contemplation of Christ Crucified. Her very presence became a "word" revealing the mystery of the Cross. Thérèse herself discreetly admitted that Christ was living His Passion again in her. One evening Pauline, Marie and Céline were all dozing at her bedside. When they awoke she pointed at them saying "Peter, James and John."

Finally during the last months of her life, Thérèse came to understand that God had ordained a posthumous mission for her. She became convinced that her heaven would be spent doing good on earth. On July 17, 1897, she noted:

> I feel that I'm about to enter into my rest, but I feel especially that my mission is about to begin, my mission of making God loved as I love Him, of giving my little way to souls. If God answers my desires, my heaven will be spent on earth until the end of the world. Yes, I want to spend my heaven in doing good on earth. This isn't impossible since from the bosom of the beatific vision, the angels watch over us."[46]

Thus, *Her Last Conversations* complements the *Story of a Soul* and renders Thérèse's self-revelation abundantly complete. In her last recorded words, one discovers Thérèse practicing her "Little Way of Spiritual Childhood" perfectly and with astonishing strength.

Thérèse's deathbed testimony reveals that the "Way" in fact, stands the test of intense physical and spiritual agony and leads to victory over all of the forces of evil. Also, these carefully recorded conversations offer penetrating insight into Thérèse's mystical graces and her final struggles with temptations against the Faith. They present Thérèse as perfectly identified with Christ in His agony and death — suffering with Him for sinners, and in par-

---

[46] *L.C.*, p. 102.

ticular, for those who had sinned against the Faith. It would be difficult to interpret Thérèse's "trial of faith" apart from *Her Last Conversations.*

General Correspondence

Thérèse, following the common practice of her day, was an avid letter writer. Fortunately, many of her letters were retained by the recipients as keepsakes after her death and then as relics after her beatification and canonization. No less then 266 letters are extant. These texts either carry her autograph or are copies of autographed texts made and authenticated during the process which preceded her beatification in 1923.

Thérèse's letters are extremely important for a number of reasons. They allow the reader to examine her personality and development from the perspective of her own communication with others. The letters, especially those written after her entry into Carmel, reveal Thérèse's understanding of God's intimate dealings with the human soul. Following the teaching of her spiritual mother, St. Teresa of Jesus, Thérèse writes always of the love of God. Hence, the letters are vehicles for the propagation of her "Little Way of Spiritual Childhood." Her ability to use images of sense to convey spiritual truths is strikingly evident in her *General Correspondence.* Thérèse's rich affectivity is manifested in her love for her family members, her Sisters in the Carmel, the novices and her missionary brothers. One is also struck by the penetrating strength of her thought.

The letters, especially those written during the final years of her life, reveal her charity, her apostolic zeal, and her deep insight into her particular mission of participating in Christ's redemptive work through vicarious suffering. Finally, we find in the letters valuable insights into Thérèse's mysterious "trial of faith" and posthumous mission.

Surprisingly enough, Thérèse refers to her "trial of faith" only three times in her letters. Each of these references is discreet and somewhat indirect. Two of the revelations were made to Mother Agnes of Jesus and one to her spiritual brother, Fr. Maurice Bellière. The first reference to the trial is found in *LT 216*, addressed to Mother Agnes, dated January 9, 1897. Interestingly this letter also contains Thérèse's first reference to her impending death:

> Dear little mother, if you only knew how much I was touched when seeing the degree to which you love me! Never would I be able to show you my gratitude here below.... I hope to go soon up above. Since "if there is *a heaven, it is for me*," I shall be rich, I shall have all God's treasures, and He himself will be *my good*; then I shall be able to return to you a hundredfold all I owe you.[47]

In his commentary on this letter, Fr. John Clarke notes:

> The words "if there is a heaven, it is for me," is a probable allusion to this verse of Soumet: "For whom would the heavens be if they were not for you." Taken from the tragedy, *Jeanne d'Arc Martyre*, third part of *Jeanne d'Arc*, national trilogy dedicated to France (1846). Thérèse introduced this passage (which she erroneously attributes to d'Avrigny) into her play of 1895, *Jeanne d'Arc, Accomplissant Sa Mission* (*RP* III). The dubious variant at the beginning: "If there is a heaven, it is for me," is the first reference, veiled, to her trial of faith in her correspondence.[48]

In *LT 230*, dated May 28, 1897, Thérèse again discreetly alludes to her "trial of faith" to Mother Agnes of Jesus: "Little mother, Jesus does well to hide Himself and talk to me only from time to time and 'through the lattices' (*Canticle of Canticles*) for I feel I would be unable to bear anymore, my heart would break, being powerless to contain so much joy.... Ah! you, the sweet Echo

---

[47] *G.C. II*, p. 1046.
[48] *G.C. II*, p. 1047, n. 2.

of my soul, you will understand that this evening the vessel of divine Mercy overflowed for me."[49]

In *LT 258*, dated July 18, 1897, Thérèse, writing to Fr. Bellière, sought to help him to understand that true Christian joy consists of selfless obedience to God's will. Revealing her love for redemptive suffering in communion with Christ, she wrote: "The thought of heavenly bliss not only causes me not a single bit of joy, but I even ask myself at times how it will be possible to be happy without any suffering. Jesus, no doubt, will change my nature; otherwise, I would miss suffering in this valley of tears."[50]

Why did Thérèse say so little about her "trial of faith" in her letters? A few reasons come immediately to mind. First of all, it is characteristic of Thérèse in her letters, to focus attention on either God's dealing with the soul or the soul's response to God's love. In her written communication, she seeks to praise God's mercy either in her life or in the life of the person to whom she is writing, or to give advice on how to practice the love of God more perfectly. The transcendent, selfless nature of all of her communications with others would militate against writing about herself and her interior struggles. Thérèse does speak and write about her personal sufferings. However, she did so in order to console some other person or to offer advice on how to render suffering pleasing to God and beneficial to souls.

If Thérèse, when speaking of her "trial of faith," feared blasphemy, would she not consider speaking freely about the trial to others as a possible cause of temptation for them? Consequently, we find in the letters only three enigmatic references to the trial, two of which were addressed to Mother Agnes of Jesus.

Secondly, the "trial of faith" was at the core of Thérèse's spiritual life. She understood it, in the strictest sense, as a matter of conscience. Hence, she revealed the trial formally to her confessors and superior — Mother Marie de Gonzague — and also to

---

[49] *G.C. II*, p. 1101.
[50] *G.C. II*, p. 1152.

her sisters — in particular to Mother Agnes of Jesus, her confidante since childhood. For Thérèse to speak about the trial at random would have been, to her mind, indiscreet and unseemly since it had to do with her intimate relationship with God.

The *Story of a Soul*, however, is another matter. As she wrote manuscript "C," shortly before her death, Thérèse was certain that the autobiographical manuscripts would do good for souls. In fact, she knew that her God-given mission would be accomplished through the publication of the *Story of a Soul*. Whereas the letters and conversations were for her loved ones, the *Story of a Soul* was for the world. Hence, she sensed the importance of candidly relating her "trial of faith" for the sake of those who struggle with faith.

Many of the letters written during the span of Thérèse's "trial of faith" — April 15, 1896 to September 30, 1897 — do reveal that she was enjoying a high degree of mystical union with Christ during this most difficult period of her life.

She admits, for instance, that in spite of her physical agony and harrowing interior trial, she experienced absolutely no fear.[51]

Writing to her "priest-brother," Maurice Bellière on June 21, 1987, Thérèse notes:

> Ever since I have been given the grace to understand, also the love of the Heart of Jesus, I admit that it has expelled all fear from my heart. The remembrance of my faults humbles me, draws me never to depend on my strength, which is only weakness, but this remembrance speaks to me of mercy and love even more. When we cast our faults with entire filial confidence into the devouring fire of love, how would these not be consumed beyond return?[52]

On June 6, 1897, writing to Sister Marie of the Trinity,

---

[51] St. John in his first letter notes: "In love there can be no fear, but fear is driven out by perfect love" (1 Jn 4:18).
[52] *G.C. II*, pp. 1133-1134.

Thérèse observes that as a result of her Oblation as a victim to the Merciful Love of God, she would die of love:

> You want to know if I am joyful at going to paradise? I would be very much so *if* I were going there, but... I do not count on the illness, it is too slow a leader. I *count only on ove.* Ask good Jesus that all the prayers being offered for me may serve to increase the Fire which must consume me.[53]

Writing to hr other "priest-brother," Adolphe Roulland, on May 9, 1897, Thérèse uses a charming image of herself as "zero" to describe her role in stimulating and supporting apostolic fecundity. Her contemplation and sufferings, she notes, will animate the priestly service of her adopted spiritual brother:

> I can do very little, or rather absolutely nothing, if I am alone; What consoles me is to think that at your side I can be useful for something. In fact, zero by itself has no value, but when placed next to a unit it becomes powerful, provided, however, that it is placed on the *right side*, after and not before! That is where Jesus has placed me, and I hope to remain there always, following you from a distance by prayer and sacrifice.[54]

Finally, Thérèse reveals in her letters her certainty of an apostolic mission after her death — a mission directly related to the communication of the gift of faith. To Fr. Bellière, for instance, she wrote:

> I do not know the future; however, if Jesus realizes my presentiments, I promise to remain your little sister up above. Our union, far from being broken, will become more intimate. Then there will no longer be any cloister

---

[53] *G.C. II*, pp. 1120-1121.
[54] *G.C. II*, p. 1095.

and grilles and my soul will be able to fly with you into distant missions. Our roles will remain the same: yours, apostolic weapons; mine, prayers and love.[55]

In summary, we might say that Thérèse's *General Correspondence* is an extremely valuable tool in plumbing the depths of Thérèse's rich personality, relationship with God, and spiritual doctrine. The letters, although containing few direct references to the "trial of faith," do offer important insights into matters relative to our subject: namely, Thérèse's love of suffering, her mystical graces, her charity, apostolic fecundity, and her certainty of a posthumous mission of spreading and/or strengthening the Catholic faith.

Recreational Plays

According to a custom established by St. Teresa of Jesus herself, the nuns of her Order would create and perform inspirational skits for the celebration of major feasts. It was the task of the novices to perform these plays on Christmas, the Feast of the Holy Innocents (December 28 — the novices' special feast day); the feast day of the Prioress of the Carmel; the Feast of St. Martha (July 29 — the feast day of the lay Sisters) and the celebration of a Sister's golden jubilee of profession.

These skits, inspirational in nature, were composed of prose, dialogue, poetry, music and audience participation. The novices would prepare the spectacle by making costumes, scenery, and props. One recalls Céline's famous photograph of Thérèse in military armor playing the role of Joan of Arc in the skit of her own composition.

During the last three years of her life, between January 1894

---

[55] *G.C. II*, p. 1060.

and February 1897, Thérèse wrote and participated in no less than eight recreational pieces. These pious skits are perhaps the least known of all of Thérèse's writings. In the past, large segments of these skits wre published in collections of Thérèse's poetry. It is interesting to note that the first critical edition of her plays appeared only in 1985.[56] These plays have yet to appear in English translation. The eight plays are:

1. The Mission of Joan of Arc or The Shepherd of Domrémy Listening to Voices (R.P. 1).

This skit was staged on January 21, 1894 to celebrate the feast day of Mother Agnes of Jesus. It reveals that Thérèse felt herself and Joan of Arc to be kindred spirits — each called to save her homeland through suffering.[57]

Regarding Thérèse's play on Joan of Arc, Guy Gaucher has noted:

> For her first "theatrical" attempt, Sister Thérèse had big ideas. There were to be two plays on Joan of Arc and she planned to devote two recreations to them: one on Joan's vocation; the other, on her suffering, death and triumph. To this end she made a serious study on Henri Wallon's recently published book (1877), which contained extracts from the trials. As author, producer and actress, Sister Thérèse did not spare herself while keeping to the story; she attributed Carmelite sentiments to her heroine.[58]

---

[56] Thérèse de l'Enfant Jésus et de la Sainte-Face, *Théâtre au Carmel: Récréations Pieuses* (Paris: Editions du Cerf-Desclée de Brouwer, 1985). See also John F. Russell, O. Carm., "Religious Plays of St. Thérèse," in *Carmelite Studies: Experiencing St. Thérèse Today*, ed. John Sullivan, OCD (Washington, DC: Institute of Carmelite Studies, 1990), pp. 41-48.

[57] Since her childhood, Thérèse had a deep devotion for Joan of Arc. See *S.*, p. 72.

[58] Guy Gaucher, *op. cit.*, p. 131.

2. *Angels at the Manger of Jesus (R.P. 2).*

This skit was performed on Christmas 1894. It starred two angels: The Angel of the Infant Jesus and the Angel of the Last Judgment. The themes of the skit were the merciful love of God manifested in the Christ Child and the desire of the Christ Child that all men and women come to eternal salvation.

3. *Joan of Arc Accomplishing Her Mission (R.P. 3).*

This play was staged on January 21, 1895, to celebrate the feast day of Mother Agnes of Jesus. The theme of the skit is Christian Death. Perhaps Thérèse reveals a presentiment of her approaching "trial of faith" and death in this composition. At the stake, Joan tells the Archangel Gabriel: "How I am consoled in seeing that my agony is like my Savior's.... However, I don't feel His divine presence and death fill me with fear."[59]

4. *Jesus at Bethany (R.P. 4).*

Performed in honor of the lay Sisters in the monastery who serve the Choir Nuns by manual labor, this play was staged on July 29, 1895. Its main theme is that Jesus is consoled more by the Christian's gift of self to Him than by many works performed without love.

5. *The Small Divine Beggar at Christmas (R.P. 5).*

Thérèse's Christmas play of 1895 actively engaged every member of the community. Each Sister was summoned to the nativity scene, invited to become a special gift offered to Jesus the "Divine Beggar" who ever seeks human love and affection.

---

[59] John Russell, O. Carm., *op. cit.*, p. 46.

6. *The Flight into Egypt (R.P. 6)*.

This play was celebrated on January 21, 1896 to celebrate again the feast day of the prioress, Mother Agnes of Jesus. The longest of all of Thérèse's theatrical pieces, the "Flight Into Egypt" deals with the value of poverty and suffering and the reward promised to those who faithfully fulfill God's will in this life. In his article entitled "Religious Plays of St. Thérèse" John Russell, O. Carm., notes:

> This play turned out to be a source of humiliation for St. Thérèse. Mother Agnes stopped the play before the performance was completed. St. Thérèse's reaction was recorded by Sister Geneviève of the Holy Face (Céline): "I surprised her back stage, secretly wiping away her tears. Then regaining possession of herself she was calm and sweet." Mother Agnes later explained her action with some sense of contrition: "I caused her grief one festive evening... in telling her bluntly that these compositions for evening recreation were too long and tired out the community."[60]

7. *The Triumph of Humility (R.P. 7)*.

This play was performed on June 21, 1896 to honor Mother Marie de Gonzague on her feast day. Its theme was the power of humility which is able to conquer all of the forces of evil. The play also exalted the Carmelite's spousal relationship with Christ as a source of holiness in the world.

8. *St. Stanislaus Kostka (R.P. 8)*.

The last of Thérèse's plays was performed on February 8, 1897 to celebrate the golden jubilee of Sister St. Stanislaus. In the play Thérèse tells the story of Stanislaus Kostka with special attention given to the death of the young Jesuit novice. The text strongly

---

[60] John Russell, O. Carm., *op. cit.*, p. 51.

suggests that after his early death, Stanislaus would continues to do good on earth through his "work" in heaven.

Commenting on this play, Fr. John Clake, O.C.D., notes:

> On February 8, 1897, in a piece composed for Sister St. Stanislaus, Thérèse made her hero, Stanislaus Kostka, ask the great question that haunts her, the only question for her from now on: "I have a desire... a desire so great that I shall be unable to be happy in heaven if it is not realized.... Tell me whether the blessed can still work for the salvation of souls.... If I cannot work in paradise for the glory of Jesus, I prefer to remain in exile and combat for Him!" The affirmative answer of the Blessed Virgin Mary then gave rise to this entreaty: "I beg you, when I am close to you in the homeland, permit me to come back to earth."[61]

Thérèse's plays, filled with engaging prose, poetry and even music, revealed the richness of her imagination and creativity. All of the main themes of the *Story of a Soul* appear in her *Pious Recreations*. These skits also illuminate for us certain aspects of her "trial of faith": her desire to give all to Jesus for love of Him and the salvation of souls, her certainty of dying the death of a martyr — the death of love — and her certainty that she would be able to continue doing good on earth from heaven after her death.

Poetry

St. Teresa of Jesus had frequently encouraged the nuns of the Carmelite Reform to sing, play msical instruments and even dance. The Mother of Carmel had understood the importance of recreation and wholesome relaxation. She also encouraged the sisters to exploit their artistic talents for the glory of God and the

---

[61] *G.C. II*, Introduction to Letters dated 12/96 to 4/97, p. 1026.

common good of the community. She recognized the value and even the need of contemplatives expressing their deep encounters with God in various forms, such as poetry, music, dance, painting, prose, etc.

After Mother Agnes of Jesus' election as Prioress on February 20, 1893, Thérèse began to understand and develop the artistic dimension of her personality. Besides naming her "assistant" to Mother Marie de Gonzague, who had become the mistress of novices, Mother Agnes, knowing her sister's love of drawing, placed Thérèse in charge of all "art work" in the cloister. She was frequently asked to sketch pictures for the nuns and she even painted a fresco for the Oratory of the sick Sisters.[62]

Until her election, Mother Agnes had written poetry, hymns and religious skits for community celebrations. As superior, she was too occupied to continue this work which she had always enjoyed very much. Thérèse, who had already shown an aptitude for such composition, was slated to take her place. After all, she had written a poem considered "lovely" by the nuns at the request of Sister Thérèse of St. Augustine. It was entitled *La Rosée Divine* and dated February 2, 1893.

This first poem of Thérèse was followed by no less than fifty-three others. Like the *Story of a Soul* and the *Pious Recreations*, most, although not all of the poems, were written as an "obedience." In other words, at the requestof the superior, Thérèse was frequently called upon to compose a poem to celebrate a feast day, birthday, anniversary, clothing, or profession of one or another of the Sisters. She became, through this obedience, the official "bard" of the Lisieux Carmel. All of these poems were originally set to music — hence, they are lyrics, properly-so-called.

In *The Story of a Life*, Guy Gaucher, commenting on Thérèse's poetry, observed: "In the language of pious clichés called religious poetry, Thérèse unburdened her innermost heart. The

---

[62] See Guy Gaucher, *op. cit.*, pp. 124-126.

means at her disposal were meager but under obedience she managed to express more and more of what was burning inside her."[63]

The major themes of the *Story of a Soul* re-emerge in Thérèse's poetry: her desire to live for God alone; her love of suffering in union with Jesus; the conviction that life in the world is exile while heaven is the Christian's true home; the importance of offering everything to God as an act of pure love; love of the Blessed Virgin; the desire for martyrdom; abandonment to Divine Providence.

Twenty-six of Thérèse's poems were written during "her trial of faith." These compositions illuminate the various dispositions of her soul during a long period of intense physical and spiritual suffering.

The profound peace that reigned in her soul during the "trial of faith" is beautifully expressed in her poem: *L'Abandon est le fruit délicieux de l'amour* (*Abandonment is the Sweet Fruit of Love —* *PN* 52, May 31, 1897):

> Every creature
> Can forsake me.
> Near you I'll know how to do without them
> Without complaining.
>
> And if you abandon me,
> O my Divine Treasure,
> Deprived of your caresses,
> I still want to smile.
>
> In peace, sweet Jesus,
> I want to wait for your return,
> Without ever ceasing
> My canticles of love.
>
> No, nothing worries me.
> Nothing can trouble me.

---

[63] Guy Gaucher, *op. cit.*, p. 126.

My soul knows how to fly
Higher than the lark.

Above the clouds
The sky is always blue.
One touches the shores
Where God reigns.

I await in peace the glory
Of that Heavenly abode,
For I find in the Ciborium
the sweet Fruit of Love![64]

A poem entitled *À Théophane Vénard* (*To Théophane Vénard* — *PN* 47, February 2, 1897), gives voice to her desires for martyrdom as well as her apostolic zeal in suffering for the salvation of souls:

I also love that infidel shore
That was the object of your burning love.
I would happily fly to it
If God called me there some day…
But in His eyes, there is no distance.
For Him the whole universe is just one speck.
My weak love, my little sufferings,
Blessed by Him, make Him loved far and wide!…

Ah! if I were a springtime flower
That the Lord soon wanted to pluck,
O Blessed Martyr! I implore you,
Descend from Heaven at my last hour.
Come embrace me in this mortal dwelling,
And I'll be able to fly with the souls
That will make up your eternal procession!…[65]

---

[64] *The Poetry of Saint Thérèse of Lisieux*, Translated by Donald Kinney, OCD (Washington DC: ICS Publications, 1996), pp. 207-208. (Henceforth cited as *Poetry*.)

[65] *Poetry*, p. 192.

In what is perhaps her greatest poem, *Pourquoi je t'aime, Ô Marie!* (*Why I Love You, O Mary* — *PN* 54, May, 1897) in which she summarizes her "Marian Sermon,"[66] Thérèse explains her wish to live like the Blessed Virgin in the simple obscurity of faith:

> The Gospel tells me that, growing in wisdom,
> Jesus remains subject to Joseph and Mary,
> And my heart reveals to me with what tenderness
> He always obeys his dear parents.
> Now I understand the mystery of the temple,
> The hidden words of my Lovable King.
> Mother, your sweet Child wants you to be the example
> Of the soul searching for Him in the night of faith.
>
> Since the King of Heaven wanted His Mother
> To be plunged into the night, in anguish of heart,
> Mary, is it thus a blessing to suffer on earth?
> Yes, *to suffer while loving is the purest happiness!*...
> All that He has given me, Jesus can take back.
> Tell Him not to bother with me...
> He can indeed hide from me, I'm willing to wait for Him
> 'Till the day without sunset when my faith will fade away...
>
> Mother full of grace, I know that in Nazareth
> You live in poverty, wanting nothing more.
> *No rapture, miracle, or ecstasy*
> *Embellish your life, O Queen of the Elect!*...
> The number of little ones on earth is truly great.
> They can raise their eyes to you without trembling.
> It's by the *ordinary way*, incomparable Mother
> That you like to walk to guide them to Heaven.
>
> While waiting for Heaven, O my dear Mother,
> I want to live with you, to follow you each day.
> Mother, contemplating you, I joyfully immerse myself,
> Discovering in your heart *abysses of love*.
> Your motherly gaze banishes all my fears.
> It teaches me *to cry*, it teaches me *to rejoice*,

---

[66] See *L.C.*, pp. 161-162: "In my Poem, *Pourquoi je t'aime, Ô Marie*, I have said all I would preach about the Blessed Virgin Mary."

Instead of scorning pure and simple joys,
You want to share in them, you deign to bless them.[67]

Finally, in the poem *Une rose effeuillée* (*An Unpetalled Rose*, *PN* 51, May 19, 1897), Thérèse expressed her joy over the prospect of living and dying for the love of Jesus:

The rose in its splendor can adorn Your feast,
Lovable Child,
But *the unpetalled rose* is just flung out
To blow away.
An unpetalled rose gives itself unaffectedly
To be no more.
Like it, with joy I abandon myself to You,
Little Jesus.

One walks *on rose petals* with no regrets,
And this debris
It is a simple ornament that one disposes of artlessly,
That I've understood.
Jesus, for your love I've squandered my life,
My future.
In the eyes of men, a rose forever *withered,*
I must *die!*...

For You, I must *die,* Child, Beauty Supreme,
What a blessed fate!
In *being unpetalled,* I want to prove to You that I love You,
O my Treasure!...
Under your *baby steps,* I want to live here below
With mystery,
And I'd like to soften once more on Calvary
Your last steps!...[68]

Commenting on Thérèse's poems, Hans Urs von Balthasar, in an article entitled "The Timeliness of Lisieux," has remarked:

---

[67] *Poetry*, pp. 218-219.
[68] *Poetry*, pp. 203-204.

Though her poetry remains, as to form, a prisoner of the taste of her time — where, after all, would she have learned the language of Péguy or of Claudel? — her mind is a bubbling spring of the most pertinent, the most original, and the most unforgettable images which, I am not afraid to say, render her the equal of the two great Reformers of Carmel in poetic power.[69]

Thérèse, over the short span of her 24 years, has left us a considerable amount of literature on the spiritual life. The major themes of her thought are all contained in the *Story of a Soul*, her masterpiece. However, her *General Correspondence*, *Her Last Conversations*, her *Pious Recreations*, and *Poetry* provide us further insight into her personal relationship with God. Also, through her literary production, we find our primary testimony regarding her mysterious "trial of faith" which is our immediate focus.

---

[69] *Carmelite Studies, op. cit.*, pp. 112-113.

Chapter III

THE SOURCES OF
THÉRÈSE'S DOCTRINE

The Formation of Thérèse within Her Family

Of primary importance in Thérèse's formation, was the influence of her family. There is no doubt that God was truly the heart and center of the Martin home. Their family life at Alençon and then at Lisieux, reflected perfectly the criteria of authentic catechesis which was described by His Holiness, Pope John Paul II, in the Apostolic Exhortation, *On Catechesis in Our Times (Catechesi Tradendae)*. In this document, the Holy Father notes that catechesis in the home is irreplaceable in the Christian formation of children: "Education in the faith by parents, which should begin from the children's tenderest age, is already being given when members of a family help each other to grow in the faith."[1]

Both of her parents were deeply committed to the Catholic faith and, whenever possible, attended daily Mass. Often in the afternoon, Louis Martin would bring the children to the parish church to adore the Blessed Sacrament. Prayer and informal discussion about God and Christian virtue were daily family occurrences. The great liturgical feasts were the high points of each

---

[1] See John Paul II, *On Catechesis in Our Times (Catechesi Tradendae)* (Vatican City State: Vatican Polyglot Press, 1979), pp. 84-90.

passing year. Both parents were acutely aware of their children's growth in virtue and cultivated this growth with special care.

Especially after her mother's death, Thérèse was very close to her father. She began to recognize his human virtue, his love of God, and his selflessness. Thérèse's love and admiration for her father helped her to grasp the goodness and love of the heavenly Father. In her tender relationship with her human father, the pattern was established for her relationship with the heavenly Father. For example, Thérèse's childhood desire to give her father pleasure by performing simple acts of love for him, became the "matrix" of her "Little Way of Spiritual Childhood." Thérèse learned from her human father that God has infinite compassion on His children especially in their experience of suffering.

It seems clear that Thérèse's understanding of the Christian's ability to save souls from eternal damnation through acts of love, developed in no small measure from her experience of the love and concern of her family members, one for the other.

A number of priests frequently visited the Martin household to engage Louis Martin and on occasions, his children, in theological and spiritual discussions. One such priest was Fr. Almire Pichon, S.J., who would become the spiritual director of Pauline, Marie and Thérèse.[2] Through his fatherly advice and direction, he, among others, helped to launch Thérèse in her youth on the "way of confidence, joy and love."[3]

In the *Story of a Soul*, Thérèse describes not only the formation in Christian virtue but also the formal catechesis she had re-

---

[2] See Lewis Gillet, OCD, "St. Thérèse of the Child Jesus and Spiritual Direction," *Carmelite Studies* (Washington, DC: ICS Publications, 1980), pp. 81-100. This is a comprehensive study of the role spiritual direction played in the formation of Thérèse of Lisieux. Gillet observes: "Of all the priests who attended to her spiritually from the age of fourteen to her death, Father Pichon is the only one to whom she gives the name of director, and the only one whom she mentions in her correspondence." For Thérèse's reference to Father Pichon, see *S.*, pp. 62, 76, 149-151, 167, 177, 239; *G.C. I*, pp. 248, 297, 468, 684; *G.C. II*, pp. 878, 999.

[3] For a sampling of Fr. Pichon's spiritual doctrine, see Almire Pichon, SJ, *Seeds of the Kingdom*, ed. and trans. Lyle Terhune, T.OCD, (Westminster: The Newman Press, 1961); see in particular, Sermon XXIX, "The Way of Confidence, Joy and Love."

ceived at home from her two elder sisters, Marie and Pauline. They had carefully prepared her for First Confession, Holy Communion, and Confirmation. Writing to Pauline, she recalled her preparation for her First Confession:

> With what care you prepared me for my first confession, telling me it was not to a man but to God I was about to tell my sins; I was very much convinced of this truth. I made my confession in a great spirit of faith, even asking you if I had to tell Fr. Ducellier I loved him with all my heart, as it was to God in person I was speaking.[4]

Thérèse, likewise, recalled the preparation Marie had given her for her first reception of Holy Communion:

> Just as famous warriors taught their children the art of war, so Marie spoke to me about life's *struggles* and of the palm given to the victors. She also spoke about the eternal riches that one can so easily amass each day, and what a misfortune it was to pass by without so much as stretching forth one's hand to take them. She explained the way of becoming *holy* through fidelity in little things; furthermore, she gave me a little leaflet called "Renunciation" and I meditated on this with delight.[5]

To the end of her life, Thérèse was convinced that this teaching that she had received at home — profound and practical — as well as the example of her parents and sisters, had been God's way of calling her to perfection.[6]

Three months before her death, Thérèse and Mother Agnes (Pauline) were walking in the cloister garden. Thérèse noticed a white hen sheltering her chicks beneath her wings. She immediately began to weep and was unable to continue her conversation

---

[4] S., p. 40.

[5] S., p. 74.

[6] Thérèse had also received formal catechetical instruction at the Benedictine Abbey School that she attended from October 1881 to March 1886.

with Mother Agnes. Later that same day, she explained her emotion. She had experienced a sudden insight into the graces God had given her through her family:

> I cried when I thought how God used this image in order to teach us His tenderness towards us. All through my life, this is what He has done for me! Earlier in the day when I was leaving you, I was crying when going upstairs; I was unable to control myself any longer and I hastened to our cell. My heart was overflowing with love and gratitude. Had you not brought me up so well, you would have seen sad things. I would never have cried when seeing the little white hen.[7]

In the past, and perhaps even today, some writers and popular preachers present Thérèse's teaching as if it were on the level of superficial piety. Others even denounce her for cloying sentimentality. Some have given the impression that her writings defend an anti-intellectual trend in spirituality. These opinions reflect a prejudice and a grave injustice against Thérèse. No doubt, individuals themselves have related to Thérèse in a sentimental and pietistic manner, but anyone who has carefully read the *Story of a Soul* would not make such statements.

Certainly Thérèse was neither a theologian in a formal sense nor was she concerned with knowledge simply for the sake of knowledge. However, she does manifest remarkable intellectual insight in her writing. It would seem that Thérèse herself never fully appreciated the force of her intellect. This power, however, generates sparks on every page of the *Story of a Soul.* Her genius is revealed in her disarming use of images to define spiritual and psychological states; in her integrated grasp of Sacred Scripture and the doctrine of the Church; in her mastery and creative recasting of the teaching of the great spiritual masters. Her genius is shown most clearly in her insights into the mysteries of the Christian share in the redemptive work of Christ and the Communion of the

---

[7] *L.C.*, pp. 60-61.

Saints. Thérèse is certainly not out of place when standing among the Doctors of the Church.[8]

A number of spiritual authors helped to form Thérèse in her relationship with God and prepared her as a "teacher" of the spiritual life. Four of these authors she specifically mentions: the author of *The Imitation of Christ*, Fr. Charles Arminjon, and of course, St. John of the Cross and St. Teresa of Jesus. We shall now investigate these influences on Thérèse's spiritual formation as well as the role Sacred Scripture had played in her spiritual development.

The Imitation of Christ

In the *Story of a Soul*, Thérèse explains the place *The Imitation of Christ* held in her spiritual life as a child and adolescent. Describing her spiritual growth, at the age of fourteen, Thérèse notes: "I was nourished for a long time on the 'pure flour' contained in *The Imitation of Christ*, this being the only book which did me any good, for as yet I had not discovered the treasures hidden in the Gospels."[9]

The Imitation of Christ, traditionally attributed to Thomas à Kempis, is certainly among the best known and loved pieces of Catholic literature. In it, the spirituality of the *Devotio Moderna*, a renewal movement of the late medieval period, finds its classical expression. Written originally for the "Brethren of the Common Life," *The Imitation of Christ* instructs the reader to practice the maxims of the Gospel in a literal manner in his daily dealings with God and neighbor. The first book of *The Imitation of Christ* offers practical suggestions on how to detach oneself from the things of this world and, thereby, to prepare for union with Christ. The reader is urged to make progress in his conversion by electing to travel "the royal road of the Cross."

---

[8] See Jean Guitton, *op. cit.*, *passim.*
[9] *S.*, p. 102.

In the second book, the author encourages all who are engaged in the following of Christ to further develop the interior life and diligently practice the virtues of Christ. Book three speaks of the incomparable consolation of union with Christ, while book four focuses the Christian on the Eucharist as the center of the spiritual life.

No doubt Christ's persistent call to self-abnegation and abandonment to Divine Providence, as recorded in *The Imitation* made a deep impression on the young Thérèse. In fact, she makes the startling statement in the *Story of a Soul* that by the age of fourteen she had committed nearly the entire text of *The Imitation of Christ* to memory:

> I knew almost all of my beloved *Imitation* by heart. This little book never parted company with me, for in summer I carried it in my pocket; in winter, in my muff. At Aunt's they used to amuse themselves by opening the book at random and telling me to recite the chapter before them.[10]

In the *Story of a Soul*, Thérèse cites *The Imitation of Christ* directly no less than twelve times; in her *Correspondence* twenty-seven times and at least three times in *Her Last Conversations*.

Thérèse used direct citations from *The Imitation of Christ* in three ways: First, she quoted the text, rooted firmly as it was in her formidable memory, as a source of personal illumination and consolation. For instance, on her pilgrimage to Rome, Thérèse met and conversed with noble, wealthy people. She admitted that for a moment her head had been turned by them. However, as she notes in the *Story of a Soul*: "I saw that 'all that glistens is not gold,' and I understood the words of the *Imitation*: 'Be not solicitous for the shadow of a name, nor for acquaintances with many, nor for the particular love of individuals.' (*Imitation of Christ*, III, 24, 2)."[11]

---

[10] *S., ibid.*
[11] *S.,* p. 121.

Secondly, Thérèse used *The Imitation of Christ* to interpret her own or others' spiritual experiences. For example, in explaining the special graces she and Céline had received as children, she observed: "As the *Imitation* says, God communicates Himself at times in the midst of great splendor or *'gently veiled, under shadows and figures.'* (*Imitation*, III, 43, 4). It was in this way He deigned to manifest Himself to our souls."[12]

Writing to Fr. Roulland on March 19, 1897, Thérèse uses the *Imitation* to elucidate his intense suffering in the missions:

> Truly, Brother, I cannot pity you since in you are realized the words of *The Imitation of Christ*: "When you find suffering sweet and when you love it for the love of Jesus Christ you will have found paradise on earth" (*Imitation*, II, 12, 11).[13]

Finally, Thérèse used the text of the *Imitation* as a vehicle for teaching her "little way." On July 11, 1897, she instructed her cousin, Marie Guérin: "I advise you, when you have struggles against charity, to read this chapter of *The Imitation of Christ*: 'We must bear with the faults of others.' You will find that your struggles will disappear; it always did me a lot of good. It's very good and very true."[14]

Since it applies directly to our subject, it is worth recalling that on the occasion of her second reception of Holy Communion, Thérèse received a very significant grace. She found herself praying a verse from *The Imitation of Christ*, a prayer that would give her direction and help her later to understand and interpret the varied and intense suffering of her life, including in particular, her "trial of faith": "O Jesus, unspeakable sweetness, change all

---

[12] *S.*, p. 104.
[13] *G.C. II*, p. 1069.
[14] *L.C.*, p. 252.

the consolations of this earth into bitterness for me" (*Imitation*, III, 26, 3).[15]

Thérèse writes that this prayer was, so to speak, placed in her mouth by God Himself. It might be also said that the prayer was "infused" and indicated Thérèse's specific mission as a victim of the Merciful Love of God. Describing this grace, so intimately bound to *The Imitation of Christ*, Thérèse observed: "This prayer fell from my lips without effort, without constraint; it seemed I repeated it not with my will but like a child who repeats the words a person he loves has inspired in him."[16]

Whereas it may be sad that Thérèse consistently used *The Imitation of Christ* to interpret her own spiritual experiences and to teach others the way of perfection, it may also be correctly asserted that Christ, Thérèse's "only teacher,"[17] used at least this one text of *The Imitation of Christ* to reveal the specific vocation He had chosen for His bride.

The copious, direct citations from *The Imitation of Christ* are by no means the only witness to the influence of that text on Thérèse's religious consciousness. Having memorized the book verbatim, Thérèse had at every moment, a rich source of meditation and contemplation; a source, as we have seen, that was not left untapped by the Lord Himself.

The *Imitation* had been so deeply imprinted on Thérèse's mind and heart that it was impossible for her not to weave its content and style into her own compositions. Above everything else, *The Imitation of Christ* helped Thérèse to understand the focus — that is, the point of gravity — of the spiritual life: union with Christ in all his mysteries — especially the mystery of the redemption.

---

[15] *S.*, p. 79; also see *L.C.*, p. 123.
[16] *S.*, pp. 79-80.
[17] *S.*, p. 179.

Father Charles Arminjon

In May of 1887, Thérèse read a book entitled *The End of the Present World and the Mysteries of the Future Life (Fin du Monde Present et Mystères de la Vie Future)*. The book, published in 1881, contained a series of doctrinal conferences that had been preached in the Chambery Cathedral by the theologian and orator, Father Charles Arminjon.

The titles of the nine conferences which Thérèse had read are:

1. On the End of the World — of Signs which are to Precede it and the Circumstances Accompanying it.
2. On the Persecution of the Anti-Christ and the Conversion of the Jews.
3. On the Resurrection of the Body and the General Judgment.
4. On the Place of Immortality or the State of the Glorious Body after the Resurrection.
5. On Purgatory.
6. On the Everlastingness of Pain and the Destiny of the Unfortunate.
7. On Eternal Bliss and the Supernatural Vision of God.
8. The Christian Sacrifice; Means of Redemption.
9. On the Mystery of Suffering in Relation with the Future life.[18]

Thérèse describes her reaction to these dogmatic treatises, which for an ordinary fourteen-year-old girl would have been heavy and dull. She said: "This reading was one of the greatest graces of my life. I read it by the window of my study and the impressions I received are too deep to express in human words."[19]

Although Thérèse had been carefully catechized in the dogmatic and moral teachings of the Catholic Church by her father and sisters, her teachers at the Abbey school and parish priests, she had not fully understood that the propositional truths of the Catho-

---

[18] Charles Arminjon, *The End of the Present World and the Mysteries of the Future Life*, trans. Martin Research Associates (Tampico, IL: Martin Books Edition, 1968).

[19] *S.*, p. 102.

lic Catechism terminate not in the abstract statement itself, but rather in the Truth Himself. Reading Arminjon's conferences on the Last Things, Thérèse was led to profound contemplation through the articles of faith:

> All the great truths of religion, the mysteries of eternity, plunged my soul into a state of joy not of this earth. I experienced already what God reserved for those who love Him (not with the eye but with the heart).[20]

Comparing the eternal joys of heaven and the momentary trials and sufferings of this life, Arminjon inspired Thérèse to unlimited generosity in her service of God:

> I wanted *to love, to love Jesus with a passion*, giving Him a thousand proofs of my love while it was possible. I copied out several passages on perfect love, on the reception God will give His elect at the moment *He* becomes their reward, great and eternal, and I repeated over and over the words of love burning in my heart.[21]

These spiritual conferences on the Last Things, scriptural and doctrinal in content, made such an impact on Thérèse that their influence is evident in many, if not most, of the major themes of her writings. The conferences also helped her to find meaning in the suffering caused by her "trial of faith."

First of all, Thérèse came to grasp, through these conferences, the broad contours of salvation history in the light of Christ's redeeming act. Arminjon explained the collapse of Christian culture which would precede the Second Coming of Christ. The masterful orator presented the signs of the parousia: the preaching of the Gospel to all nations; the conversion of the Jewish people; the apostasy of the Christian nations; the "legalization" of atheistic

---

[20] S., *ibid.*
[21] S., pp. 102-103.

humanism as the "religion" of the new age; the manifestation of the Anti-Christ in the final bloody persecution of the Church.

This view of the "end times" had a number of effects on Thérèse: Arminjon had carefully listed all the places in the world where the ministers of the Gospel had not yet penetrated. He pointed out the scriptural truth that Jesus would not return in glory until all the peoples of the earth had received the Gospel. This truth filled Thérèse with a burning zeal for the missionary activity of the Church. This zeal would later become evident both in her concern for her two spiritual brothers, each a missionary, and also in her desire to give her life in order to animate and fecundate the Church's work of evangelization in pagan lands.

This "world view" also helped Thérèse to understand the apostasy from the Faith which had marred her homeland since the days of the French Revolution. Thérèse, it must be noted, gives no evidence of apocalyptic tendencies in her thoughts. She never declared that her times were in fact, the end times, or that she was living during the time of the Anti-Christ. Rather, she came to understand that as the world proceeds closer to its conclusion, the faith, violently attacked and opposed, would be abandoned by many Christians. Throughout her years in Carmel, the desire to help those who would live in the days of the Anti-Christ grew in her heart. She herself longed to bear witness to the true faith in the midst of the great apostasy which was to take place. She gives voice to this desire in manuscript "B" of the *Story of a Soul*: "When thinking of the torments which will be the lot of Christians at the time of the Anti-Christ, I feel my heart leap for joy and I would that these torments be reserved for me."[22]

Father Arminjon helped to solidify and strengthen Thérèse's view of the joys of heaven. He deepened her grasp of this article of faith by providing her with teaching on the physical resurrection of the dead on the last day and the union of the elect with the Holy Trinity in their glorified bodies.

---

[22] S., p. 193.

One passage of Arminjon's teaching moved Thérèse immensely. Comparing the sufferings of the present life to the joys of eternity, as well as the Christian's gift of self to God in this life and God's gift of Himself to the elect in heaven, Arminjon encouraged his congregation to make every sacrifice while there is still time to do something significant for the Lord. He said:

> Oh! the Lord cannot forget that the saints, when they lived long ago on the earth, paid Him homage and the total deliverance of their peace and quiet, of their joys and of their whole being; that they would have wished a perennial blood in their veins to shed as a living and inexhaustible proof of their faith; that they would have desired a thousand hearts in their breasts to consume them with the inextinguishable fires, to possess a thousand bodies to hand them over to martyrdom, like hosts endlessly being reborn. And the bountiful God cries out: "Now it's my turn. To the gift which the saints had made me of themselves, can I respond otherwise than by giving of Myself without restriction or limitation."[23]

This teaching of Arminjon had made such an impression on Thérèse, that she mentioned it in at least five of her letters to Céline. For instance, encouraging Céline to bear up under the strain of her father's illness, she wrote on July 23, 1888:

> Jesus is looking at us and He is *begging* this sorrow, this agony from us. He needs it for souls and for our soul. He wants to give us such beautiful recompense, and His ambitions for us are very great. But how can He say: "My turn," if ours hasn't come, if we have given Him nothing? Alas, it does pain Him to give us sorrows to drink, but He knows this is the only means of preparing us to know Him as *He knows Himself* and to become *gods ourselves.*[24]

---

[23] Charles Arminjon, *op. cit.*, Conf. VII, p. 22.
[24] *G.C. I*, p. 450. See *LT* 94, 107, 157, 169 all written to Céline.

Arminjon spoke eloquently of God's desire to communicate Himself totally to every human person in an "eternal face to face vision."[25] The preacher's ardent words filled Thérèse with the desire to make every sacrifice to help satisfy God's desire for man's eternal salvation. This seventh conference inspired Thérèse to limitless generosity in her Oblation to God for the salvation of souls. The knowledge that man's proper end is the enjoyment of God in heaven and that God also earnestly desires this union, animated Thérèse throughout the rest of her life to work tirelessly in union with Christ for the salvation of all mankind. So ardent was this desire, that Thérèse was unable to fathom the concept of eternal rest after the death of the body. She desired to continue in heaven her work — Jesus' work — of saving souls.

Arminjon gave Thérèse a solution to this issue which had preoccupied her for a long period of time. He noted in one of his conferences that the angels both enjoy the beatific vision and help us as our guardians and guides.

> The angels enjoy a perfect bliss and they see eternally the face of their Father who is in heaven. Nevertheless they dispose and coordinate the material elements; they preside over the movement of the stars and they are not heedless of the presence of God when they help us in our pilgrimage or enlighten us with their inspirations.[26]

This insight of Arminjon had made such an impression on Thérèse that nearly ten years later, writing to Fr. Roulland, she

---

[25] See Charles Arminjon, *op. cit.*, Conf. VII, p. 22: "I must be the soul of their soul, says the Lord, and penetrate them and have them drink of my divinity as fire consumes iron; that, by showing me their soul, unclouded without veil, without a thinking intermediary, I may unite myself to them in an eternal face to face; may my glory illuminate them, that it may transpire and shine through the pores of their being in order that 'knowing me as I know them, they may become "gods" themselves.'" See also Thérèse's "Act of Oblation to Merciful Love," *S.*, p. 276-77, that echoes these ideas of consuming and transforming fire and the "Eternal Face to Face."

[26] Charles Arminjon, *op. cit.*, p. 29.

cites the text as a support for her desire to spend her heaven doing good on earth:

> I really count on not remaining inactive in heaven. My desire is to work still for the Church and for souls. I am asking God for this and I am certain He will answer me. Are not the angels continually occupied with us without ever ceasing to see the divine Face and to lose themselves in the Ocean of Love without shores? Why would Jesus not allow me to imitate them.[27]

Thérèse had obviously found her answer in Arminjon's explanation of the angels' "work" in heaven. If the angels are able to enjoy the Lord's presence and at the same time govern the material universe and act as guardians of souls, what could stop her, in the Communion of Saints, from both seeing God face to face and, at the same time, working to establish His kingdom on earth?

In summary, then, Arminjon provided a number of invaluable services for Thérèse. He gave her a broad view of history in the Christian perspective, taught her the doctrine of the Second Coming of Christ and the resurrection of the dead on the last day. He explained the "signs" of the end and inspired in her a great desire to help those who would, in fact, live in the time of the Anti-Christ. He also inspired her to "work" through prayers and penance to quench Christ's thirst for souls in an "eternal face to face union." Finally, in his digression on the angels, Arminjon helped Thérèse to formulate her dynamic concept of heaven in which the elect, in union with Christ, continue to "work" for the salvation of all.

Arminjon prepared Thérèse in several ways for her "trial of faith."[28] He helped her to suspect, at least, that her trial might be

---

[27] *G.C. II*, p. 1142.

[28] Ida F. Görres, *op. cit.*, p. 406: "The powerful influence of the *Imitation of Christ* never abated no more than did that of Abbé Arminjon."

akin to the sufferings the elect would undergo in the last days. He also inspired her to offer her trial as a kind of martyrdom to expiate the sins of those who would deny Christ through the rejection of the Catholic Faith.

Whereas *The Imitation of Christ* had consciously made Christ the central focus of her spiritual way, so Arminjon's conferences had made heaven — heaven for herself and for others — the conscious motive of her self-oblation in Carmel. Thérèse had read Arminjon's conferences in May of 1887, the very month in which she sought permission from her father to enter Carmel. She notes:

> All of the great truths of religion, the mysteries of eternity, plunge my soul into a state of joy not of the earth.... I wanted *to love, to love Jesus with a passion*, giving Him a thousand proofs of my love while it was still possible.[29]

St. Teresa of Jesus

Thérèse first mentions St. Teresa of Jesus in Chapter II of the *Story of a Soul*, when she describes the first sermon she understood as a young child:

> The first sermon I *did understand* and which *touched me deeply*, was a sermon on the Passion preached by Father Ducellier and since then I've understood all the others. When the preacher spoke about St. Teresa, papa leaned over and whispered: "Listen carefully, little queen, he's talking about your patroness."[30]

St. Teresa of Jesus is, however, much more than the "patron saint" of Thérèse of Lisieux. She is, in the deepest sense of the term, Thérèse's spiritual mother. There is a striking monument to this

---

[29] S., p. 102.
[30] S., p. 42.

truth which stands in the hospital of St. Thérèse de Villeneuve-Sur-Lot. It is a sculpture by the Parisian artist Collamarini of St. Teresa of Jesus and St. Thérèse of Lisieux. The two women are not standing side by side; the artist does not present them simply as teacher and disciple. Rather St. Teresa of Jesus is depicted as giving birth to her Daughter, St. Thérèse of Lisieux.

Stated simply, it is not possible to understand Thérèse and her spiritual doctrine apart from the teaching of the foundress of the Discalced Carmelites. Also, as we shall later see, Thérèse's writings clarify and, in a sense, simplify many of the ascetical and mystical teachings of both St. Teresa of Jesus and St. John of the Cross, the parents and Doctors of the Carmelite Reform. Thérèse renders their doctrine, which is often perceived as lofty and formidable, accessible to Christians in every state of life.

Thérèse rarely cited the works of St. Teresa of Jesus in a direct way. She mentioned her spiritual Mother only six times in the *Story of a Soul*, thirteen times in her *General Correspondence*, and seven times in *Her Last Conversations*. Only on one occasion does Thérèse directly praise St. Teresa's doctrine. In the *Story of a Soul*, she observes:

> O Mother, how different are the ways through which the Lord leads souls! In the life of the saints we find many of them who don't want to leave anything of themselves behind after their death, not the smallest souvenir, not the least bit of writing. On the contrary, there are others, like our Holy Mother St. Teresa, who have enriched the Church with their lofty revelations, having no fears of revealing the secrets of the King.[31]

The fact that the Daughter quotes infrequently from the writings of the Mother should not be used to dismiss St. Teresa of Jesus as a major influence in the spiritual life of Thérèse. It would seem that Thérèse had read the life of St. Teresa of Jesus and her

---

[31] S., p. 207.

complete works before her entry into Carmel at the age of fifteen.[32]
This early exposure of Thérèse to St. Teresa of Jesus' thought not
only prepared Thérèse for her life in Carmel but also served as the
perfect introduction to the spiritual doctrine of St. John of the
Cross.

After her entry into Carmel, Thérèse lived her remaining years
immersed daily in Teresian spirituality. Every facet of her life was
formed "in the school of St. Teresa" through the faithful observance of the Rule and Constitutions of Carmel.[33] The careful study
of St. Teresa of Jesus' *Way of Perfection* and her other spiritual writings was an integral part of Thérèse's formation as a religious.[34]
Mother Agnes of Jesus, during the canonical process, attested to
the fact that Thérèse had been devoted to the study of the writings of St. Teresa of Jesus.[35] Furthermore, St. Teresa of Jesus exerted a daily influence on her Sisters through their daily reading
of the Rule and Constitutions and other spiritual writings. The oral,
lived tradition of Carmel made "La Madre" ever present in the
daily routine of her daughters. Thus, Thérèse had been thoroughly
formed in the school of Teresian spirituality simply by living the
life of Carmel.

It is interesting to briefly compare the lives of the two great
Saints, mother and daughter. St. Teresa of Jesus (1515-1582) was
a Spanish woman of Castilian origin who lived at the beginning

---

[32] *Histoire de Sainte Thérèse*, d'après Les Bollandistes, ses divers historiens et ses
oeuvres complètes.

[33] *Règle Primitive et Constitutions des Religieuses de l'Ordre de Notre-Dame du Mont
Carmel*, Selon la Reformation de Sainte Thérèse pour les Monastères de son ordre
en France (Poitiers: 1865). See Pierre Descouvemont, *Sainte Thérèse de l'Enfant
Jesus et son Prochain* (Paris: P. Lethielleux, 1959), p. 249.

[34] Available for her use in the Lisieux Carmel was: *Oeuvres de Sainte Thérèse*,
Traduites d'après les manuscrits originaux par Marcel Bouix, SJ: Vol. I: *Vie* Ecrite
par elle-même (Paris: 1884); Vol. II: *Livre des Fondations, Exclamations, Avis
Spirituels* (Paris: 1885); Vol. III: *Chemin de la Perfection, Fragment du Livre sur le
Cantique des Cantiques, Chateau Interieur* (Paris: 1884); see Pierre
Descouvemont, *op. cit.*, p. 258.

[35] See Pierre Blanchard, "Saint Teresa of Avila and Saint Thérèse of Lisieux,"
Spiritual Life (9:159-173), Fall 1963, p. 161.

of the sixteenth century; St. Thérèse (1873-1897), a French woman from Normandy who lived at the end of the nineteenth century. Teresa came from a middle class family. She had nine brothers and three sisters. Thérèse's family was also among the middle class of her time. She grew up in the company of four sisters. Teresa of Jesus lost her mother at the age of thirteen; Thérèse at the age of four. Teresa died at the age of 67; Thérèse at the age of 24.

The personality of St. Teresa of Jesus is complex. She relates in her *Life* a number of "conversions" leading up to her quest for perfection. Thérèse is simple in her outlook and determined, by the age of fourteen, to become a saint. After her "conversion" on Christmas Eve, 1886, Thérèse notes that she was never again overcome in any combat. Her spiritual director, Fr. Pichon, assured her as a novice in Carmel that she had never seriously offended God.

Teresa of Jesus had traveled far and wide across Spain to establish the houses of her Order. She frequently met with the highest dignitaries — theologians, bishops, papal nuncios, kings, men and women of the world. Thérèse lived an obscure life within the walls of Carmel. When she died, she was known only by her family and religious community and a few friends.

Teresa of Jesus experienced a multitude of mystical phenomena during her life: ecstasies, transports, flights of the spirit, locutions, divine wounds, levitation, etc. Thérèse, on the other hand, although no stranger to mystical phenomena as we shall see, was primarily graced with an abundance of divine love received without the accompanying phenomena or consolations.

Both suffered ill health: Teresa was seriously ill for three years at the very beginning of her religious life. In fact, shortly after she entered the Convent of the Incarnation she became mortally ill, was in a comatose state, pronounced dead and prepared for burial. During most of her adult life she suffered various illnesses: pains in the back, headaches, toothaches, fevers, liver and kidney problems, and violent hemorrhages at the end of her life. As noted in Chapter I, Thérèse, too, suffered ill health throughout most of her life.

Teresa's personal vocation was the reform of her Order and the establishment of a pattern of spirituality for all Carmelites. Thérèse's personal vocation was to draw souls to share in her love and confidence in God. Her call was to "popularize," in the best sense of that word, the spirituality of the Carmelite Reform and to make it accessible to Christians of every state of life.

Finally, Teresa of Jesus is considered one of the greatest writers of Christian literature and has been named a Doctor of the Church. However, many find her writings disorganized and her thoughts scattered. Thérèse, on the other hand, although tied down by a style considered by many as excessively sentimental, is clear, to the point, and didactic in the best sense of that term.

In spite of these differences and as a result of the influence Teresa had exerted on Thérèse in her religious formation, the Saints have a great deal in common: Teresa and Thérèse possessed powerful intellect and wills, as is evident in both their lives and writings. The faculties of each were riveted to God and the accomplishment of His Will. In a letter to her spiritual brother, Fr. Roulland, Thérèse notes that St. Teresa of Jesus, a woman of "manly strength" would never have accepted her into Carmel had she remained a weak, oversensitive child. Speaking of her "conversion" Thérèse notes:

> Jesus transformed me in such a way that I no longer recognized myself. Without this change, I would have had to remain for years in the world. St. Teresa, who said to her daughters: "I want you to be women in nothing, but in everything may you equal strong men," would not have wanted to acknowledge me as her child if the Lord had not clothed me in His divine strength, if He had not Himself armed me for war.[36]

Thérèse admired St. Teresa's strength of character and her will to die to every human attachment and inclination in order to

---

[36] *G.C. II*, pp. 1016-1017.

be united to God alone. In each of her struggles in Carmel and in particular, in her "trial of faith," Thérèse revealed that she truly shared in her Mother's "manly" spirit of strength, determination, courage and generosity in Christian combat.

In his excellent article entitled: "Teresa of Avila and Thérèse of Lisieux," the Canon Pierre Blanchard notes: "Though Thérèse seldom quotes St. Teresa, she is often inspired by her — consciously or unconsciously. Sometimes it is difficult to know which things to classify as borrowed."[37]

Blanchard gives two revealing examples: In manuscript "B" Thérèse, to underscore her weakness and total dependency upon the power of Jesus, presents the image of herself as a "little bird" who was unable to fly into the sun, i.e., the life of the Holy Trinity. She then describes how her "union" will be accomplished:

> As long as You desire it, O my beloved, Your little bird will remain without strength and without wings and will always stay with its gaze upon You.... One day I hope that You, the adorable Eagle, will come to fetch me, Your little bird, and ascending with it to the Furnace of Love, You will plunge it for all eternity into the burning Abyss of that Love to which it has offered itself as a victim.[38]

Did Thérèse, as many presume, cast this image of the little bird from her knowledge of Scripture? For instance, from Exodus 19:4 or Deuteronomy 32:11: "Like an eagle watching its nest, hovering over its young, he spreads out his wings to hold him, he supports him on his pinions." Or rather, is Thérèse's inspiration directly drawn from the writings of St. Teresa of Jesus? In the *Life*, St. Teresa describes the mystical rapture thus: "...without any forethought or any help there frequently comes a force so swift and powerful that one sees and feels this cloud or mighty eagle raise it up and carry it aloft on its wings."[39]

---

[37] Pierre Blanchard, *op. cit.*, p. 167.
[38] *S.*, p. 200.
[39] St. Teresa of Avila, *The Collected Works*, Vol. I: *The Book of Her Life*, trans. Kieran

Thérèse of Lisieux had also practiced the "little virtues" in imitation of her Mother, St. Teresa of Jesus. Describing her practice, for instance, of the virtue of charity during her first years in Carmel, Thérèse offers an example: "I applied myself to practicing little virtues, not having the capacity of practicing the great. For instance, I loved to fold up the mantles forgotten by the Sisters and to render them all sorts of little services."[40]

St. Teresa of Jesus relates an identical occurrence in her *Life*:

> So, with respect to humility it occurred to me, upon seeing that all were advancing except myself — for I was never good for anything — to gather up all their mantles when they left the choir. It seemed to me I was serving those angels that were praising God there. I did this until — I don't know how — they came to know about it. This caused me no little embarrassment because my virtue hadn't reached the point of desiring that they know these things; and this wasn't out of humility but lest they laugh at me, since these things were such trifles.[41]

These are only two obvious points of textual comparison. The influence of St. Teresa is also discernible in every major theme explicated in Thérèse's writings: understanding her Foundress' goals perfectly, Thérèse saw her vocation as a call to contemplative love of God. For both Mother and Daughter, the Carmelite vocation was not primarily a call to penance or victimhood, but rather, it was a call to the perfection of love through specific means: namely, prayer, penance and the common life lived within the enclosure.

However, like her spiritual Mother, Thérèse never separated the contemplative love of God from the love of neighbor. Teresa

---

Kavanaugh, OCD, and Otilio Rodriguez, OCD (Washington, DC: ICS Publication, 1987), p. 173. (Henceforth cited as *Life*.)

[40] *S.*, 159.
[41] *Life*, p. 275.

had taught Thérèse that contemplative love, if it be authentic, will overflow and have a healing and elevating effect in the Church. Teresa's admonition to her Sisters to spare nothing for the salvation of souls was not left unheeded by Thérèse. She had come to understand the teaching of St. Teresa of Jesus: that the most ardent desires to work and suffer with Christ for the salvation of souls are possessed by those who attain to the mystical marriage — the highest degree of contemplative union with Christ attainable in this life.[42]

St. Teresa's *Way of Perfection* had impressed on Thérèse the importance of "working" for the sanctification of priests. In this book, St. Teresa of Jesus states:

> Since we would all be occupied in prayer for those who are the defenders of the Church and for preachers and for learned men who protect her from attack, we could help as much as possible this Lord of mine Who is so roughly treated by those for whom He has done so much good.[43]

St. Teresa of Jesus also clearly points out in the *Way of Perfection* that apart from this "end," Carmel would make no sense:

> And when your prayers, desires, disciplines and fasts are not directed towards obtaining these things I mentioned, reflect on how you are not accomplishing or fulfilling the purpose for which the Lord brought you here together. And may the Lord, because of Who His majesty is, never allow you to forget this.[44]

---

[42] See St. Teresa of Avila, *The Collected Works of St. Teresa of Avila*, Vol. I: *The Interior Castle*, trans. Kieran Kavanaugh, OCD, and Otilio Rodriguez, OCD (Washington, DC: ICS Publications, 1980), pp. 427-452. (Henceforth cited as *Interior Castle*.)

[43] St. Teresa of Avila, *The Collected Works of St. Teresa of Avila*, Vol. II: *The Way of Perfection*, trans. Kieran Kavanaugh, OCD, and Otilio Rodriguez, OCD (Washington, DC: ICS Publications, 1976) p. 42. (Henceforth cited as *The Way of Perfection*.)

[44] *The Way of Perfection*, p. 52.

It is interesting to note that Thérèse believed St. Teresa of Jesus had chosen her "spiritual brothers" for her:

> It was our holy Mother, St. Teresa, who sent me my first little brother as a feast day gift in 1895. I was in the laundry, very much occupied by my work, when Mother Agnes of Jesus took me aside and read a letter she had just received. It was from a young seminarian, inspired, he said, by St. Teresa of Avila. He was asking for a Sister who would devote herself especially to the salvation of his soul and aid him through her prayers and sacrifices when he was a missionary so that he could save many souls. He promised to remember the one who would become his sister at the Holy Sacrifice each day after he was ordained. Mother Agnes of Jesus told me she wanted me to become the sister of this future missionary.[45]

In another article also entitled "Teresa of Avila and Thérèse of Lisieux," Father Agapito Dias Cabrera lists those qualities which Thérèse not only held in common with Teresa, but to be more precise, those characteristics which Teresa, through her Constitutions and writings, formed in the soul of Thérèse. These points summarize well the essential role St. Teresa of Jesus had played in the spiritual formation of Thérèse. They also help us to understand her role as a "source" of Thérèse's spiritual doctrine:

— The spirit of prayer;
— The love of Jesus Christ, based on the indestructible foundation of the Humanity of Our Savior;
— Missionary zeal for the salvation of souls;
— Sisterly charity made up of minute daily details;
— The spirit of humility;
— The practical feeling of gratitude;
— The love and devotion for the sanctification of priests, together with personal friendship and sisterly affection with a

---

[45] S., p. 251.

number of them. (St. John of the Cross and Father Gracián on the one hand and Fathers Bellière and Roulland, on the other.)[46]

St. John of the Cross

In Thérèse's time, the writings of St. John of the Cross were popular in France. In 1876, three years after Thérèse's birth, two different translations of the works of St. John of the Cross were published: one by a Father Charles Mary, C.S., and the other by the Carmelites of Paris. The Carmelite version was well received and by 1922 had been reprinted four times.[47]

Thérèse revealed that she had some contact with the writings of St. John of the Cross even before her entry into Carmel. Writing of her spiritual bond with her sister Céline, at the age of fourteen, Thérèse quotes St. John of the Cross' *Spiritual Canticle*:

> Jesus wanting to have us advance together, formed bonds in our hearts stronger than blood. He made us become *spiritual sisters*, and in us were realized the words of St. John of the Cross' *Canticle* (speaking to her spouse, the bride exclaims):

> > Following your footprints
> > Maidens run lightly along the way,
> > The touch of a spark,
> > The special wine,
> > Cause flowings in them from the balsam of God.[48]

---

[46] Agapito Dias Cabrera, "Teresa of Avila and Thérèse of Lisieux," *Sicut Parvuli* (Vol. XLIV, No. 2, 5/82), p. 50.

[47] See Gabriel of St. Mary Magdalen, OCD, "St. Thérèse's Little Way and the Teachings of St. John of the Cross," *Spiritual Life* (Vol. 2, No. Z-6/56), p. 75.

[48] S., p. 103.

Later in Carmel, in the midst of aridity, interior trials, and conflicts within the community, and as she failed to be understood by her religious superior, novice mistress and spiritual directors, Thérèse found consolation and direction chiefly in the writings of St. John of the Cross. She notes: "Ah! how many lights have I not drawn from the works of our Holy Father, St. John of the Cross. At the age of seventeen and eighteen, I had no other spiritual nourishment."[49]

There is no record of Thérèse ever having met a Carmelite friar — neither as spiritual director, retreat master or instructor in ascetico-mystical theology. Many priests passed through the Carmel — Jesuits, Franciscans, missionaries of various societies, diocesan priests — but never the mention of a Carmelite. Yet as we have noted already, Thérèse was Carmelite to the very marrow of her bones. This may only be explained by the "culture" created by her faithful observance of the Carmelite Rule and the Constitutions of St. Teresa of Jesus as well as her precocious and graced assimilation of the spiritual doctrine of the Reformers of Carmel.

During her years in Carmel, Thérèse had a copy of the *Spiritual Canticle* and the *Living Flame of Love* for her personal use.[50] The complete works of the Saint were in the library of the Lisieux Carmel at Thérèse's disposal.[51] Thérèse kept her copy of the *Spiritual Canticle* and the *Living Flame of Love* near her bedside during her last months in the infirmary of the Lisieux Carmel. She consulted these works frequently and marked off several passages which we shall carefully pursue later in this book.[52]

During the canonical process, several witnesses highlighted Thérèse's devotion to St. John of the Cross and his writings. For instance, Sr. Marie of the Trinity said: "She had a filial love of St.

---

[49] *S.*, p. 179.
[50] Pierre Descouvemont, *op. cit.*, pp. 256, 257.
[51] *Ibid.*, p. 257.
[52] See *L.C.*, pp. 245, 246.

Teresa and St. John of the Cross. The latter's writings especially filled her with love."[53]

Thérèse quotes St. John of the Cross frequently in all of her writings: fourteen times in the *Story of a Soul*; twenty-one times in her *General Correspondence*; and eight times in *Her Last Conversations*. Significantly, Thérèse cites the *Ascent of Mount Carmel* and *Dark Night of the Soul* only rarely; for example, she does so only once in her *General Correspondence*, whereas she cites the *Spiritual Canticle* twelve times in her letters. Also, *Her Last Conversations* are filled with references, both direct and oblique, to the content of the *Spiritual Canticle*.

Venerable Anne of Jesus, the foundress of Carmel in France, was the one who had asked St. John of the Cross to write a commentary on his poem, the *Spiritual Canticle*. It was the same Venerable Anne of Jesus who "appeared" to Thérèse in a dream to console her in her "trial of faith."[54] The *Spiritual Canticle* was to be one of the chief supports of Thérèse in her trial and the "tool" which helped her to interpret her mysterious suffering. As we shall see, it is highly significant that Thérèse turned to the *Spiritual Canticle* for help in her "trial of faith" rather than to the *Ascent of Mount Carmel* or the *Dark Night*.

Three major themes of St. John of the Cross' writings are at the core of Thérèse's spirituality and teaching: the necessity of detachment from creatures in order to attain union with God; the primacy of love in the spiritual life; and the apostolic fecundity of contemplative prayer.

In the *Ascent of Mount Carmel* and the *Dark Night of the Soul*, St. John of the Cross explains how God seeks to detach the soul through various trials from disordered attachment to relationships, material things, and even from that self-seeking, which accompanies the imperfect love of God and neighbor. The Christian, moved by divine grace, must seek to enter the "active night"

---

[53] *P.*, p. 242.
[54] *S.*, pp. 190-191.

in which he progressively rejects mortal sin, then venial sin and deliberate faults and thus struggles to attain deeper self-knowledge through the imitation of Christ's virtues. Then at a time ordained by God, the Christian soul is further purified in the "passive nights" which effect mystical union.

Although Thérèse did not speak in a systematic way of active or passive purgation in her life, she did frequently state that God in His goodness had preserved her from attachment to creatures:

> How can I thank Jesus for making me find *"only bitterness in earth's friendships"*! With a bent such as mine, I would have allowed myself to be taken and my wings to be clipped and then how would I have been able to *"fly and be at rest"*? How can a heart given over to the affection of creatures be intimately united with God? I *feel* this is not possible. Without having drunk the empoisoned cup of a too ardent love of creatures, I feel I cannot be mistaken. I have seen so many souls seduced by this *false light* fly like poor moths and burn their wings, and then return to the real and gentle light of *love* that gives them new wings which are more brilliant and delicate so that they can fly towards Jesus, that divine fire "which burns without consuming."[55]

Thérèse frequently spoke of detachment as a means to the true end of all spirituality: the selfless love of God and neighbor. Thérèse's doctrine is identical to that of her spiritual father. As one author has noted:

> It is clear that Thérèse did not intend to diminish the demands of St. John of the Cross; she, no less than he, is a soul vibrating with a spirit of totality. This totality she finds in giving. The mystical doctor says: "To love is to strip

---

[55] *S.*, p. 83.

oneself for God of all that is not God!" Thérèse says: "To love is to give all and even oneself!" Is there any difference between these two definitions? In substance, no: in shadings; yes. The word "stripping" has a more negative aspect than "giving" which indicates, instead, a positive act.[56]

In other words, the "*nada*" of St. John of the Cross is translated by Thérèse as "total giving" or as "giving all." In her "Little Way," perfect union with God is attained through "total generosity in active detachment and docility to the Will of God in passive detachment."[57] In other words, to attain perfect union with Jesus, the Christian must be ready to make every sacrifice and abandon himself to every manifestation of the Will of God. Through this giving which causes death to self, the Christian encounters the healing and transforming presence of Christ.

In the teaching of St. John of the Cross, love holds absolute primacy in the spiritual life. Active and passive purgation, penance, prayer — every means given by God for the attainment of holiness — if it is authentic, will lead to the sincere and sacrificial love of God and neighbor. Writing in the *Spiritual Canticle* of the person who has attained perfect union with God, St. John of the Cross observes: "All of the ability of my soul and body (memory, intellect and will, interior and exterior senses, appetites of the memory and spiritual parts) move in love and because of love. Everything I do, I do with love, and everything I suffer, I suffer with the delight of love."[58]

For Thérèse, love is the only force able to move her into action. This theme, always at the forefront of Thérèse's mind, becomes even more dominant during the last year and a half of her life. She notes frequently, citing St. John of the Cross, that she is

---

[56] Gabriel of St. Mary Magdalen, OCD, *op. cit.*, p. 88.

[57] *Ibid.*, p. 90.

[58] *Spiritual Canticle*, p. 586.

literally being consumed by the love of God. Less than a month before her death, Thérèse told Mother Agnes: "Ah! it is incredible how all my hopes have been fulfilled. When I used to read St. John of the Cross, I begged God to work out in me what he wrote; that is, the same thing as though I were to live to be very old; to consume me rapidly in love. And I have been answered!"[59]

It was St. John of the Cross who empowered Thérèse to understand and articulate the significant mystical graces she had received in her life. Her vocabulary of mysticism is his. She had revealed to Mother Agnes that throughout her life, she had experienced extended periods of "quietude," "transports of love," "flights of the spirit," and the "mystical wound of love."

St. John of the Cross' teaching that those who had attained to the mystical marriage would "die of love" gae Thérèse light and consolation as she endured her physical illness and the "trial of faith." Affirming repeatedly that she would die of love, Thérèse revealed that she had attained the highest degree of union with God possible in this life. Her interpretation and explanation of St. John of the Cross' concept of the "death of love" manifests her genius in the realm of spirituality.

Lastly, it was St. John of the Cross who had taught Thérèse the value of contemplative prayer in the life of the Church and, consequently, the deep meaning of her Carmelite vocation:

> Until the soul reaches this state of union of love, she should practice love in both the active and contemplative life. Yet once she arrives, she should not become involved in other works and exterior exercises that might be of the slightest hindrance to the attentiveness of love toward God, even though the work be of great service to God. For a little of this pure love is more precious to God and the soul and more beneficial to the Church even though it seems one is doing nothing, than all these other works put together.[60]

---

[59] *L.C.*, p. 177.
[60] *Spiritual Canticle*, p. 587.

In conclusion Thérèse's teachings on asceticism and mysticism, as well as her stress on the primacy of love in the spiritual life, developed organically from the doctrine of St. John of the Cross in every respect. It is impossible to understand Thérèse apart from John. It might also be said that Thérèse renders St. John of the Cross' spiritual doctrine palpable and accessible to the Christian seeking holiness in the midst of the world today.

Sacred Scripture

Thérèse's primary source of inspiration, however, was the inspired Word of God. Before her entry into Carmel, Thérèse's exposure to Sacred Scripture was minimal — limited to the texts read during Mass and to the fragments of Scripture found in *The Imitation of Christ*, the writings of St. Teresa of Jesus and other spiritual books. Thérèse confesses her ignorance of Scripture before her entry into Carmel. Speaking of her love of *The Imitation of Christ* and Fr. Arminjon's conferences, she noted: "I was nourished for a long time on the 'pure flour' contained in *The Imitation of Christ*, this being the only book which did me any good, for as yet I had not discovered the treasures hidden in the Gospels"[61] She admitted that since her eighteenth year, the Scriptures, and in particular the Gospels, became her one source of meditation and contemplation. Explaining her inability to read and benefit from spiritual books after her eighteenth year, Thérèse explains:

> If I open a book composed by a spiritual author (even the most beautiful, the most touching book) I feel my heart contract immediately and I read without understanding, so to speak. Or if I do understand, my mind comes to a standstill without the capacity of meditating. In this helplessness, Holy Scripture and *The Imitation* come to my

---

[61] *S.*, p. 102. See Pierre Descouvemont, *op. cit.*, pp. 253-254, for a complete survey of the translations of Sacred Scripture used by Thérèse in Carmel.

aid; in them I discover a solid and very *pure* nourishment. But, it is especially the *Gospels* which sustain me during my hours of prayer, for in them I find what is necessary for my poor little soul. I am constantly discovering in them new lights, hidden and mysterious meanings.[62]

By Thérèse's own admission, we know that the Scriptures became her daily food during the hours of mental prayer and spiritual reading in Carmel. Literally every page of the *Story of a Soul*, the *General Correspondence*, and *Her Last Conversations* contains either a direct quote from the Sacred Scriptures or is, at least, filled with thoughts and sentiments of the inspired texts. Thérèse, through her daily immersion in Scripture, thought in its categories, spoke and wrote under its direct influence and always "broke the bread" of the Divine Word in her communication with others.

All of Thérèse's writings reveal that she had acquired a keen intellectual penetration of the Old and New Testaments. Considering the sad neglect of the inspired text common in her day, her knowledge of the Word of God was admirable and, in fact, formidable. Most, if not all of her insights into the spiritual life had their genesis in her relentless quest to root her personal relationship with Christ firmly in His Word.

Interestingly, Thérèse had "aspired" to formal scriptural scholarship. Shortly before her death she said to Mother Agnes:

It's only in heaven that we will see the whole truth about everything. This is impossible on earth. Thus even regarding Holy Scripture, isn't it sad to see so many translations! Had I been a priest, I would have learned Hebrew and Greek and wouldn't have been satisfied with Latin. In this way I would have known the real text dictated by the Holy Spirit.[63]

---

[62] *S.*, p. 179.
[63] *L.C.*, p. 132.

Thérèse had revealed her desire to comment on the text of the Canticle of Canticles (or Song of Songs) o her cousin Marie Guérin, then a novice in Carmel: "If I had the time I would like to make a commentary on the *Canticle of Canticles*; I have found in this book such profound things about the union of the soul with its Beloved."[64]

In his article entitled "The Song of Songs and Thérèse," Roland Murphy, O. Carm., observes:

> There are many reasons to admire Thérèse's desire to prepare this commentary: For one thing, the ease with which she accepts and even yearns to comment on a biblical book (to my knowledge she has said this of no other book in the Bible). Can we make a surmise about the missing commentary? What would it have been like? I would suggest the "Sermons" of Bernard of Clairvaux. He wrote eighty-six sermons for his confrères at Clairvaux over a period of eighteen years (1135-1153) in a century that could count some thirty works dealing solely with the "Song of Songs."[65]

Reflecting on Thérèse's desire to comment upon Scripture, it is tempting to suggest that each manuscript of the *Story of a Soul* may simply be a commentary on various texts of Sacred Scripture. For instance, manuscript "A" which reveals Thérèse's discovery of her "Little Way" may be read as her commentary on three Old Testament passages which illuminated the specific path to divine union prepared for her by God. These texts frequently surface whenever Thérèse teaches her "Little Way": "Whoever is a little one, let him come to me" (Proverbs 9:4); "For to him that is little, mercy will be shown" (Wisdom 6:7); "As one whom a mother

---

[64] Quoted in Guy Gaucher, *op. cit.*, p. 141.

[65] Roland Murphy, O. Carm., "The Song of Songs and Thérèse," *Carmelite Studies*, ed. John Sullivan, OCD (Washington, DC: ICS Publications, 1990), p. 9.

caresses, so will I comfort you; you shall be carried at the breasts, and upon the knees they shall fondle you" (Isaiah 66:12-13).[66]

Manuscript "B" explains the discovery of Thérèse's unique vocation in the pages of Sacred Scripture. Unable to fully comprehend her "immense desires" to suffer and work for Christ's glory, Thérèse turned to the Word of God and found her answer in St. Paul's description of the Church as the Mystical Body of Christ and his hymn to charity in chapters 12 and 13 of the First Letter to the Corinthians.[67]

Thérèse will use Scripture texts later in manuscript "C" in order to buttress her image of the "Divine Elevator." For the little one, she explained, Jesus' arms become the "lift" to heaven. All the "little one" has to do is acknowledge his powerlessness and abandon himself with full confidence to the embrace of Jesus.[68]

But above all, manuscript "C" is in reality Thérèse's masterpiece on supernatural charity. Weaving into the text both her doctrine of the "Little Way" and her awareness that her vocation is to be "Love in the heart of the Church," Thérèse offers a profound commentary on the twofold commandment of Christ. It is in fact, her hymn to love.

Long before Scripture scholars came to realize the immense Christological significance of the Servant Songs of Isaiah (Isaiah 42:1-9; 49:1-7; 50:4-11; 52:13-ch. 53), Thérèse of Lisieux had discovered them and placed them at the very center of her spirituality.[69] These texts revealed to Thérèse the abandonment of Christ to the Will of the Father in taking upon Himself the sins of the whole world. They, likewise, revealed to her His salvific love as the motive of His vicarious suffering for human sins.

These texts of Isaiah, discovered by Thérèse during her early years in Carmel, were to form the foundation of her devotion to

---

[66] See *S.*, p. viii.

[67] See *S.*, p. 193 ff.

[68] See *S.*, pp. 207, 208.

[69] See *L.C.*, pp. 5-33 for an excellent treatment of the place of these texts in Thérèse's spiritual development.

the Holy Face of Jesus. It was precisely this devotion which allowed her to identify herself with Christ in the mystery of His suffering for others. The prophet Isaiah helped her in the midst of her own intense suffering caused by her father's illness to understand that it is possible not only to suffer for others, but through suffering, to bring healing and salvation to them. In these passages, Thérèse began to grasp that her personal sufferings were an actual participation in the Passion of Christ.

In this context she found great comfort in the contemplation of the Face of Jesus in His Passion. In the *Story of a Soul*, Thérèse thanked Mother Agnes for introducing her to this devotion. She noted that her devotion to the Holy Face had helped her to supernaturalize the intense sufferings she had experienced during her first years in the convent: "Ah! I desired that, like the Face of Jesus, 'my face be truly hidden, that no one on earth would know me.' I thirsted after suffering and I longed to be forgotten."[70] It must be underscored here that Thérèse's devotion to the Face of Christ was, in her mind, rooted firmly in the texts of the Suffering Servant of Yahweh in which she savored the mystery of co-redemption.

On January 10, 1889, when Thérèse was clothed in the Habit of Carmel, she added the title "of the Holy Face" to her religious name. Shortly after Thérèse's entrance, her father suffered his physical and mental breakdown. In the *Story of a Soul*, Thérèse compares her father's suffering to the Passion of Jesus. She also recognized that his illness offered his daughters the opportunity of entering deeply into the Paschal Mystery of the Lord. Thérèse had felt very close to her father in his suffering. She wanted to help her sisters understand that this experience was permitted by God in order to unite them more closely to Christ in His Passion. Many of her letters to Céline during this period centered in on the Suffering Servant as the model of the Christian's vicarious suffering for others.

---

[70] *S.*, p. 152.

Céline, who was then preparing to enter Carmel, cared for Louis Martin during his final illness. On July 18, 1890, Thérèse wrote to her and sent her the text of Isaiah 53. She urged her sister to recognize Christ's sufferings reflected in her own. She also suggested that Céline see the mercy of God in the cross that He had sent to their family. She wrote: "Jesus has sent us the best chosen Cross that He was able to find in His immense love... how can we complain when He Himself was looked upon as a man struck by God and humbled!..."[71]

As she was dying, Thérèse confided to Pauline the great part these texts had played in her spiritual life:

> These words of Isaiah: "Who has believed our report? There is no beauty in him, no comeliness, etc." have made the whole foundation of my devotion to the Holy Face, or, to express it better, *the foundation of all my piety.* I, too, have desired to be without beauty, alone in treading the winepress, unknown to everyone.[72]

These words are highly significant. In them Thérèse reveals that the Suffering Servant of Yahweh, i.e., Jesus in His "kenosis" bearing all human sins as if they were His own, had been the foundation of her spiritual way. Thérèse intimates in this passage what she had explained frequently throughout her life to Mother Agnes: the suffering that she had experienced was at a level far deeper than her physical and mental agony and was, in a sense, ineffable. Thérèse believed that only in the next life would others understand the degree of her union with Christ in His Passion. For instance on July 30, 1897, Thérèse, pointing to a glass containing a very distasteful medicine that looked like a red-currant liqueur, said:

---

[71] *G.C. I,* pp. 629-635.
[72] *L.C.,* p. 135.

This glass is an image of my whole life. Yesterday, Sister Thérèse of St. Augustine said: "I hope you are drinking some good liqueur!" I answered: "Oh, Sister Thérèse, it is the worst possible thing to drink!" Well, little mother, this is what happens in the eyes of creatures. It has always seemed to them I was drinking exquisite liqueurs and it was bitterness. But no! My life hasn't been bitter because I know how to turn all bitterness into something joyful and sweet.[73]

In her spirituality, which had been firmly built upon the texts of Isaiah, Christological and soteriological in content, Thérèse found the means of interpreting and sanctifying her many physical and spiritual trials. She also found in these texts the means of offering her sufferings in hidden union with Christ, in His Passion, for others. Contemplating the Suffering Servant of Yahweh, stricken for the sins of His people, Thérèse realized that if she united her sufferings to the perfect self-offering of Christ, He would bring many souls to His Father through her.

The fourth song of the Suffering Servant became very important to Thérèse throughout all of her religious life, but especially in her final and physical sufferings. In the words of the prophet applied properly, of course, only to the Messiah, but, in an adapted and participatory sense, to herself also, Thérèse grasped the full meaning of co-redemption:

And yet ours were the sufferings He bore, ours the sorrows He carried. But we thought of Him as someone punished, struck by God and brought low. Yet He was pierced through for our faults, crushed for our sins. On Him lies a punishment that brings us peace and through His wounds we are healed (Isaiah 53:4-5).

As in her name, Sister Thérèse of the Child Jesus and of the

---

[73] *L.C.*, p. 119.

Holy Face,[74] so also in her scriptural spirituality, Jesus in His kenosis is central — Jesus, the beloved Son always doing the Father's Will; Jesus, rejected and crucified, bearing personally the guilt of human sin.

Conclusion

A number of different influences helped to form Thérèse in her own spiritual life and prepared her to communicate the fruit of her contemplation to others in her refreshing presentation of evangelical holiness.

From her family, Thérèse had received the gift of wholesome human formation as well as a grounding in the fundamental truths of the Catholic Creed, moral law, divine worship, and personal prayer. In fact, the formation she had received in her family was at the foundation of her profound holiness.

From *The Imitation of Christ*, Thérèse had learned the value of renunciation for the sake of the love of Christ. This work also helped her to understand intellectually the fundamental Christocentricity of any authentically Catholic spirituality. In Fr. Arminjon's conferences, her already elevated concept of heaven was expanded. The preacher was perhaps the first to demonstrate to Thérèse the role of dogmatic truth in the human person's relationship to God. Arminjon's description of heaven remained Thérèse's only consolation during the difficult years in Carmel and was, in a sense, the very object that was assaulted in her "trial of faith."

St. Teresa of Jesus and St. John of the Cross provided definitive orientation for Thérèse's spiritual life, vocation and teaching. In fact, her analysis of her spiritual growth was always carried

---

[74] It is to be noted that Thérèse, with very few exceptions, always signed her religious name as "Sister Thérèse of the Child Jesus *of* the Holy Face." See *G.C. I*, p. 520, note 2; also Guy Gaucher, *op. cit.*, p. 99.

out within the parameters of the spirituality of the Carmelite Reform. As we have seen and as we shall later see in greater depth,
Thérèse always understood and explained the spiritual life in the
framework of the teachings of St. John of the Cross and St. Teresa
of Jesus.

However, Thérèse frequently insisted that, in spite of these
formative influences, Jesus alone, through His Word, had taught
her the Little Way of Spiritual Childhood. She notes:

> Jesus has no need of books or teachers to instruct souls;
> He teaches without the noise of words. Never have I heard
> Him speak, but I feel that He is within me at each mo-
> ment; He is guiding and inspiring me with what I must
> say and do. I find just when I need them certain lights
> which I had not seen until then, and it isn't most frequently
> during my hours of prayer that these are most abundant,
> but rather in the midst of my daily occupation.[75]

While admitting influences on Thérèse's thought, all of which
were ordained by Divine Providence, Thérèse's conviction must
be respected: it was Christ Himself, through His Word, who
formed her and prepared her for her teaching mission. Not without deep significance has the Church chosen the entrance anti-
phon for the Mass in honor of Thérèse: "He led her about and
taught her, and He kept her as the apple of his eye. As the eagle
He spread his wings and has taken her on his shoulder. The Lord
alone was her leader." (Deuteronomy 32:10-11)

---

[75] S., p. 179.

Chapter IV

THÉRÈSE'S SPIRITUAL DEVELOPMENT IN FAITH

In my treatment of Thérèse's life (Chapter I), I highlighted her desire to give God pleasure through the willing acceptance of every manifestation of His Will. It had been Thérèse's wish to reproduce in her life, through her cooperation with grace, all of the dispositions of Christ — in particular, His love of the Father and His thirst for the salvation of all men and women. Clearly, nothing else concerned her. Apart from faith, Thérèse's life is rendered incomprehensible and meaningless.

In Chapter II, through a general analysis of Thérèse's writings, we penetrated into the mystery of supernatural faith at a deeper level in her soul. Each writing of the Saint, from her simplest letter to the sublime manuscript "C" of the *Story of a Soul*, reveals some facet of her personal journey of faith. In this context, I analyzed what Thérèse had revealed in her writings about her "trial of faith" — the horrific experience that, at first sight, seems to have marred the landscape of faith in which Thérèse lived.

Then, having sought in Chapter III the "sources" of Thérèse's doctrine in general and, in particular, all those things that had aided her in comprehending and explaining her mysterious "trial of faith," I asserted that it is impossible to understand either Thérèse's development or spiritual vision apart from the ascetico-mystical theology of St. Teresa of Jesus and St. John of the Cross. This theology in reality is, as is every authentically Catholic spirituality, only an attempt to apply the Word of God as transmitted by the Church to human existence.

Consequently, in this chapter, my goal will be to discern the virtue of faith in the spiritual development of Thérèse of Lisieux. Two different and controverted questions, each essentially related to the other, must be addressed: (1) When and how did Thérèse experience the "passive nights"? (2) Did Thérèse attain to the transforming union? After demonstrating that Thérèse had, indeed, entered the transforming union, either before or on the occasion of her "Oblation to the Merciful Love of God," I shall seek, in the teachings of both St. John of the Cross and St. Teresa of Jesus, confirmation of the truth that profound sufferings and trials are by no means incompatible with the mystical marriage, but rather offer the recipient the opportunity of perfect union with Christ in His redemptive work.

The Virtue of Faith and Active Purification in the Life of Thérèse of Lisieux

As explained in detail earlier in this book, Thérèse had received the gift of the Catholic Faith as the Church ideally wishes that gift to be received — at the hearth of a Christian family. From the dawning of her consciousness, Thérèse had been taught by her parents and sisters to love God and to do everything to please Him. Thérèse revealed, in the *Story of a Soul*, that as a small child she had already acquired a concept of eternal life that became the sole motivating goal of her life.[1]

---

[1] See *S.*, p. 17. Later in the *Story of a Soul*, Thérèse reveals: "The first word I was able to read without help was 'heaven'" (p. 36). Also, it is clear, that from the age of four, the truths of the Church in their catechetical format had been securely and fruitfully planted in Thérèse's memory. The following is a quotation from a letter written by Mme. Martin to Pauline on May 10, 1877: "Our two little dears, Céline and Thérèse, are angels of benediction, little cherubs.... Céline said the other day, 'How is it that God can be present in a small host?' Thérèse said: 'That is not surprising, God is all-powerful.' 'What does all-powerful mean?' 'It means He can do what He wants!'" (*S.*, p. 27).

Thérèse also relates that her earliest recollections of child-hood were replete with instances of personal formation in Christian holiness based on the data of revealed truth. In the *Story of a Soul* and in her other writings, Thérèse states that both the instruction and formation she had received as a child and adolescent, primarily from her family and then secondarily from her parish priests and instructors, were the graced "means" through which she had received the gift of faith. Through this instruction, Thérèse remained loyal to the laws of God and His Church throughout her entire life. She notes that her nature, so drawn to seek its end in earthly beauty, would have been defaced and perhaps even lost eternally were it not for God's preservative grace operating through human instruments. She observes, for instance, in the *Story of a Soul*:

> With a nature such as my own, had I been reared by par-ents without virtue or even if I had been spoiled by the maid, Louise, as Céline was, I would have become very bad and perhaps have even been lost. But Jesus was watch-ing over his little fiancée. He had willed that all turn out for her good, even her faults, which, corrected very early, stood her in good stead to make her grow in perfection.[2]

It will be worthwhile to examine briefly Thérèse's experience of the Church's fourfold ministry of the word: that is, *evangeliza-tion*, *catechesis*, *liturgical preaching* and *theology*. This ministry is described in the Church's *General Catechetical Directory*.[3]

Thérèse, called by God to perform a definite service in the Church, received special graces of the Holy Spirit at a tender age for her doctrinal mission. Also, the Christian witness of her fam-ily, as well as the extraordinary human formation she had received

---

[2] *S.*, pp. 24-25. See also *L.C.*, pp. 60, 61.

[3] Sacred Congregation of the Clergy, *The General Catechetical Directory* (*Directorum Catechisticum Generale*), (Vatican City State, Polyglot Press, 1971).

at home, prepared her to accept the Word of God into excellent "soil" and bear an abundant harvest.

Thérèse began to be carefully evangelized by her parents and sisters in the warmth and security of their Christian home. The goal of this "work" of *evangelization* was to lead her to accept, know and love Jesus Christ as the "holy one of God" — that is, as God's only Son and her Savior. The evangelization Thérèse had received from her family brought her to discover as a child that Christ is the "mystery which for ages was hidden in God, the Creator of all" (Ephesians 3:9).

In particular, Louis Martin led Thérèse and each of his daughters not to a vague ideological notion of Christ, but rather, to a concrete, immanent knowledge of Him as truly present in the Sacrament of the Eucharist. He reinforced his children's faith in the mystery of Christ by bringing them each day to visit and adore Him in the Blessed Sacrament of the altar. Thérèse observes: "Each afternoon I took a walk with papa. We made our visit to the Blessed Sacrament together, going to a different church each day."[4]

Thérèse's formal *catechesis*, which led her to a deeper and more comprehensive knowledge and self-surrender to Christ, began in her home and was supplemented by the instruction she received from her parish priests as well as from the Benedictine Sisters who instructed her at school. Three points may be made regarding the exceptionally complete catechesis Thérèse had received as a child:

1. It was comprised of instructions on the articles of Catholic Faith and morality, the Eucharistic Sacrifice and the sacraments of the Church and Christian prayer. The proximate source of Thérèse's catechetical instruction was the *Catechism of the Council of Trent* also known as the *Roman Catechism*. This instruction imparted knowledge of: (a) the God of revelation (the Creed); (b) the way of life that pleases him (the Commandments); (c) the supernatural means of grace at

---

[4] *S.*, p. 36.

man's disposal to help him faithfully practice God's law in imitation of Christ (the Mass, sacraments and prayer);

2. The instruction did not seek to introduce Thérèse to theological truths for the simple purpose of imparting knowledge, but rather through the medium of the propositions, to unite her to the Divine Persons themselves;

3. The instruction at every level was accompanied by solid human and supernatural formation through familial and pedagogic discipline, the witness of Christian virtue, admonitions to holiness and even to heroism in virtue.

This instruction strengthened Thérèse's personal knowledge of God and helped her to anchor her life in the mystery of Christ, present in the Blessed Sacrament. It is not difficult to see how this instruction, which explained the articles of the Catholic Faith, formed the solid foundation of Thérèse's growth in holiness.

Liturgical preaching was also a powerful means through which Thérèse's faith was strengthened and deepened. She relates in the *Story of a Soul* that the first sermon she had comprehended as a child was on the Passion and Death of Christ: "I listened attentively to the sermons which I understood very poorly. The first *I did understand* and which *touched me deeply*, was a sermon preached by Father Ducellier and since then I've understood all the others."[5] Thérèse asserts that her marvelous contemplative grasp of the mystery of Christ was imparted to her specifically through a consideration of Christ's suffering.

It is evident from our previous treatment of Thérèse's growth in the spiritual life that she had had contact, albeit unsystematic, with the *theological form of the ministry of the Word*, specifically through at least three sources: the conferences of Fr. Arminjon and

---

[5] *S.*, p. 42. Throughout the rest of her life, Thérèse was at times critical of preachers because they did not convey the accurate content of Scripture and were given to excesses and exaggerations (see *L.C.*, pp. 161-162; 166; 235). Several of the great graces of Thérèse's life came through liturgical preaching; for example, the retreat preached by Father Alexis Prou from October 8-15, 1891.

the works of St. John of the Cross and St. Teresa of Jesus. These writings, all of which Thérèse had read and comprehended by her eighteenth year strengthened her catechetical formation and helped her to live in more intimate company with the hidden "mystery of Christ."

Fr. Arminjon led her to understand in clear theological categories the mysteries of the Beatific Vision enjoyed by the souls in heaven, the Second Coming of Christ, the end of the present world, the resurrection of the dead, the general judgment and the definitive establishment of the Kingdom of God. St. John of the Cross and St. Teresa of Jesus, now Doctors of the Church, helped Thérèse above all others to apply the Gospel of Christ to her personal life so that she might live for Him alone. As mentioned earlier, Thérèse's deep intellectual penetration of Sacred Scripture and, in particular, her discovery of the Songs of the Suffering Servant of Yahweh in the book of the prophet Isaiah, shed light on the great trial she would experience near the end of her life. Her theological prowess is evident in each of her descriptions of the spiritual life.

Thérèse's knowledge of God led her, at an unusually tender age, to open herself to Him in prayer. By the age of four she was already able to find Him through the mediation of His creation:

> There were beautiful days for me, those days when my "dear king" took me fishing with him. I was very fond of the countryside, flowers, birds, etc. Sometimes I would try to fish with my little line but I preferred to go *alone* and sit down on the grass bedecked with flowers, and then my thoughts became very profound, indeed! Without knowing what it was to meditate, my soul was absorbed in real prayer. I listened to distant sounds, the murmuring of the wind, etc. At times the indistinct notes of some military music reached me where I was, filling my heart with a sweet melancholy. Earth then seemed to be a place of exile and I could dream only of heaven.[6]

---

[6] S., p. 37.

Thérèse discovered early in life that all of the things of this world are transitory and pass away. This truth led her to yearn for eternity. As a child of barely five years, Thérèse was raised to the contemplation of eternity by a stale piece of bread:

> The afternoon sped by quickly and soon we had to return to Les Buissonnets. Before leaving, I would take the lunch I had brought in my little basket. The *beautiful* bread and jam you had prepared had changed its appearance: instead of the lively colors it had earlier, I now saw only a light rosy tint and the bread had become old and crumbled. Earth, again, had seemed a sad place and I understood that in heaven alone joy will be without any clouds.[7]

By the age of ten, Thérèse was already uniting herself to God in a form of mental prayer, which, by all appearances, seems to have been affective in nature:

> At this time in my life nobody had ever taught me how to make mental prayer, and yet I had a great desire to make it. Marie, finding me pious enough, allowed me to make only my vocal prayers. One day, one of my teachers at the Abbey asked me what I did on my free afternoons when I was alone. I told her I went behind my bed in an empty space which was there, and that it was easy to close myself in with my bed curtain and that, "I *thought*." "But what do you think about?" she asked. "I think about God, about life, about ETERNITY.... I *think!*" I understand now that I was making mental prayer without knowing it and that God was already instructing me in secret.[8]

Holy pictures elevated her to a simple form of contemplation. For instance, before her first reception of Communion, she was given a picture of a little flower standing before a tabernacle. Reflecting upon this image, she wrote to Pauline:

---

[7] S., *ibid.*
[8] S., pp. 74-75.

I owe to the beautiful pictures you gave me as rewards, one of the sweetest joys and strongest impressions which aided me in the practice of virtue. I was forgetting to say anything about the hours I spent looking at them. The *little flower* of the Divine Prisoner, for example, said so many things to me that I became deeply recollected. Seeing that the name of *Pauline* was written under the little flower, I wanted Thérèse's name to be written there also and I offered myself to Jesus as His *little flower.*[9]

Thérèse confesses that in their childhood, she and her "soul friend," Céline, were often raised in a deep union with God through their spiritual conversations. Of special interest is a passage from the *Story of a Soul*, in which Thérèse speaks about faith and its relationship to charity:

I don't know if I'm mistaken, but it seems to me the out-pourings of our souls were similar to those of St. Monica with her son, when, at the Port of Ostia, they were lost in ecstasy at the sight of the Creator's marvels! It appears we were receiving graces like those granted to the great saints. As *The Imitation* says, God communicates himself at times in the midst of great splendor or "*gently veiled under shadows and figures.*" In this way He deigned to manifest Himself to our souls, but how *light* and *transparent* the veil was which hid Jesus from our gaze! That was impossible; faith and hope were unnecessary, and *Love* made us find on earth the one whom we were seeking. "*Having found us alone, He gave us his kiss, in order that in the future no one could despise us*" (Song of Songs, 8:1).[10]

From childhood, her faith matured prodigiously toward mystical union. As we shall see later in this chapter, Thérèse may well have experienced passive purification in her prayer prior to her entry into Carmel. In any event, it may be affirmed here that the prayer, which issued from her life of faith, and grew so beautifully and

---

[9] S., p. 71.
[10] S., p. 104.

effortlessly during her childhood, continued to develop to perfection within the enclosure of Carmel. This growth was particularly evident in her ever-deepening awareness of Jesus' presence at the depth of her soul where He adored His Father's will and worked for the salvation of souls.

Thérèse's life of prayer, which served the growth of charity in her soul, never waned but rather grew stronger with each passing day. This is particularly true of the final year and a half of her life when she suffered her "trial of faith" without relief. In the midst of her trial she continued to be firmly rooted in the "homeland of faith," to make all of her judgments based on faith, and to relate with the Father, Jesus and Mary in an ineffable intimacy. In faith, Thérèse would offer her life in her "Oblation to the Merciful Love of God," especially for those who had lost the Faith.

Thérèse's knowledge of God in faith led her also to be assiduous in recognizing and rooting out sin and all imperfection in her life and in practicing the virtues in imitation of Christ. In other words, Thérèse's faith prompted her to initiate in herself, at an early age, what St. John of the Cross has termed "the active night of the senses and of the spirit."

Describing Thérèse's spirit of renunciation as a child, François Jamart, O.C.D., notes:

> From her earliest years, Thérèse had applied herself to the practice of sacrifice. She had learned this first of all from her sisters but later she was led to it by a special grace from God. At the age of three she had already her "beads of mortification" on which she counted her acts of renunciation. When some article was taken from her, she let it go without complaining. If she was accused, she preferred to keep silence instead of offering excuses. She also applied herself to the task of curbing her self-will. She refrained from answering back as children are so prone to do and rendered little services to others without seeking an acknowledgment of them.[11]

---

[11] François Jamart, OCD, *The Complete Spiritual Doctrine of St. Thérèse of Lisieux*, trans. Rev. Walter Van DePutte (New York: Alba House, 1961), p. 111.

Thérèse, like all members of our fallen human race, did not initially find renunciation easy or pleasurable. Her chief human weakness, as I have pointed out in Chapter I of this book,[12] was the tendency to form a sentimental attachment to family members and the concomitant inability to function apart from such a dependent relationship, especially outside of the family.[13] Thérèse recognized in herself a related tendency toward hypersensitivity, moodiness, and touchiness.[14] Precisely in the experience of her human weakness in this regard, she came to know the power of Christ's healing love — first in the "Smile of the Virgin" which imparted health and peace of mind to a child traumatized by the loss of both her natural and surrogate mother, and then in the "grace of Christmas" which wrought healing at a far deeper level to the personality of an emotionally wounded child and opened the floodgates of supernatural charity for her.[15]

In these two experiences of grace, Thérèse "touched" and understood what would become the core of her spiritual doctrine: in acknowledgment of her human abnegation and dereliction, she would encounter the healing and elevating grace of Christ. Consequently, Thérèse penetrated the truth that the "active nights" of both the senses and the spirit are absolutely dependent upon the grace of Christ. Her activity in the active night was the humble acknowledgment of her powerlessness and her receptivity to Christ's sovereign grace. For Thérèse, human weakness became not only an occasion for spiritual transformation, but also a means of profound union with Christ in His saving work.

Thérèse would recognize the residue of her fallen tendencies later in her life as a Carmelite. From the beginning of her re-

---

[12] See Chapter I, pp. 6-14.

[13] See S., pp. 82-83, for Thérèse's account of her relationships with her peers.

[14] See S., p. 97: "I was really unbearable because of my extreme touchiness; if I happened to cause anyone I loved some little trouble, even unwittingly, instead of forgetting about it and not *crying*, which made matters worse, I *cried* like a Magdalene and then when I began to cheer up, *I began to cry again for having cried*. All arguments were useless, I was quite unable to correct this terrible fault."

[15] See Chapter I, pp. 9-25.

ligious life, she carefully avoided treating her blood sisters in the community differently from the other Sisters. She also refused to indulge her tendency to seek affirmation and affection from the superior, Mother Marie de Gonzague, who was so prone to indulge her own needs for affective relationships.

In his work, *The Complete Spiritual Doctrine of St. Thérèse of Lisieux*, François Jamart, O.C.D., enumerates the main forms of renunciation or active purgation practiced by Thérèse throughout her entire religious life: (1) heroic mortification as a result of fasting; (2) the habitual choosing of the most painful and disagreeable tasks; (3) deprivation of certain things that helped her in her spiritual life, for the sake of others; (4) continued and heroic acts of penance and abnegation even during her terminal illness.[16] I might add to this list: (5) the denial of beautiful things to which she was legitimately entitled; (6) heroic charity towards all of her Sisters and, in particular, towards the most disagreeable; (7) her readiness to correct any Sister, including the prioress, for violations of either the letter or the spirit of the Rule of Carmel.

Thérèse practiced heroic self-abnegation throughout her entire religious life, not solely as a form of asceticism through which she brought herself under the dominion of Christ, but also as a form of voluntary mortification offered to God for the salvation of souls and, in particular, for the formation and sanctification of priests.

Thérèse, then, having studied St. Teresa of Jesus' doctrine on detachment before her entry into Carmel and St. John of the Cross' teaching on active purgation by the beginning of her eighteenth year, put her faith into action by practicing self-abnegation aimed, in particular, at her specific human weaknesses. She practiced this form of active purgation throughout her life as a Carmelite, without relaxation, as a means of obtaining graces for others.

My goal in this section has been simply to demonstrate that

---

[16] François Jamart, OCD, *op. cit.*, pp. 112-120.

Thérèse's faith, imparted by the Holy Spirit through the Church's ministry of the Word, led her to evaluate all reality in its luminous aura. The Faith, likewise, initiated in her a progressive life of prayer and contemplation as well as a systematic program of active purification of the senses and the spirit.

As we progress in our treatment of Thérèse's spiritual development, several temptations should be carefully avoided. One is to assert that Thérèse had experienced the full gamut of passive purification as a child and adolescent, or, in any event, before her entry into Carmel. As we shall see, there are several striking indications of passive purification in the course of Thérèse's religious life. On the other hand, the opposite temptation should also be avoided: the assertion that until her entry into Carmel, Thérèse had lived in the ascetical way and then, sometime after her entry, had begun to enjoy the mystical way. As we have already seen, Thérèse had experienced a number of mystical graces long before she embraced the religious life.

André Combes perceptively warns the student of Thérèse's spirituality to avoid haste in forming judgments on the saint's development apart from her own written testimony of God's activity on her behalf: "Even before she was twelve, the state of Thérèse's soul was too complex to be classified under our everyday categories.... It is not enough to observe her external conduct; we must pay the fullest attention to what she tells us."[17]

As I have demonstrated in Chapter I, it is certain that after her reception of the Sacraments of the Holy Eucharist and Confirmation, Thérèse was given to understand, in a supernatural manner, that her special mission from God would be to suffer in union with Christ for the conversion of sinners — in short, to be a victim soul. Before her entry into Carmel and as a direct result of the close association she had experienced with the clergy on the pilgrimage to Rome, Thérèse's mission was further clarified: she

---

[17] André Combes, St. Thérèse and Suffering, p. 43.

understood that God was calling her to offer her life to Him for the sanctification of priests.

Also, near the end of her life, Thérèse intuited that she had also been assigned a definite "doctrinal mission" by God. She had been called to teach a new "way of perfection" firmly rooted in the Carmelite school of spirituality. This way was to be directed specifically to "little souls" who followed the ordinary path of love without mystical phenomena. As Thérèse approached death and reflected upon her autobiographical memoirs, she realized that she herself was the content of her doctrinal mission; she grasped that God willed His manifold graces in her life to be revealed in the *Story of a Soul*, for the edification and spiritual guidance of other Christians. Hence, her mission may correctly be explained in terms of exemplarity: every major detail of her life possessed a spiritual and pedagogic significance.

This fact, among others, obviously renders a clear-cut analysis of Thérèse's spiritual development according to the Carmelite school difficult and, in a sense, impossible. Suffice it to say that in spite of the extraordinary graces Thérèse had received as a child and adolescent, by the time of her entry into Carmel, she had been well prepared for passive purification, properly-so-called, and the resulting transforming union. This preparation had taken place through her early exposure to the Word of God, the human and spiritual formation she had received at home, and by her heroic personal efforts of offering God the creaturely homage of her prayer and evangelical self-reformation.

Passive Purification

The first indication of passive purification in Thérèse's life is found in the period between May 29, 1887, the day on which she received permission from her father to enter Carmel and April 9, 1888, the actual date of her entry into the enclosure. During these months of waiting, Thérèse experienced many disappointments and setbacks: the initial opposition of her uncle, Isidore Guérin; the reluctance of several diocesan officials, including the clerical "superior" of the monastery, to approve of her entry into Carmel; the hesitation of Bishop Hugonin; the journey to Rome and sad discovery of the disarray of the French clergy; the refusal of Pope Leo XIII to grant her a dispensation and, finally, after a favorable decision had been rendered by the Bishop, the postponement of her entry date by Mother Marie de Gonzague herself.

Since Thérèse was certain that God willed her to enter Carmel to work for the conversion of sinners, she presumed her entry would be effected by God immediately, without effort or human opposition. In the midst of her external tribulations, she suddenly lost the consolations she had previously enjoyed in her intimate relationship with Jesus in prayer. In this context, Thérèse elicits two images to describe the darkness of her soul: Jesus asleep in her boat and herself as Jesus' toy. Speaking of the state of her soul in the wake of her uncle's opposition to her entry into Carmel at the age of fifteen, Thérèse writes:

> O! never have I understood so well as during this trial, the sorrow of Mary and Joseph during their three-day search for the divine Child Jesus. I was in a sad desert, or rather my soul was like a fragile boat delivered up to the mercy of the waves and having no pilot. I knew Jesus was there sleeping in my boat, but the night was so black it was impossible to see Him; nothing gave me any light, not a single flash came to break the dark clouds. No doubt, lightning is a dismal light, but at least if the storm had broken out in earnest I would have been able to see Jesus for one passing moment. But it was night! The dark night of the soul! I felt I was all alone in the garden of Gethsemane like Jesus and I found no consolation on earth or from heaven; God Himself seemed to have abandoned me.[18]

This image is extremely important in any analysis of Thérèse's contribution to Christian mysticism. She notes the various com-

---

[18] S., p. 109.

ponents of passive purification in this passage: "I was in a sad desert." This relates, of course, to the aridity she discovered in her prayer and inability to find consolation in anything created or uncreated. Again, "nothing gave me any light" indicates that under the impulse of a higher understanding, Thérèse was unable to draw light from her previous perception of God and His way of dealing with her. "But it was night! The dark night of the soul!" Thérèse found her soul in distress and turmoil. Jesus was beyond her sight and she felt abandoned by God. She herself, as a mature religious who has carefully studied St. John of the Cross, did not hesitate to call this experience of internal suffering the "dark night of the soul." However, and this is a point of great importance, Thérèse not only knew that "Jesus was sleeping in her boat" (i.e., in her soul), but profoundly experienced His presence precisely as mystery in the midst of her darkness and suffering.

Writing of her pilgrimage to Rome, Thérèse describes herself for the first time as Jesus' toy:

> I had offered myself, for some time now, to the Child Jesus as his *little plaything*. I told Him not to use me as a valuable toy children are content to look at but dare not touch, but to use me like a little ball of no value which He could throw to the ground, push with His foot, *pierce*, leave in a corner, or press to His heart if it pleased Him; in a word, I wanted to *amuse little Jesus*, to give Him pleasure; I wanted to give myself up to His *childish whims*. He heard my prayer.[19]

This image, as stated, does not yet relate directly to the dark night. It simply reveals Thérèse's great devotion to the Child Jesus and her desire to please Him by doing His will in all things. However, in the next paragraph of her text, Thérèse uses the image to describe the state of her soul in the dark night:

---

[19] *S.*, p. 136.

> At Rome, Jesus pierced His little plaything; He wanted
> to see what there was inside it and having seen, content
> with His discovery, He let his little ball fall to the ground
> and He went off to sleep. What did He do during his
> gentle sleep and what became of the little abandoned ball?
> Jesus dreamed He *was still playing* with his toy, leaving it
> and taking it up in turns, and then having seen it roll quite
> far, He pressed it to His heart, no longer allowing it to
> ever go far from His little hand.[20]

At first sight Thérèse seems to be saying that Jesus' activity on her behalf had ceased. He is asleep and she is cast aside, abandoned. In reality, through this image, Thérèse indicates that Jesus continues to dwell within her and to love her. However, His presence and activity are perceived as incomprehensible and far beyond her previous experiences of the Divine Presence. Void of understanding, Thérèse trusts that her exterior and interior trials, mysteriously related, have significance in her sanctification and her mission. André Combes sees in this image a "complete distinction, a duality. On one side Jesus; on the other, his little ball. What He wills she does not know. The toy is pierced and makes no resistance, but it does not understand the designs of its owner. It does not delight in suffering."[21]

The painful aridity Thérèse experienced before her entry into Carmel was to continue uninterruptedly after her entry into religious life until her death. This fact alone has led some authors to conclude that Thérèse had spent her entire life as a "beginner" in the purgative way. In this context it will be valuable to seek out several statements of Thérèse's which seem to indicate passive purification and, then, to analyze her spiritual state in the light of her growth in charity. However, before embarking on this path, four related truths must be noted — truths highlighted by Thérèse in her description of her entry into Carmel.

First of all, the fifteen-year-old Thérèse, as soon as she had

---

[20] *Ibid.*

[21] André Combes, *St. Thérèse and Suffering*, p. 77.

set foot within the monastic enclosure, experienced, as she testified, "a *PEACE* so sweet, so deep, it would be impossible to express it." Shortly before her death she manifested the state of her soul: "For seven years and a half that inner peace has remained my lot, and has not abandoned me in the midst of the greatest trials."[22] The masters of the spiritual life have universally taught that deep spiritual peace is a sure sign of the presence and activity of God and a clear indication that an individual is accomplishing His Will.[23]

Second, Thérèse states that along with profound peace, suffering was her constant lot in Carmel from the day of her entry. She also makes it clear that all of her interior sufferings are offered to God for the conversion of sinners and especially for priests.[24] Describing her first perceptions of Carmel, Thérèse says: "Yes, suffering opened wide its arms to me and I threw myself into them with love.... When one wishes to attain a goal, one must use the means: Jesus made me understand that it was through suffering that He wanted to give me souls, and my attraction for suffering grew in proportion to its increase. This was my way for five years."[25]

Third, Thérèse indicates that her suffering was far deeper and more comprehensive than seemingly warranted by both external circumstances and the ordinary forms of active and passive purgation: "Exteriorly nothing revealed my suffering which was all the more painful since I alone was aware of it. Ah! what a surprise we shall have at the end of the world when we shall read the story of souls! There will be those who will be surprised when they see the way through which my soul was guided!"[26] Thérèse in this text

---

[22] *S.*, p. 148.

[23] See Ignatius of Loyola, *The Spiritual Exercises*, trans. Louis J. Puhl, SJ (Chicago: Loyola University Press, 1951); see in particular St. Ignatius' "Rules for the Discernment of Spirits," pp. 141-150.

[24] Describing the day of her entry, Thérèse remarked: "I had declared at the feet of Jesus-victim, in the examination preceding my Profession, what I had come to Carmel for: 'I come to save souls and especially to pray for priests.'" *S.*, p. 149.

[25] *S.*, p. 149.

[26] *Ibid.*

states that the sufferings she endured in Carmel were inexplicable and, in fact, mysteriously granted to her by God Himself.

Fourth, in her discussion of her entry into religious life, Thérèse relates the story of the general confession she had made to Father Pichon several months after her entry. In that sacramental moment, the Jesuit provided Thérèse with one of the most consoling lights of her life. He said to her solemnly: "In the presence of God, the Blessed Virgin, and all the saints I declare that you have never committed a mortal sin."[27]

Later in life, Thérèse would come to realize that her purity of soul was the result of a special "preservative grace" of God — a grace resembling, from afar, the grace of the Virgin Mary.[28] Thérèse's sanctity then, allowed her and, in fact, propelled her to draw very close to Jesus in His suffering. Through the graces she had received from God from childhood she had been prepared for a special mission of sharing in Christ's redemptive love for all people.

This point is made within the modality of analogy. Needless to say, the Blessed Virgin Mary alone, among all women, was preserved by God from original sin and, by another special grace, from all actual sin. Thérèse, a daughter of Eve, had inherited Adam's sin and all of the dire effects of that sinful condition. She was subject to concupiscence, actual sin, and imperfections of all kinds, as she amply admits. However, as both her confessor and her conscience affirmed, she had never grievously offended God and had indeed reached moral perfection at a tender age. This fact led her to stand in awe before God's grace that had accomplished this wonder in her. Frequently, in the *Story of a Soul*, Thérèse confesses that apart from that grace, she would have become the greatest of sinners. Also, she understood that her purity, itself exclusively God's work, enabled her to enter very deeply into Christ's redemptive work for the salvation of the world.

---

[27] *Ibid.*

[28] See Hans Urs von Balthasar, *Thérèse of Lisieux: The Story of a Mission*, pp. 35-36.

[29] See Chapter I, pp. 26-29.

As I have noted in Chapter I of this book,[29] Thérèse, in her experiences of physical and affective powerlessness as a child, had come to recognize that suffering was to be her means of attaining mystical union with the Crucified. As a result of her moral purity, she was particularly apt to be an instrument of his work. She also recognized that God's grace had prepared her to be a living model of sanctity for others. It seems impossible to understand Thérèse apart from her purity, her call to co-redemptive love and her mission of exemplarity. As Hans Urs von Balthasar has pointed out:

> Thérèse wished God to grind down every single particle of her being until she became his grain. Her mission is to praise God with her whole being in the presence of the Church. And this *confessio* cannot be a confession of sin — because God has preserved her from sin — it has to be a *confessio* of God's grace in her. For Thérèse, to display herself is a token of her own poverty.[30]

It is worthwhile to list these four points that became anchors during Thérèse's "trial of faith": (1) Since her entry into Carmel and throughout her religious life, Thérèse, in spite of harrowing physical and spiritual trials, experienced the peace of Christ. This peace, in the depths of her soul, she rightly interpreted as the presence and affirmation of God's activity. (2) Thérèse sensed early in life, well before her entry into Carmel, that her vocation was to suffer vicariously for the salvation of others — for sinners and most specifically, for priests. (3) Thérèse's sufferings may not be adequately explained either by difficult external circumstances or by the assaults of active and passive purification. Her suffering was of the nature of a supernatural gift for others. (4) Thérèse's moral and spiritual purity prepared her for vicarious suffering in close union with the Crucified for the salvation of the world.

A point which is crucial to this thesis must now be made: every instance of purgation in Thérèse's life, from as early as the

---

[30] von Balthasar, pp. 35-36.

Pranzini experience until her death, was of the nature of vicarious suffering for the Church. As a result of a marvelous bestowal of grace, there was hardly a trace of sinfulness in Thérèse that called for purification. Hence, her purgation, as it healed the wounds of her fallen nature and elevated her to supernatural life, concomitantly became from the beginning a powerful source of healing and elevation for others.

It is interesting to note that shortly after her entry into Carmel, Thérèse discovered her devotion to the Holy Face of Jesus — a devotion she would later link to the "theology" of the Suffering Servant Songs of Isaiah. As we have pointed out in Chapter III,[31] these prophetic texts not only led Thérèse to understand that Christ had taken to Himself the guilt of the entire world in His Passion, but also that she, in union with Him, was capable of being a source of salvation for others through her suffering.[32]

In the twenty-month period of her novitiate (January 10, 1889 to September 8, 1890), Thérèse reveals signs of intense spiritual purgation and also of illumination. It was precisely during this period that Louis Martin had suffered his breakdowns. Her inability to be with her father caused Thérèse tremendous anguish of heart and further complicated her suffering. She says: "My desire for suffering was answered, and yet my attraction for it did not diminish. My soul soon shared in the sufferings of my heart. Spiritual aridity was my daily bread and, deprived of all consolations, I was still the happiest of creatures since my desires had been satisfied."[33]

---

[31] See Chapter III, pp. 123-127.

[32] See *S.*, pp. 151-152: "The little flower transplanted to Mt. Carmel was to expand under the shadow of the Cross. The tears and blood of Jesus were to be her dew, and her Sun was His adorable Face veiled with tears. Until my coming to Carmel, I had never fathomed the death of the treasures hidden in the Holy Face.... I understood what *real glory* was. He whose kingdom is not of this world showed me that true wisdom consists of 'desiring to be unknown and counted as nothing,' (*Imitation of Christ*, I, II, III), in 'placing one's joy in the contempt of self' (*Imitation of Christ*, 49:7). Ah! I desired that, like the Face of Jesus, 'my face be truly hidden, that no one on earth would know me' (Isaiah 53:3). I thirsted after suffering and I longed to be forgotten."

[33] *S.*, p. 157.

Having completed her canonical novitiate, Thérèse was informed that her profession would be postponed for nearly another year. In her disappointment, Thérèse discovered attitudes in herself that needed purification: "One day, during my prayer, I understood that my intense desire to make Profession was marked with a great self-love. Since I had *given* myself to Jesus to please and console Him, I had no right to oblige Him to do *my will* instead of His own."[34]

Thérèse continued to live in uninterrupted spiritual dryness up to her profession on September 8, 1890:

> The retreat preceding my Profession was far from bringing me any consolations since the most absolute aridity and almost total abandonment were my lot. Jesus was sleeping, as usual in my little boat; ah! I saw very well how rarely souls allow Him to sleep peacefully within them. Jesus is so fatigued with always having to take the initiative and to attend to others that He hastens to take advantage of the repose I offer to Him. He will undoubtedly awaken before my great eternal retreat, but instead of being troubled about it, this only gives me extreme pleasure.[35]

On the eve of her profession, Thérèse, fearing that she had come to Carmel to do her own will rather than God's, doubted her vocation and was prepared to leave the monastery. She says: "The darkness was so great that I could see and understand only one thing: I didn't have a vocation."[36] Having confided her internal turmoil to both the novice mistress and the prioress, Thérèse understood that her doubt was, indeed, a temptation to forsake God's Will: "The act of humility I had just performed put the devil to flight since he had perhaps thought that I would not dare ad-

---

[34] *S.*, p. 158.
[35] *S.*, p. 165.
[36] *S.*, p. 166.

mit my temptation. My doubts left me completely as soon as I finished speaking."[37]

In a letter written to Mother Agnes of Jesus around August 30-31, 1890, during her profession retreat, Thérèse even more clearly described the purgation she was enduring:

> My fiancé says nothing to me, and I say nothing to Him either except that *I love Him more than myself,* and I feel at the bottom of my heart that it is true, for I am more His than my own! I don't see that we are advancing toward the summit of the mountain since our journey is being made underground, but it seems to me that we are approaching it without knowing how. The route on which I am has no consolations since Jesus is the One who chose it and I want to console Him alone.[38]

Thérèse states in the *Story of a Soul* that she pronounced her Vows in profound peace: "On the morning of September 8, I felt as though I was flooded with a river of peace and it was in this peace 'which surpasses all understanding' (Philippians 4:7), that I pronounced my holy Vows. My union with Jesus was effected not in the midst of thunder and lightning; that is, in extraordinary graces, but in the bosom of a light breeze similar to the one our father, St. Elias, heard on the Mount (1 Kings 19:12-13)."[39]

Two weeks later Thérèse received the veil although neither her father nor the Bishop were able to be with her and many other things conspired against her besides.[40] Thérèse said, "and still *peace,* always *peace,* reigned at the bottom of the chalice."[41]

It is valuable to consider the prayer Thérèse had prepared for her profession day and which she carried on her heart.[42] Address-

---

[37] *Ibid.*

[38] *G.C. I,* p. 652.

[39] *S.,* pp. 166, 167.

[40] Thérèse states: "In a word, everything was sadness and bitterness." *S.,* p. 167.

[41] *Ibid.*

[42] The prayer in its entirety is found in the Appendix in *S.,* p. 275.

ing Jesus as her "Divine Spouse," she immediately asks Him to preserve the second robe of her Baptism; that is, the innocence and holiness merited by the profession of her vows. She also asked that He preserve her from ever committing the slightest voluntary fault and that "creatures be nothing and Jesus be *everything*." She asked for four graces: (1) Peace, "Jesus, I ask you for nothing but peace"; (2) Love, "infinite love without any limits other than Yourself; love which is no longer I but You, my Jesus. Jesus, may I die a martyr for You. Give me martyrdom of heart or body, or rather, give me both"; (3) Grace, "to fulfill my Vows in all their perfection" and "may Your will, Jesus, be done in me perfectly"; (4) Finally, Thérèse asked that she be allowed "to save very many souls."

During the same period, as I have indicated, Thérèse experienced many interior lights and graces and even mystical phenomena. Besides receiving tremendous consolations in her understanding of the mysteries of the Incarnation and the Redemption, she became more markedly attracted to penance and self-denial:

> I was taken up, at this time, with a real attraction for objects that were both very ugly and the least convenient. So it was with joy that I saw myself deprived of a pretty *little jug* in our cell and supplied with another large one *all chipped*. I was exerting much effort, too, and not excusing myself, which was very difficult for me, especially with our Novice Mistress from whom I didn't want to hide anything.[43]

Also during this period of her novitiate, Thérèse came to a new level of interior mortification that had charity towards the other Sisters as its end: "I applied myself to practicing little virtues, not having the capability of practicing the great. For instance... I loved to render them all sorts of little services."[44]

---

[43] *S.*, p. 159.
[44] *Ibid.*

Mother Agnes of Jesus explained several of the mystical graces Thérèse had received during her novitiate. She notes specifically "flights of the spirit" and "the prayer of quiet."[45] Thérèse herself relates a mystical grace, mediated through the Blessed Virgin, that she had received in the month of July 1889: "It was as though a veil had been cast over all the things of this earth for me.... I was entirely hidden under the Blessed Virgin's veil. At this time, I was placed in charge of the refectory, and I recall doing things as though not doing them; it was as if someone had lent me a body. I remained that way for a whole week."[46]

By way of summary, during the initial period of her religious life, Thérèse seems to have struggled with neither the virtue of faith nor sin. In fact, although suffering from painful aridity in her prayer, she continued to live in an external and internal milieu of peace. Struggles with family attachments, anxiety over her father's health and the discovery of internal problems in her religious community provided Thérèse with ample reasons to wrestle with that common tendency of fallen human nature to seek self-gratification above all else. However, there is no hint in her writings or in the testimony of those who had known her of any serious temptation to grievous sin or even to deliberate venial sin. Certainly there were no temptations against the theological virtues. In the midst of external trials and internal aridity, Thérèse continued to grow prodigiously in all of the virtues. Also, there is evidence during this period that she experienced mystical graces commonly received by those in the unitive way.

We must now consider the period that spans the five years between her profession and her "Oblation to the Merciful Love of God"— September 8, 1890 to June 9, 1895. This period (and also the preceding years within the cloister) may be called Thérèse's

---

[45] See *L.C.*, p. 88.
[46] *L.C.*, p. 88. For St. Teresa of Jesus' treatment of the "prayer of quiet," see St. Teresa of Avila, *The Collected Works, Vol. II: Meditations on the Song of Songs*, trans. Kieran Kavanaugh, OCD, and Otilio Rodriguez, OCD (Washington, DC: ICS Publications, 1980), pp. 242-247.

"hidden life." In the *Story of a Soul* she speaks little of her interior life, her struggles and her suffering during this period. Because of the paucity of details provided by Thérèse, it is difficult, if not impossible, to pinpoint the various stages through which she must have journeyed. However, through consideration of her virtue it is abundantly clear that God had prepared her not only for the transforming union but also for a distinct doctrinal mission in the Church, specifically as a result of her aridity and other trials.

During this period Thérèse found herself strongly attracted to the sanctity of the aged foundress of the Lisieux Carmel, Mother Geneviève of St. Teresa. Thérèse, prone at this stage of her development to the religious fads of her times, went one Sunday to Mother Geneviève, who had unexpectedly spoken some words of consolation to her a few days previously, and inquired whether she had received any other revelation. Thérèse notes:

> She assured me she had received *none* at all, and then my admiration was greater still when I saw the degree to which Jesus was living within her and making her act and speak. Ah! that type of sanctity seems the *truest* and the *most holy* to me, and it is the type that I desire because in it one meets with no deception.[47]

Interestingly, Thérèse distinguished an extraordinary and an ordinary type of sanctity. The "extraordinary" is comprised of visions, revelations and, in fact, of all sorts of mystical paraphernalia. The "ordinary" type of holiness is total self-surrender to Jesus in faith, hope and charity, for Thérèse's union with God reached perfection in the union of wills accomplished in the darkness of faith. In this union of wills, transformation in Christ is accomplished. Thérèse perceived this highest level of union with God as the ordinary and safest way of Christian sanctity.

The memory of Mother Geneviève moved Thérèse to reveal the quality of her dreams. Therein one discovers the beautiful psy-

---

[47] *S.*, pp. 169-170.

chological and affective health of the eighteen-year-old Carmelite. The account taken along with her previous description of Mother Geneviève's holiness, provides insight into Thérèse's doctrine on Christian mysticism:

> I attached no importance to dreams; besides, I have rarely had any meaningful dreams, even wondering why it is that I think of God all day long and yet am so little occupied with Him in my sleeping hours. I dream usually about such things as woods, flowers, streams, and the sea; I see beautiful children almost all the time; I catch butterflies and birds the likes of which I have never seen before. You can see, dear Mother, that though my dreams are rather fanciful, they are never mystical. One night after Mother Geneviève's death, I had a very consoling dream: I dreamed she was making her last will and testament, giving each of the Sisters something which she possessed. When my turn finally came, I thought I would get nothing as there was really nothing left to give; however, she said: "To you I leave my *heart*." She repeated this three times with great emphasis.[48]

In reality, in giving Thérèse her heart, Mother Geneviève was giving the young girl Jesus, living and acting deep in her interior, transforming her in His grace.

Thérèse's nineteenth birthday marked the beginning of an influenza epidemic which claimed the lives of several of the Lisieux Carmelites. During the epidemic, Thérèse single-handedly kept the monastery in operation, tended the sick, and prepared the dead for burial.[49] Her strength during those difficult weeks came from the daily reception of Christ in the Eucharist — a luxury rarely, if ever, permitted in those days.

---

[48] S., pp. 170, 171.

[49] The entire Community was confined to bed with the exception of Sr. Marie of the Sacred Heart, Sr. Martha (a lay-Sister) and Thérèse. Her courageous conduct during these trying days earned her the belated respect of Fr. Delatroëtte, the superior, who had always shown doubts about her suitability for the life of Carmel. See Guy Gaucher, *op. cit.*, p. 120.

Besides describing her method of preparing for Communion[50] and her desire to give Jesus pleasure in her reception of the Eucharist,[51] Thérèse also reveals, along with the fact of her habitual aridity, an interior struggle which was the harbinger of her great "trial of faith": "At the time (of the retreat in 1891) I was having great interior trials of all kinds, even to the point of asking myself whether heaven really existed."[52]

Having sought counsel and absolution from Fr. Alexis Prou, who preached the Carmelite retreat from October 8-15, 1891, Thérèse had received assurance. She was concerned whether her faults and imperfections were causing God pain. Explaining Fr. Prou's reaction, Thérèse says: "He launched me full sail upon the waves of *confidence and love* which so strongly attracted me, but upon which I dared not advance. He told me that *my faults caused God no pain, and that holding as he did God's place*, he was telling me *in His name* that God was very much pleased with me."[53]

This fact manifests the simplicity and purity of Thérèse's soul at this period of her religious life. Her concern was not with mortal sin — although she always knew with penetrating insight that apart from God's grace, she could be entangled in grievous sin — nor with deliberate venial sin, but rather, with her faults and imperfections. Add to these two facts (Thérèse's aridity and interior trials, on the one hand, and her preoccupation with not offending God, on the other) a third, i.e., Thérèse's profound maternal desire to give birth to souls through suffering[54] and one is able to

---

[50] See *S.*, p. 172.

[51] Thérèse, discussing her Eucharistic practice, notes: "I can't say that I frequently received consolations when making my thanksgiving after Mass; perhaps it is the time when I receive the least. However, I find this very understandable since I have offered myself to Jesus, not as one desires of her own consolations in his visit, but simply to please Him who is giving Himself to me." *S.*, p. 172.

[52] *S.*, p. 173.

[53] *S.*, p. 174.

[54] See *S.*, p. 174: "I see that *suffering alone* gives birth to souls and more than ever before the sublime words of Jesus unveil their depths to me: '*Amen, amen I say to you, unless the grain of wheat falls into the ground and dies, it remains alone; but if it dies, it will bring forth much fruit.*'"

discern a profound instance of passive purgation of an apostolic nature.

February 20, 1893, is an important date in the spiritual history of Thérèse of Lisieux. On that day the Conventual Chapter elected Mother Agnes of Jesus, Thérèse's "second mother," as prioress of the Carmel to replace Mother Marie de Gonzague. One of the first acts of the newly-elected prioress was the appointment of Thérèse as assistant mistress of novices. Also at this same time, largely through the encouragement of Mother Agnes, Thérèse realized her talent of expressing her deep thoughts in verse, drama and painting.

For almost any other person, Pauline's election would have been received as a summons to freedom, license, and the little privileges that accrue to family relationships. Such, however, was not the case with Thérèse. Discussing her reaction to her sister's election, André Combes notes:

> Her purification had been too thorough. Her fidelity under trials had been too clear-sighted and generous, for a change of superiors to affect her religious character, or to lead her into relaxation of her ideals or her practices.... She was glad that God had given to the community so good a Prioress but for her part she was supernaturally indifferent to the person in whom was vested the authority of the divine Lord, whom she obeyed. So detached was she from all consolation that, of all the nuns, she was the one who most rarely had recourse to Mother Agnes. In her responsible charge she saw but a motive of humility, for trust in God, for prayer and zeal. As to her poetry, that was written merely out of charity for others. Thus Thérèse, never for an instance, relaxed her strivings after the highest perfection.[55]

During this period of her life, which is marked by the death of her father (July 29, 1894) and the entry of Céline into Carmel

---

[55] André Combes, *St. Thérèse and Suffering*, p. 90.

(September 14, 1894), Thérèse already begins to show signs of the attainment of the mystical marriage: Her only desire was to do the Will of God:

> Neither do I desire any longer suffering or death, and still I love them both, it is *love* alone that attracts me.... I possessed suffering and believed I had touched the shores of heaven.... now, abandonment alone guides me. I have no other compass! I can no longer ask for anything with fervor except the accomplishment of God's will in my soul without any creature being able to set obstacles in the way.[56] And again, "how sweet is the way of love! How I want to apply myself to do the will of God always with the greatest self-surrender."[57]

Thérèse also experienced the presence of Jesus in her soul teaching and directing her at every moment:

> Jesus has no need of books or teachers to instruct souls; He teaches without the noise of words. Never have I heard Him speak, but I feel that He is within me at each moment; He is guiding and inspiring me with what I must say and do. I find just when I need them, certain lights which I had not seen until then, and it isn't most frequently during my hours of prayer that these are most abundant, but rather in the midst of my daily occupations.[58]

Suffice it to say, by way of summary, that there are indeed indications of passive purification in Thérèse's life both before and after her entrance into Carmel. As she prepared to enter the monastery, she experienced confusion regarding the way God was leading her and, concomitantly, a purifying dryness in her prayer. Jesus, she noted, was present within her and she was ever capable of dis-

---

[56] S., p. 178.
[57] S., p. 181.
[58] S., p. 179.

cerning (in her words, "feeling")[59] His presence. However, He was present as one asleep — and, as asleep, dreaming of Thérèse.

After her entry into Carmel, her aridity in prayer continued, along with a constant inability to make use of the tried methods of prayer, including discursive meditation, meditation upon the mysteries of the rosary, and thanksgiving after Holy Communion. However, her awareness of Jesus present within her as asleep continued and became progressively more vivid. Less than five years after her entrance into the monastery, she was able to say that Jesus within her was her constant teacher and guide.

Thérèse also recognized in herself, through the gift of understanding, a need for healing and purification — especially in the areas of self-love and her natural desires for affirmation from others and, in particular, from her Prioress, Mother Marie de Gonzague. However, after her entry into Carmel, although she continued to receive the sacrament of Penance regularly, her struggles seemed centered upon her imperfections and faults rather than sins.

Her moral and spiritual purity, acknowledged by Thérèse as God's gift, equipped her for a life of vicarious suffering for others. Hence, the purgation of the senses and of the spirit which she experienced, always had about it the characteristic of reparation. As early as 1890, Thérèse revealed to Mother Agnes of Jesus her understanding of the expiatory nature of her purification. She wrote: "I don't understand the retreat I am making; I think of nothing, in a word, I am in a very dark subterranean passage! Oh! ask Jesus, you who are my light, that He not permit souls to be deprived of lights that they need because of me, but that my darkness serve to enlighten them."[60]

---

[59] See François Jamart, OCD, *op. cit.*, pp. 244-246: here the author explains Thérèse's frequent use of the verb "to feel" in terms of the operation of the gift of wisdom: "Thérèse ordinarily uses the term 'to feel' to designate the lights she received during her meditation or at other times. This is important, for 'to feel' in this context does not mean a sensible impression, but, as we shall see, it is a knowledge that springs from love."

[60] *G.C. I*, p. 658.

Thérèse and the Transforming Union

As Thérèse finished manuscript "A" of the *Story of a Soul* in January of 1896, six months after her "Oblation to the Merciful Love of God," she chose two stanzas (St. 26 and 28) of St. John of the Cross' *Spiritual Canticle* to explain her state of soul.[61] As François Jamart, O.C.D. remarks in his work *The Complete Spiritual Doctrine of St. Thérèse of Lisieux*, Thérèse chose these sections because they speak of the mystical marriage: "In these verses of the *Spiritual Canticle*, St. John of the Cross describes the life of the soul that is transformed in its twofold phase: the phase in which the soul enjoys high transports, and the ordinary phase in which all life is love and when all the soul's faculties act solely for God under the motion of the Holy Spirit."[62]

With this fact in mind, I shall now examine Thérèse's "Act of Oblation to the Merciful Love of God," which both revealed and furthered her mystical union with Christ. I shall then evaluate her development beyond the point of her Oblation in the light of the teaching of St. John of the Cross and St. Teresa of Jesus on the transforming union. Finally, I shall briefly examine Thérèse's explanation of the transforming union, which had developed organically from her apostolic understanding of passive purgation.

Thérèse had been inspired to offer herself to the merciful love of God on Trinity Sunday, June 9, 1895, during the seventh year of her religious life. Both Thérèse and Céline actually made the "act" on June 11, 1895. As noted in Chapter I: "This oblation held a paramount place in Thérèse's spiritual life. She understood it as the culmination of her spiritual life and the existential perfection of her religious vocation."[63]

In this act of divine worship, Thérèse, already possessed by the love of God, asked that the Lord, abandoned and rejected by

---

[61] *S.*, pp. 178-179.
[62] François Jamart, OCD, *op. cit.*, p. 253.
[63] See Chapter I, p. 42.

so many of His children, pour out His unrequited love on her.[64] In the Act of Oblation, Thérèse stated that she desired to "live in one single act of perfect Love." She also said: "I OFFER MYSELF AS A VICTIM OF HOLOCAUST TO YOUR MERCIFUL LOVE, asking You to consume me incessantly, allowing the waves of *infinite tenderness* shut up within You to overflow into my soul, so that thus I may become a *martyr* of Your *Love*, O my God."[65]

Well schooled in the spiritual teaching of St. John of the Cross, Thérèse asked in the Oblation to ultimately die of the love of God. She had been well aware that in the Sanjuanist scheme, only those who have attained the mystical marriage actually die of the love of God. Consequently, in asking to die of love, Thérèse reveals that she had already entered into the transforming union or, at least, expected to enter the mystical marriage through the Oblation: "May this martyrdom, after having prepared me to appear before You, finally cause me to die and may my soul take its flight without delay into the eternal embrace of *Your merciful love*."[66]

In her offering, Thérèse asked God for three specific favors — graces which would perfect her union with Christ for the remaining years of her life and even into eternity.

First, she prayed that the Eucharistic presence of Christ remain perpetually within her: "I cannot receive Holy Communion as often as I desire, but, Lord, are You not *all powerful*? Remain in me, as in a tabernacle, and never separate Yourself from Your little victim."[67] Does this aspiration of Thérèse not indicate that she desired to be possessed by Christ in His sacred Humanity and to participate as fully as possible in His redemptive act for the salvation of the human race? It seems clear that in her request, moti-

---

[64] The text of the "Act of Oblation to the Merciful Love of God" is found in the Appendix of *S.*, pp. 276-277.

[65] *S.*, p. 277.

[66] *Ibid.*

[67] *S.*, p. 276.

vated as she was by the love of the human race, Thérèse asked to share as completely as possible in the *kenosis* of Jesus.

Second, in order to expiate the sins, coldness and ingratitude of people who had lost the Faith, Thérèse asked again for what she had prayed on the day of her first reception of Holy Communion: "I beg of You to take away my freedom to displease You."[68] Here again, she asks to participate comprehensively in Christ's work of redeeming the world through obedience to the Father's Will and through suffering.

Third, Thérèse asked for the gift of Christ's stigmata in her glorified body:

> I thank you, O my God! for all the graces You have granted me, especially the grace of making me pass through this crucible of suffering. It is with joy I shall contemplate You on the Last Day carrying the scepter of Your Cross. Since You deigned to give me a share in this very precious Cross, I hope in heaven to resemble You and to see shining in my glorified body, the sacred stigmata of Your Passion.[69]

When asked at the process of Thérèse's beatification whether her sister had meant these requests in a literal sense, or rather in some metaphorical way, Mother Agnes of Jesus answered: "She often enlarged on these ideas when speaking to me and I am certain she meant them literally. Her loving confidence in Our Lord made her extraordinarily daring in the things she asked Him for. When she thought of His all-powerful love, she had no doubt about anything."[70]

Since this Oblation had held such a prominent place in Thérèse's spiritual life and seems to be directly related to her "trial of faith," it is worthwhile to pause and analyze the significance of the self-offering.

A number of the nuns of the Lisieux Carmel, borrowing a

---

[68] *Ibid.*
[69] S., p. 277.
[70] P., p. 46.

popular devotion of the day, offered themselves as victims to the justice of God. In other words, for the sake of the salvation of sinners, these generous souls invoked upon themselves the punishment for the sins of others. François Jamart, O.C.D., in his *The Complete Spiritual Doctrine of St. Thérèse of Lisieux* notes that an author who was popular among some of the Sisters in the Carmel, held wrongly that the oblation to the divine justice was one of the purposes for the foundation of the Carmelite order.[71]

Thérèse found nothing appealing in this practice which exercised a particular attraction on persons of a Jansenistic mindset. Rather, she was drawn to offer herself as a victim to the merciful love of God. For her, the focus of the doctrine of the redemption was Christ's human love for every person. It was this love "unto folly" which drove Him to embrace each human sin as if it were His own on the Cross. Jesus' thirst (John 19:28), which Thérèse had come to understand years before, was His desire for the love of those redeemed in his Blood.

In her Oblation, Thérèse invoked upon herself the unrequited love pent up in the Heart of the Crucified for indifferent, sinful souls. She desired to give Our Lord pleasure by allowing Him to love her in place of all those who had rejected His love. She also begged Him to create in her an infinite supernatural love for God and the salvation of souls.

It is important to underscore the fact that Thérèse had offered her life for the sanctification of the clergy. It may be suggested that the "Oblation to the Merciful Love of God" was specifically made for priests. Thérèse would certainly have considered it indiscreet to speak or write about priests who had lost the Catholic Faith. We might recall that she had been preoccupied, up to her death, with the apostate priest, Hyacinthe Loyson, for whom she would offer her last Holy Communion.

In requesting the binding of her freedom, the real presence of Jesus habitually in her soul, and the revelation of the stigmata

---

[71] See François Jamart, OCD, *op. cit.*, p. 149.

of Christ in her glorified flesh, Thérèse was, in effect, asking to be totally possessed and transformed by Christ. In reality, through her prayer, Thérèse formally and solemnly invited Christ to offer His sacrifice again in her for the salvation of the world.

Hence, she asked to experience His death of love. It is interesting to note that when she was in the last stages of pulmonary tuberculosis, Thérèse was certain that she would not die of the disease but rather of the love of God. In this conviction, as we shall examine in more detail later, Thérèse revealed beyond any doubt that she had already experienced the mystical marriage and would actually die of the love of God.

Shortly after offering herself to the merciful love of God, Thérèse had a mystical experience that confirmed the conviction that she had indeed entered the state of mystical marriage. She related this grace to Mother Agnes shortly before her death. Responding to her sister's question, "What happened when you made the Act of Oblation to the Merciful Love of God?" Thérèse answered:

> Well, I was beginning the Way of the Cross; suddenly I was seized with such violent love of God that I can't explain it except by saying it felt as though I were totally plunged in fire. Oh! what fire and what sweetness at one and the same time! I was on fire with love, and I felt that one minute more, one second more, and I wouldn't be able to sustain this ardor without dying. I understood, then, what the saints were saying about these states which they experienced so often.... At the age of fourteen I also experienced transports of love. Ah! how I loved God! But it wasn't at all as it was after my Oblation to Love, it wasn't the real flame that was burning me.[72]

One might be tempted to see in this mystical fire, the purification of the second passive night. However, Thérèse herself does not understand the experience in that way. Rather, she perceived

---

[72] *L.C.*, p. 77.

the fire as the love of God which was joined mystically to the substance of her soul, transforming her into itself and causing spiritual delight. Spiritual writers have seen in this mystical experience the imparting of the "wound of love" which, according to St. John of the Cross, is rarely granted.[73]

St. John of the Cross amply discusses the "wound of love" experienced only rarely by those in the transforming union. He explains:

> It will feel that a seraphim is assailing the soul by means of an arrow or a dart that is all afire with love.... The soul feels its ardor strengthen and increase and its love become so refined in this ardor, that seemingly there are seas of loving fire within it, reaching to the heights and depths of the earthly and heavenly spheres, imbuing all with love.[74]

The mystical Doctor also explains the reason God so wounds the soul with love: "Few persons have reached these heights. Some have, however, especially those whose virtue and spirit was to be diffused among their children. For God accords to founders, with respect to the first fruits of the spirit, wealth and value commensurate with the greater or lesser following they will have in their doctrine and spirituality.[75]

Following this teaching of St. John of the Cross, it may be affirmed that Thérèse had not only personally attained the mystical marriage but had also been chosen by God to pass on her "Way" of spiritual light to many others in the Church. As I have already indicated, Thérèse's specific mission is twofold: to suffer with Christ as a victim of the love of God and, through a remarkable exemplarity, to be a model and teacher of Christian holiness for others in times of apostasy from the Faith.

According to both St. John of the Cross and St. Teresa of

---

[73] See François Jamart, OCD, *op. cit.*, p. 253.
[74] *Living Flame of Love*, p. 661.
[75] *Living Flame of Love*, p. 662.

Jesus, the person who enjoys the transforming union lives always in the presence of God and enjoys the most intimate relationship with Him. In fact, the human will and the divine will are so unified in this marriage that rarely, if ever, does the human subject offend God. Rather, he or she seeks to give God pleasure by every human act.[76]

Less than a year after her "Oblation to the Merciful Love of God," and her experience of the "wound of love" Thérèse entered her mysterious "trial of faith." Each of the characteristics of the mystical marriage, so readily discernible in Thérèse's life, especially after the Oblation, not only perdured but were intensified, as we shall see, during her final months. This is important to keep in mind since my aim is to demonstrate that Thérèse's trial is perfectly compatible with the mystical marriage and, in fact, is a staggering manifestation of transforming union. Consequently, from this point forward, my focus shall be the state of Thérèse's soul from her Oblation (June 11, 1895) through the initiation of the "trial of faith" (April, 1896) until her death (September 30, 1897). These last months of her life were, in her own words, the beginning of her mission[77] — in other words, her "hour."

The primary sign of the transforming union, as we have seen, is the tranquil and intimate awareness of the presence of God in the soul. Although St. John of the Cross states that it is impossible in this life to continually perceive and directly enjoy divine union, the soul in the mystical marriage nonetheless does enjoy "a state of habitual sweetness and tranquility which is never lost or lacking."[78] Besides the habitual awareness of God's presence,

---

[76] St. John of the Cross held that the person in the transforming union was confirmed in sanctifying grace. St. Teresa of Jesus, while affirming the profound unity of the human will and the divine will in the mystical marriage, held that there is no "confirmation in grace" in this life. For an excellent treatment of this "controversy," see Reginald Garrigou-Lagrange, *The Three Ages of the Interior Life*, Vol. II, trans. by Sr. M. Timothea Doyle, OP (St. Louis: B. Herder Book Co., 1948), pp. 533-539.

[77] *L.C.*, p. 102.

[78] *Spiritual Canticle*, p. 567. See also Thomas Dubay, SM, *Fire Within* (San Francisco: Ignatius Press, 1989), pp. 191-192.

the person in the transforming union is so surrendered to the divine Will that his or her every act is, in effect, a direct response to God's Will — in other words, God living and acting in and through the human subject.

Manuscripts "B" and "C" of the *Story of a Soul* bear ample evidence of Thérèse's perception of the divine presence in her soul as well as her awareness of Jesus acting in and through her by means of charity. Writing at the worst moment of her "trial of faith," Thérèse said: "Yes, I feel it.[79] When I am charitable, it is Jesus alone who is acting in me and the more united I am to Him, the more also do I love my Sisters."[80]

Thérèse was also capable of experiencing and reverencing Jesus living by grace in the souls of others. In fact, in her "Little Way," this mystical presence is the primary motive of charity. Writing of the Sister who was, humanly speaking, most disagreeable to her, Thérèse says: "One day at recreation this Sister asked in almost these words: 'Would you tell me, Sister Thérèse of the Child Jesus, what attracts you so much toward me; every time you look at me I see you smile.' Oh! what attracted me is Jesus hidden in the depths of her soul; Jesus Who makes sweet what is most bitter."[81]

Thérèse, likewise, was able to perceive Jesus' presence in the soul of her superior. She observes that her "trial of faith" helped her to perfect this perception: "Since the time He permitted me to suffer temptation against the *faith*, He has greatly increased the *spirit of faith* in my heart, which helps me to see in you, Mother, not only a loving mother but also Jesus living in your soul and communicating His Will to me through you."[82]

Describing her "method" of instructing and directing the novices in her charge, Thérèse beautifully reveals the union of her will and God's Will:

---

[79] See p. 157, note 59, above.
[80] *S.*, p. 221.
[81] *S.*, p. 223.
[82] *S.*, p. 219.

When I was given the office of entering into the sanctuary of souls, I saw immediately that the task was beyond my strength. I threw myself into the arms of God, as a little child, and hiding my face in His hair, I said: "Lord, I am too little to nourish Your children. If You wish to give through me what is suitable for each, fill my little hand and without leaving Your arms or turning my head, I shall give Your treasures to the soul who will ask for nourishment. If she finds it according to her taste, I shall know it is not to me but to You she owes it; on the contrary, if she complains and finds bitter what I present, my peace will not be disturbed, and I shall try to convince her this nourishment comes from You and be careful not to seek any other for her.[83]

So united was she to God's Will, that Thérèse was able to affirm without hesitation that her desires and God's were always in harmony. It is even possible to go beyond this assertion — for Thérèse, God communicated His Will to her specifically through her desires. She said, for instance, two months before her death: "God always made me desire what He wanted to give me."[84]

As she approached death, Thérèse manifested another characteristic of the mystical marriage: she lost all preferences and desired only what God manifested to her as His Will in the "sacrament of the present moment." Describing the mystical marriage, St. Teresa of Jesus writes: "The soul experiences strange forgetfulness for, seemingly, the soul no longer is or would want to be anything in anything, except when it understands that there can come from itself something by which the glory and honor of God may increase even one degree... the desire left in these souls that the will of God be done in them reaches such an extreme that they think everything His Majesty does is good... not only do they not desire to die but they desire to live very many years suffering the greatest trials if through these they can help that the Lord be

---

[83] *S.*, pp. 237-238.
[84] *L.C.*, p. 94.

praised... nor do they think of the glory of the saints... Their glory lies in being able some way to help the Crucified..."[85]

Thérèse frequently expressed such abandonment to God's Will; for instance, shortly before her death, she was able to say: "I am resigned to remain sick for several months, as long as God wills it."[86] As she was dying, Thérèse was asked innumerable inane questions by her religious and blood sisters. These questions, however, elicited answers which permit us to understand the perfect resignation of Thérèse's will to the divine will. On one occasion, Thérèse was asked if she would choose to suffer the "death agony" or not. Thérèse answered simply: "I would choose nothing."[87]

In the *Living Flame of Love*, St. John of the Cross teaches that the person in the transforming union understands, without the slightest trace of vanity or self-aggrandizement, that God has accomplished great things in his or her soul for the good of the Church: "God permits the soul in this state to see its beauty and He entrusts to it the gifts and virtues He has bestowed."[88]

While acknowledging her own powerlessness, Thérèse affirmed the great things God had done in her through His grace. In this respect, Thérèse had entered deeply into the Blessed Virgin's *Magnificat* and made its spiritual truth her own. For instance, on August 4, 1897, she said: "No, I don't believe I am a great saint. I believe I am a very little saint; but I think God has been pleased to place things in me which will do good to me and to others."[89]

In this area, as in so many others, Thérèse insisted upon a precise definition of St. John of the Cross' teaching. She did assert that those in the mystical marriage perceive their own beauty, but, however, she insisted that the cause of this beauty is God's grace alone. On August 9, 1897, she said, for instance: "No, I'm not a saint. I've never performed the actions of a saint. I'm a very

---

[85] *Interior Castle*, pp. 438-439.
[86] *L.C.*, p. 89.
[87] *L.C.*, p. 190.
[88] *Living Flame of Love*, p. 592.
[89] *L.C.*, p. 131.

little soul upon whom God has bestowed graces; that's what I am. What I say is the truth; you'll see this in heaven."[90]

The very next day, the nuns were saying that souls who reach the transforming union, as Thérèse had, recognize their beauty. Thérèse responded with clarity and firmness: "What beauty? I don't see my beauty at all; I see only the graces I've received from God. You always misunderstand me; you don't know, then, that I'm only a little seedling, a little almond."[91] On the day of her death, Thérèse made a staggering assertion: "Yes, it seems to me I've never sought anything but the truth; yes, I have understood humility of heart."[92]

Another characteristic of the transforming union is consummation and transformation in the love of God. Describing the state of her soul to Mother Agnes, Thérèse wrote:

> You permitted me, dear Mother, to offer myself in this way to God, and you know the oceans of grace which flooded my soul. Ah! since that happy day, it seems to me that *Love* penetrates and surrounds me, that each moment this *Merciful Love* renews me, purifying my soul and leaving no trace of sin within it... Oh! how sweet is the way of love! How I want to apply myself to doing the will of God always with the greatest self-surrender![93]

Supernatural love penetrated and possessed Thérèse's soul after her Oblation. This love grew to infinite proportions during the two remaining years of her life. One year after the Oblation she experienced the desire to do great things for Christ in His Church — in fact, to do everything out of love for Him and for souls: "I feel the *vocation* of THE WARRIOR, THE PRIEST, THE APOSTLE, THE DOCTOR, THE MARTYR."[94] And again: "*Martyrdom* was the dream of my youth and this dream has grown

---

[90] *L.C.*, p. 143.
[91] *L.C.*, p. 144.
[92] *L.C.*, p. 205.
[93] *S.*, p. 181.
[94] *S.*, p. 192.

within me within Carmel's cloisters. But here again, I feel that my dream is folly for I cannot confine myself to desiring *one kind* of martyrdom. To satisfy me, I need *all!*"[95]

In the midst of these incomprehensible desires, Thérèse came to comprehend her precise vocation through meditation on St. Paul's description of the Church as the mystical body of Christ: "O Jesus, my love.... My *vocation,* at last I have found it.... MY VOCATION IS LOVE!.... Yes, I have found my place in the Church and it is You, O my God, who have given me this place; in the heart of the Church, my Mother, I shall be *Love.* Thus I shall be everything and thus my dreams will be realized."[96]

It is important to remember that Thérèse discovered her vocation and wrote these words in the midst of her "trial of faith." In fact, from her Oblation until her death, it was the mystery of supernatural charity which absorbed her. During this period, Thérèse confidently asked all of the inhabitants of heaven for a "double portion" of their spirit so that she might indeed "be Love in the heart of the Church." At the request of her superior, she adopted two missionary brothers, one a priest, the other a seminarian. She worked most effectively with her novices, forming them in faith and charity in the midst of her internal agony. She also courageously embraced both her terminal illness and her mysterious and torturous "trial of faith" as perfect opportunities for loving God and saving souls in union with the Redeemer.

It was during this period (1895-97), that Thérèse wrote the *Story of a Soul* in the form of three distinct manuscripts, as noted earlier. Manuscript "A" is a commentary on the development of her "little way" of spiritual childhood; manuscript "B," a description of Thérèse's discovery of her vocation as "Love in the heart of the Church"; and manuscript "C" which, as I have noted in Chapter III of this book, is her "masterpiece on supernatural char-

---

[95] S., p. 193.
[96] S., p. 194.

ity.... A profound commentary on the twofold commandment of Christ... Her hymn to love."[97]

Shortly before her death, as she endured the ravages of her "trial of faith," Thérèse wrote of the depth, the immensity and the ineffability of the love God had created in her soul:

> You know, O my God, I have never desired anything but to *love* You and I am ambitious for no other glory. Your love has gone before me, and it has grown with me, and now it is an abyss whose depth I cannot fathom. Love attracts love and my Jesus, my love leaps towards Yours; it would like to fill the abyss which attracts it, but alas! it is not even like a drop of dew lost in the ocean! For me to love You as You love me, I would have to borrow Your own love, and then only would I be at rest. O my Jesus, it is perhaps an illusion but it seems to me that You cannot fill the soul with more love than the love with which You have filled mine.... I cannot conceive a greater immensity of love than the one which it has pleased You to give me freely, *without any merit on my part.*[98]

Finally, as I have already amply noted in Chapters I, II, and III of this book, Thérèse was convinced during the final years of her life that, having attained the transforming union, she would literally die of the love of God. In the preceding chapters of this book, I quoted extensively from St. John of the Cross on the theme of the "death of love." His thought is well summarized in the following passage from the *Living Flame of Love*: "A person, having reached this stage (of transforming union), knows full well that it is characteristic of God to take to Himself, before their time, souls that love Him ardently, perfecting them in a short while by means of that love."[99]

According to the teaching of St. John of the Cross (and St.

---

[97] See Chapter III of this book, p. 123.

[98] *S.*, p. 256.

[99] *Living Flame of Love*, p. 656.

Francis de Sales),[100] the person who has attained the transforming union, having been purged of sin and its root in the soul, is separated from full fruition in God only by the thin veil of the flesh.

After Thérèse's death, her sisters found at her bedside a volume containing the *Spiritual Canticle* and the *Living Flame of Love*. She had marked off those passages in the latter which described the death of love. André Combes, in his work, *St. Thérèse and Suffering*, notes that St. John of the Cross had taught four important lessons to Thérèse: "First, that the secret of growth and perfection is the constant exercise of love; Second, that such an exercise normally leads to the speedy attainment of the Beatific Vision; Third, that by its own power, love prematurely breaks the bond of such a perfect life; and Fourth, that this breaking of the bonds is of the nature of a sudden disruption and not a gradual erosion."[101]

It is evident in *Her Last Conversations*, that Thérèse believed she would die of the love of God. She understood her own torturous death as a participation in the "death of love" Our Lord endured on the Cross. Thérèse frequently cited the *Living Flame of Love* during her last months and used images from St. John of the Cross' writings to describe the impending encounter with Christ that would free her from the bondage of this life. For instance, on July 27, 1897, she recalled the words: "Tear through the veil of this sweet encounter" and related them to herself: "I have always applied these words to the death of love that I desire. Love will not wear out the veil of my life; it will tear it suddenly."[102]

Returning to this theme on September 2, Thérèse used St. John of the Cross' words as a prayer: "Oh! yes, I desire heaven! 'Tear the veil of this sweet encounter,' O my God!"[103] On another

---

[100] See St. Francis de Sales, *Treatise on the Love of God*, Vol. II, trans. Rt. Rev. John K. Ryan (New York: Doubleday & Company, Inc., 1963), pp. 37-55, for another treatment of the phenomenon of the "death of love."

[101] André Combes, *St. Thérèse and Suffering*, p. 119; *L.C.*, p. 113.

[102] *L.C.*, p. 113.

[103] *L.C.*, p. 181.

occasion, Thérèse told Mother Agnes of Jesus that, in spite of her "trial of faith" and intense physical sufferings, she continued to be certain that she would die of the love of God. She also intimated that she was experiencing profound mystical union in the depths of her soul: "I shall have to say that 'joy and transports' are at the bottom of my heart. But it wouldn't be so encouraging to souls if they didn't believe I suffered very much."[104]

Thérèse's frequently articulated conviction that she would die of love and the testimony of those who actually witnessed her death, are sufficient to substantiate the claim that she had attained to the transforming union well before her demise. With great insight, André Combes observes: "With Thérèse it is death itself, this universal experience, that is invested with the highest mystic value. Her faith has taught her that death must be regarded as a punishment by God's justice, yet she sees in it a design of God's infinite mercy, and, more profoundly still, the last question that His love puts to her."[105]

There are many indications in her writings that Thérèse had attained to the mystical marriage before her "Oblation to the Merciful Love of God" on June 11, 1895. The Oblation itself is a testimony to the degree of union she had attained at that time. It also acted as an impetus for her further growth in supernatural love. The testimony of the witnesses at the process of her beatification amply justifies the claim that she had entered the mystical marriage at least by the time of her "Oblation to the Merciful Love of God."

Depending upon her writings and the testimony of those who had known her personally, we have focused upon several characteristics of Thérèse which clearly indicate the attainment of the spiritual marriage: (1) Thérèse had a vivid and habitual experience of God dwelling and acting in her soul. This mystical awareness of the divine presence was uninterrupted during the "trial of faith."

---

[104] *L.C.*, p. 148
[105] André Combes, *St. Thérèse and Suffering*, p. 123.

She also habitually experienced the divine presence in the souls of her Sisters and, in a special way, in her religious superior; (2) Thérèse's will was so united to the divine will, that, in the words of St. Teresa of Jesus: "The soul, seemingly, no longer is... there is a great detachment from everything... she lives with a remembrance and tender love of Our Lord."[106] Also, Thérèse was convinced that her desires manifested God's Will to her. In this and the previous characteristic, the presence of the gift of wisdom is plainly discernible;[107] (3) Thérèse tranquilly recognized that God had worked great wonders of grace in her soul. She was convinced in an absolute sense, that this was entirely the work of God and apart from His grace, she would have become a great sinner. In other words, claiming none of God's gifts as her own, Thérèse acknowledged her creaturehood in an absolute and comprehensive way; (4) The affective love of God and effective love of other people so absorbed Thérèse, that at the end of her life she was unable to comprehend a greater bestowal of supernatural charity and was certain that love alone would be the supernatural cause of her death. The "wound of love" she perceived in the aftermath of her "Oblation to the Merciful Love of God" indicated both her specific vocation and her mission of communicating her "Way of Spiritual Childhood" in the Church.

A number of ascetico-mystical theologians of the highest caliber have demonstrated that Thérèse of Lisieux had attained to the transforming union before the initiation of her "trial of faith." For instance, François Jamart states:

> It is our opinion that Thérèse did attain transforming union. Everything points to the fact: She suffered passive purifications; she was favored with special graces of mental prayer that prepared for such a union, and she enjoyed the fruits of such a union. Her sisters have testified that her virtues developed in a way that was unique. Her love,

---

[106] *Interior Castle*, pp. 438, 440.

[107] See François Jamart, OCD, *op. cit.*, pp. 241-246, for an excellent treatment of the gift of wisdom as the source of Thérèse's mystical life.

especially, burned with a singular intensity. Thérèse herself confessed that she was unable to fathom its depth.... She has also recorded for us that, from the day of her Oblation to Merciful Love, love surrounded and permeated her, renewed and purified her, leaving no trace of sin in her.... She boldly affirmed that no praise bestowed on her could produce in her even the shadow of vanity; that she then understood what is meant by humility of heart and knew that she was a little saint.... She was favored with the wound of love, a grace, which, according to St. John of the Cross, is rarely granted to souls. She had been chosen to teach souls a simple way of holiness. How then could we consider it possible that she herself did not realize holiness in its perfection?[108]

Describing Thérèse's trial, M.V. Bernadot, O.P., also argues that Thérèse had attained the transforming union: "Thérèse's trial undoubtedly belonged to the unitive life, where it was rather a consequence of transforming love than a preparation for it.... She suffered because she was transformed into Jesus crucified, and with Him and in Him was redeeming her brethren."[109]

In his classical work on Carmelite spirituality entitled *I Am a Daughter of the Church*, Fr. Marie-Eugène, O.C.D., criticizes those who, in their treatment of mysticism, concentrate on extraordinary phenomena and neglect the essential, i.e., the union of the human will and the divine. He states: "Confusions between the mystical phenomenon and the reality are frequent, in favor of the phenomenon, which is sought out and emphasized as if it were the principal element. This is because the mystical phenomenon that marks the summit generally exercises a strong attraction on the mass of the faithful, eager for signs and for the extraordinary and the miraculous."[110]

---

[108] François Jamart, OCD, *op. cit.*, pp. 249-253.

[109] M.V. Bernadot, OP, *St. Teresa of the Child Jesus*, trans. by a Dominican of Headington (London: Burns, Oats and Washburn, Ltd., 1926) pp. 59-60.

[110] Fr. Marie-Eugène, OCD, *I Am a Daughter of the Church: A Practical Synthesis of Carmelite Spirituality*, Vol. II, trans. Sister M. Verna Clare, CSC (Chicago: Fides Publishers, 1955), p. 568.

In this context, Fr. Marie-Eugène, O.C.D., addresses the question of Thérèse's spiritual development:

> The judgments passed on St. Thérèse and her spirituality have brought to light the incorrectness of these notions and allow us to guess the harmful influences they could exercise on the spiritual life of souls. Actually, some hesitated to recognize in St. Thérèse of the Child Jesus, the highest states of the spiritual life, because in her they were not accompanied and proven by the mystical phenomena that they thought to be inseparable from these states. And yet, the little Saint of Lisieux took care to warn us that when perfection is in question, appearing perfect is of small importance compared with being so.[111]

In his monumental study of ascetico-mystical theology, *The Three Ages of the Interior Life*, Reginald Garrigou-Lagrange, O.P., writes of a "reparatory night of the spirit." He notes:

> The reading of the works of St. John of the Cross leads one to consider the night of the spirit chiefly as a personal passive purification which prepares the soul for the perfect union with God, called the transforming union.... The winter of the night of the spirit seems followed by a springtime and a perpetual summer, after which there would no longer be autumn.[112] However, the lives of some great servants of God, especially dedicated to reparation, make one think of a prolongation of the night of the spirit even after their entrance into the transforming union. In such a case, this trial would no longer be chiefly purificatory; it would be above all, reparative.[113]

Fr. Garrigou-Lagrange holds up St. Paul of the Cross, the founder of the Passionists, as the model of this reparatory night

---

[111] Fr. Marie-Eugène, OCD, *op. cit.*, pp. 568-569.
[112] Reginald Garrigou-Lagrange, OP, *op. cit.*, Vol. II., pp. 502-503.
[113] *Ibid.*, p. 503.

of the spirit. However, in a note, the theologian includes St. Vincent de Paul, the Curé of Ars, and St. Thérèse of Lisieux among those who have experienced "reparatory nights of the spirit" to some extent. Regarding Thérèse, he notes: "What she wrote at the end of her life is quite revealing and should be re-read."[114]

Discussing Thérèse's "trial of faith," Simon Tugwell, O.P., observes: "The most striking thing about this sudden transformation is that Thérèse sees it, not as a kind of 'dark night' any student of St. John of the Cross may have predicted, but as a way of identifying herself totally with unbelievers and sinners."[115] Tugwell also asserts that Thérèse ascended to the heights of mysticism by descending into Christ's *kenosis*: "It is precisely in this way that she came to know the reality of love, and to enter into her apostolate of love. All that is left, finally, after the consolations have gone, is the desolate cry: "*J'ai soif!* I thirst!'"[116]

Each of these authors proposes Thérèse as a mystic from various vantage points: Jamart strictly demonstrates his point by having recourse to Teresian and Sanjuanist categories of spiritual development. Both Bernadot and Tugwell envision Thérèse's mysticism in terms of union with the Crucified in His work of redemption. Fr. Marie-Eugène, O.C.D., in his attempt to minimize the importance of mystical phenomena, maximizes the value of sacrificial love and thereby secures mystical status for Thérèse. Fr. Garrigou-Lagrange, although barely mentioning Thérèse by name, and admittedly not placing her in the same category as St. Paul of the Cross, does nonetheless cogently argue for the existence of a reparatory night of the spirit experienced by some who have attained the mystical marriage.

---

[114] *Ibid.*, p. 510.

[115] Simon Tugwell, OP, "St. Thérèse of Lisieux," *Doctrine and Life*, July-August, 1983, p. 343.

[116] Simon Tugwell, OP, *op. cit.*, p. 344.

Objections

The assertion that Thérèse had attained the mystical marriage, however, has not gone unchallenged. Defining mysticism in terms of the "mystical phenomena" described by St. John of the Cross and St. Teresa of Jesus, Hans Urs von Balthasar has stated categorically: "One cannot say that Thérèse crossed the threshold into what is known as mysticism."[117] He also states:

> Thérèse *deliberately rejects* mysticism. And here she takes an astonishingly independent line, in direct opposition to the great Spaniards. For whether they admit it or not, the Spaniards' whole attitude is an invitation to enter the world of mysticism, which they range over and map out with such assurance that one eventually feels as if Christian perfection is impossible without mystical experience.[118]

Pierre Blanchard, seizing upon Thérèse's temptation against the faith, presumes, as do many other writers, that these are incompatible with the transforming union. He notes: "Thérèse's ordinary state (especially during her last years) was the dark night of the soul. This is clearly the case since she was frequently assailed by temptations against the faith."[119]

Norbert Cummins, O.C.D., in an article entitled "The Night of Faith" which appears in the anthology, *The Mind of St. Thérèse of Lisieux*, observes that in the original *Story of a Soul*, Chapter 9 had been entitled "The Night of the Soul."[120] The author says: "The concern of St. Thérèse in this part of her autobiography was, not strictly speaking, the Night of the Spirit, which will come later, and which has its place, for the most part, among those pages of her story which will never be read upon earth."[121]

---

[117] Hans Urs von Balthasar, *op. cit.*, p. 252.

[118] von Balthasar, *op. cit.*, pp. 252-253.

[119] Canon Pierre Blanchard, *op. cit.*, p. 165.

[120] The title of Chapter 9 was not written by Thérèse herself. It is very likely that Mother Agnes of Jesus had chosen the chapter title not to specify a grade of mystical experience but rather to present a general idea of the theme of the section of the *Story of a Soul*.

[121] See Thomas M. Curran, ed., *The Mind of St. Thérèse of Lisieux* (Dublin: Carmelite Center of Spirituality, 1977), p. 37.

These authors articulate three major objections to the thesis that Thérèse had attained to the mystical marriage prior to the initiation of her "trial of faith." The positions may be stated and summarized thus:

1. The mystical phenomena that ordinarily precede the transforming union, such as raptures, flights of the spirit, ecstasies, are not evident in Thérèse's spiritual development. Therefore, according to the categories of both St. John of the Cross and St. Teresa of Jesus, Thérèse is not a mystic;

2. According to the spiritual doctrine of St. John of the Cross and St. Teresa of Jesus, the absence of trials and accompanying interior peace are all marks of the transforming union. Since Thérèse had spent the last year of her life embroiled in a horrendous interior struggle with faith, it is obvious that she died before attaining the mystical marriage;[122]

3. The third position is a variant of the second: Thérèse's interior struggles during her life in Carmel are all to be understood as instances of passive purgation. The "trial of faith" must be interpreted as the final stage of the purification of the spirit. Therefore, Thérèse experienced the mystical marriage only at the moment of her death.[123]

---

[122] A hasty reading of both St. John of the Cross and St. Teresa of Jesus would lead to this conclusion.

[123] A certain superficial reading of Mother Agnes' account of Thérèse's death, apart from other documentary evidence of her spiritual development, might well lead to this interpretation. See *L.C.*, pp. 206-207: "Her face had regained the lily-white complexion it always had in full health; her eyes were fixed above, brilliant with peace and joy. She made certain beautiful movements with her head as though someone had divinely wounded her with an arrow of love, then had withdrawn the arrow to wound her again.... The ecstasy lasted almost the space of a Credo, and then she gave her last breath... after her death, she had a heavenly smile. She was ravishingly beautiful."
Interestingly, von Balthasar will not even grant Thérèse the grace of mystical marriage in her passing: "For the time, in the history of mysticism, we find a privileged soul who has passed through the passion but whose resurrection is put off into the next world. She hangs there suspended unto death: 'I shall never know how to die!... I cannot go on!... I can't breathe, I can't die.'" (Hans Urs von Balthasar, *op. cit.*, p. 202).

In order to answer the first objection raised by Hans Urs von Balthasar (i.e., as a result of the absence of the mystical phenomena outlined by the Carmelite Doctors, Thérèse may not be classified among those who have attained the transforming union), one need only point to Thérèse's own testimony as found in her writings. There is striking evidence that she had been the recipient of mystical graces at every stage of her life.

In Chapter I of this book, I considered in detail three foundational graces, directly related to her development in charity, that Thérèse had received as a child: the "Smile of the Virgin" (1883); the infused desire to suffer abundantly for the salvation of souls which was received in the wake of her second reception of the Holy Eucharist (1884); and the "Christmas Grace of Conversion" (1886). Another grace might also be included in this group: Thérèse's "prophetic vision" as a child of her father's future mental collapse (1879 or 1880).[124]

As a novice in Carmel, Thérèse continued to be favored with the mystical graces: the prayer of quiet and the sleep of the senses both associated with a mystical encounter with the Virgin;[125] the awareness of having been plunged in the consuming and transforming love of God,[126] ecstasies and flights of the spirit and the "wound of love" reserved for those called to a doctrinal mission in the Church.[127]

Above all, Thérèse, even before her entry into Carmel, vividly experienced Jesus at the core of her being. At first, for at least five years, she experienced Him in her soul, but asleep and dreaming of her. Later, after her "Oblation to the Merciful Love of God" and throughout the course of her "trial of faith," Thérèse even more vividly experienced Jesus as living, guiding, instructing and, above all, suffering in the interior of her soul. This infused aware-

---

[124] Chapter I, pp. 9-26; for Thérèse's "prophetic vision," see *S.*, pp. 45-46.

[125] *L.C.*, p. 88; Flights of the spirit, raptures and ecstasies experienced, as she related, "are at the bottom of my heart"; see *L.C.*, p. 148.

[126] See *L.C.*, p. 77.

[127] *Ibid.*

ness of Christ's presence and activity existed in her along with all of the essential signs of the transforming union: profound peace in spite of difficulties; a tranquil and intense union of the human and divine wills; an habitual, loving awareness of God's presence as mystery and the concomitant absence of self-consciousness and vanity regarding graces and spiritual gifts; and the consuming desire to give everything and do anything for God's glory and the salvation of souls.

It may be granted that Thérèse does not give evidence of each and every external manifestation of mystical union as outlined in the writings of St. John of the Cross and St. Teresa of Jesus. As François Jamart, O.C.D., observes:

> Her mystical life differs considerably from the description which St. John of the Cross gives of that kind of life. Thérèse's Way is much simpler; it is much less favored with mystical graces than that of souls about whom the holy Doctor speaks in his works. Again, classification of the states of prayer described by St. Teresa of Jesus are not found in Thérèse of the Child Jesus. We know that she received mystical graces of a high order, but these were rare.[128]

Two points must be made in any valid consideration of Thérèse's experience of mystical phenomena. First, both St. John of the Cross and St. Teresa of Jesus insist that God leads each soul on a unique and unrepeatable journey of faith. The mystical Doctors of Carmel did not expect each Christian who seeks perfection to travel an identical, stereotyped route. In fact, each insists that a spiritual director is competent only if he is able to discern God's particular means of leading an individual soul. For St. John of the Cross and St. Teresa of Jesus, mystical phenomena are by-products of the union of the soul with God through faith and charity. Thérèse therefore grasped and brilliantly articulated the truth that

---

[128] François Jamart, OCD, *op. cit.*, p. 253.

volitional union and the savor of the divine presence are the only essential components of mysticism.

Second, Thérèse admitted that she had experienced mystical phenomena; however, in the light of her doctrinal mission and her vocation to exemplarity, and perhaps also in reaction to the trend of her fellow religious to understand spirituality in esoteric and Gnostic categories, she consistently minimized the importance of mystical phenomena in favor of faith and charity.

For instance, Thérèse frequently insisted that the Blessed Virgin and St. Joseph lived a very simple and ordinary life in the obscurity of faith and, nonetheless, attained the pinnacle of union with God:

> What does me a lot of good when I think of the Holy Family is to imagine a life that was very ordinary.... How many troubles, disappointments! How many times did others make complaints to good St. Joseph! How many times did they refuse to pay him for his work! Oh! how astonished we would be if we only knew how much they had to suffer![129]

Thérèse understood that in "ordinariness" and the humble acceptance of God's design, a Christian may reach the heights of divine union in imitation of the Virgin Mary, Mother and model of faith. On another occasion she said:

> For a sermon on the Blessed Virgin to please me and do me any good, I must see her real life, not her imagined life. I'm sure that her real life was very simple. They show her to us unapproachable but they should present her as imitable, bringing out her virtues, saying that she lived by faith just like ourselves, giving proofs of this from the Gospel, where we read: "And they did not understand the words which He spoke to them."[130]

Similarly, Thérèse brilliantly recast the teaching of St. John of the Cross on the "death of love" by excising the spectacular

---

[129] *L.C.*, p. 159.
[130] *L.C.*, p. 161.

and riveting her focus on the essential component — the love of the Crucified for His Father and for the fallen human race. In this, as in all else, Christ was her model: "Our Lord died on the Cross in agony, and yet this is the most beautiful death of love. This is the only one that was seen; no one saw that of the Blessed Virgin. To die of love is not to die in transports. I tell you frankly, it seems to me that this is what I am experiencing."[131]

Finally, in the context of Thérèse's recasting of mysticism, it must be noted that she consciously minimized the importance of mystical phenomena in her life so as to be more able to console and edify all who struggle to serve God in integrity of heart. Shortly before her death, Thérèse told Mother Agnes: "I shall have to say that 'joy and transports' are at the bottom of my heart. But it wouldn't be so encouraging to souls if they didn't believe I suffered very much."[132]

As noted earlier, Hans Urs von Balthasar justified his position that Thérèse had never entered the mystical way by pointing to the absence of mystical phenomena in her life. Another prominent theologian of the twentieth century, Louis Bouyer of the Oratory, well-aware that Thérèse does not fit exactly into the patterns established by St. John of the Cross and St. Teresa of Jesus, addresses von Balthasar's position and reaches quite a different conclusion regarding Thérèse's spiritual development.[133]

---

[131] *L.C.*, p. 73.

[132] *L.C.*, p. 148.

[133] See "Thérèse of Lisieux," in *Light from Light*, ed. Louis Dupré and James A. Wiseman, OSB (Mahwah: Paulist Press, 1988), p. 393. Discussing Bouyer's definition of mysticism, Dom James Wiseman, OSB, notes: "One should recall that in its original Christian usage, the word 'mystical' referred to the objective but 'hidden' (*mystikos*) reality of Christ in Scripture, in the sacraments, and in all of history. An immediate and at times overwhelmingly ecstatic consciousness of this real presence, had indeed often been found in those who have dedicated themselves in a particularly singlehearted way to the following of the Gospel. But this kind of experience did not belong to the essence of the mystical as this was originally understood by writers like Origen, Gregory of Nyssa and Maximus the Confessor. According to that more objective understanding, as Louis Bouyer observes in the concluding chapter of his long and excellent study *Mysterium*: 'The main thing is to be fully convinced that Christ is living in us and especially to act accordingly, not to experience more or less directly the feeling that this is indeed so.'"

Asserting that the Christian mystery is the hidden presence of Christ experienced through faith and charity in Word, Sacrament, the mystery of grace and the indwelling Trinity, in the community of the Church, and in the poor and suffering, Bouyer notes that true mysticism is comprised of a loving awareness of the mystery of Christ and total surrender to that mystery in sacrificial love.

Significantly, this is the position taken in the *Catechism of the Catholic Church* (#2014): "Spiritual progress tends toward ever more intimate union with Christ. This union is called 'mystical' because it participates in the mystery of Christ through the sacraments — 'the holy mysteries' — and, in him, in the mystery of the Holy Trinity. God calls us all to this intimate union with him, even if the special graces or extraordinary signs of this mystical life are granted only to some for the sake of manifesting the gratuitous gift given to all."

Discussing Thérèse, Bouyer notes: "She gave us the most convincing proof that mysticism does not consist so much in ecstasies or 'visions,' even of the divine essence, appearing to raise us above the level of faith, as simply in complete abandonment to naked faith, becoming one, through an effective love of the Cross, with the very love of the Crucified God, even in the depths of obscurity."[134]

To answer the second objection (i.e., that Thérèse's "trial of faith" discredits the assertion that she had attained the mystical marriage), it is valuable to turn to the seventh chapter of St. Teresa of Jesus' *Interior Castle* in which she explains the characteristics of a soul in the transforming union. Although we have touched many of these points already, this excursus into the writings of the Mother of Carmel will help clarify the objection that interior struggles are a clear sign of a need for further purification.

The first effect of the transforming union that St. Teresa of Jesus mentions is self-forgetfulness. The soul, she teaches, is so

---

[134] Louis Bouyer, Cong. Orat., *The Christian Mystery* (Edinburgh: T&T Clark, 1990), pp. 257-258.
[135] *Interior Castle*, p. 438.

perfectly united to Christ that it "seemingly no longer is or would want to be anything in anything, except when it understands that there can come from itself something by which the glory and honor of God may increase even one degree."[135]

Thérèse manifested this effect of union with God all throughout her life. One recalls the beautiful description of her First Holy Communion: "Thérèse had simply disappeared like a drop lost in the ocean." One also recalls her "conversion" which was precisely a graced act of forgetting self and her hurt feelings in behalf of her father. The "Way of Spiritual Childhood," in fact, is based on the conviction, among others, that self-love must be annihilated in order to discover and accomplish the Will of God. It is impossible to read the *Story of a Soul* and not detect Thérèse's constant, loving preoccupation with the person of the Savior and His redemptive work.

St. Teresa of Jesus also notes that the soul in the transforming union experiences a great desire to suffer for God. However, the soul in this state is so abandoned to the Will of God, that it is not disturbed by the absence of suffering as it previously had been. St. Teresa of Jesus observes: "The desire left in these souls that the will of God be done in them reaches such an extreme that they think everything His Majesty does is good. If He desires the soul to suffer, well and good; if not, it does not kill itself as it used to."[136]

It is also certain that Thérèse manifested this disposition of soul. During the final year of her life, her only desire was to fulfill God's Will through her suffering and death. During the early stages of her illness, it often appeared as if Thérèse was recovering. Her sisters annoyingly probed her attitude toward death. They asked her if "she would prefer to die or recover?" Thérèse offered one, consistent response: "I prefer only the Will of God."

On August 30, 1897, Mother Agnes asked Thérèse if she would be happier to die than to continue her intense suffering.

---

[136] *Interior Castle*, p. 439.
[137] *L.C.*, p. 175.
[138] *L.C.*, p. 183.

Thérèse responded: "Oh! no, I wouldn't be at all happier. What makes me happy is only to do the Will of God."[137] On September 4 of that same year, Mother Agnes asked: "Do you prefer to die rather than to live?" Thérèse said: "O, little mother, I don't love one thing more than another; I could not say like our Holy Mother, St. Teresa: 'I die because I cannot die.' What God prefers and chooses for me, that is what pleases me more."[138]

St. Teresa of Jesus also notes that the soul, enjoying the mystical marriage, experiences great apostolic zeal: "Their glory lies in being able some way to help the Crucified, especially when they see He is so offended and that few there are who, detached from everything else, really look after His honor."[139] It is impossible not to recognize this zeal in the life of Thérèse. One recalls her desires to be an apostle, a priest, a doctor, a missionary, a martyr — all for the glory of God and the salvation of souls. Thérèse often admitted that the value of all of her good works and sacrifices had been offered to God for the sake of others. She refused to keep the value of any of her merit for herself.

St. Teresa of Jesus, furthermore, observes that in the transforming union, the mystical phenomena previously experienced are now experienced only rarely, and in a very peaceful way. She notes: "The desires these souls have are no longer for consolations or spiritual delight, since the Lord Himself is present with these souls and it is His Majesty Who now lives."[140]

Thérèse was always very restrained in discussing her personal experiences of God. On occasions she mentioned to Mother Agnes, as we have noted, that she had experienced such phenomena as transports of love, ecstasies, raptures and wounds of love. Also, as mentioned above, she confided to her that during her "trial of faith" she continued to experience joy and transports deep in her soul.

During the canonical process that preceded Thérèse's beati-

---

[139] *Interior Castle*, p. 439.
[140] *Interior Castle*, p. 440.
[141] *P.*, pp. 63-64.

fication, nearly all of the witnesses mentioned her great tranquility and recollection in the midst of intense physical sufferings. Those who had known her the best also noted that mystical phenomena — for instance, her experience of the prayer of quiet — did not impede her from fulfilling the demands of the Rule and charity.[141]

However, Thérèse always desired to walk the ordinary path of perfection for the edification of others. Following the teaching of St. John of the Cross, she consistently resisted spiritual consolations in favor of a naked and selfless love of God offered for the salvation of others. This Christ-like love is most evident, especially during the final months of her life.

This brings us to the final effect of the mystical marriage. St. Teresa of Jesus teaches: "There are almost never any experiences of dryness or interior disturbance, but the soul is almost always in quiet."[142] This teaching of the Mystical Doctor is, in fact, the source of the objection voiced by Pierre Blanchard and many others.

Thérèse often admitted in her writings that she experienced aridity in prayer. She also confessed that her "trial of faith" had caused her great, almost unbearable, interior suffering. This disturbance has led a number of authors to question whether Thérèse ever entered the mystical marriage. However, it must be pointed out that throughout the *Story of a Soul*, Thérèse insists, again and again, that *nothing* (her father's illness, the hostility of some of the Sisters in the monastery, the pain experienced in prayer, the temptations posed by Satan himself, physical agony, and her "trial of faith") ever disturbed the peace which reigned in that deepest part of her soul, where she experienced intimate communion with God.

The following statement of Thérèse made on July 14, 1897, echoes the sentiment which she had expressed innumerable times throughout her short life and especially in the midst of her "trial of faith": "My heart is filled with God's will and when someone pours something on it, this doesn't penetrate its interior; it's a

---

[142] *Interior Castle*, p. 441.
[143] *L.C.*, pp. 97-98.

nothing which glides off easily, just like oil which can't mix with water. I remain always at profound peace in the depths of my heart; nothing can disturb it."[143]

St. Teresa of Jesus does not teach that souls enjoying the mystical marriage are free of all trials and disturbances. Rather, she teaches that these trials no longer have power to disturb the union of the soul with God after the attainment of the mystical marriage. She writes: "The Cross is not wanting but it doesn't disquiet these souls or make them lose peace."[144]

She also uses the brilliant image of a king in his castle besieged by enemies in order to explain the effects of suffering on these chosen souls:

> The King is living in His palace and there are many wars in the kingdom and many painful things going on, but not on that account does he fail to be at his post. So here, even though in those other dwelling places there is much tumult and there are many poisonous creatures and the noise is heard, no one enters that center dwelling place and makes the soul leave. Nor do the things the soul hears make it leave; even though they cause it some pain, the suffering is not such as to disturb it and take away its peace. The passions are now conquered and have a fear of entering the center because they would go away from there more subdued.[145]

After discussing the mystical marriage, St. Teresa of Jesus concludes the *Interior Castle* with a simple exhortation to apostolic zeal. Reasserting the end and purpose of the spiritual life, she reminds the reader that the transforming union is nothing other than the perfect transformation of the soul in Christ. Consequently, the transformed soul manifests its union with the Lord by wholeheartedly participating in His redemptive mission.

Sharing both Christ's experience of the world and re-living His mysteries in their fullness, the soul will indeed find many for-

---

[144] *Interior Castle*, p. 443.
[145] *Interior Castle*, p. 437.

midable obstacles to the fulfillment of God's Will. However, united with Christ in the "interior castle," the soul will accomplish the Will of God in union with Christ and perform wonderful works: "His Majesty could not grant us a greater favor than to give us a life that would be an imitation of the life His beloved Son lived. Thus I hold for certain that these favors are meant to fortify our weakness, that we may be able to imitate Him in His great sufferings."[146]

A careful study of Thérèse of Lisieux's writings reveal all of the effects of the mystical marriage in her life as outlined by St. Teresa of Jesus in the *Interior Castle*. This brief excursus helps us to understand with clarity that trials are by no means incompatible with the state of the mystical marriage and, in fact, provide an opportunity for the soul in that state to participate more deeply in Christ's redemptive sacrifice for the salvation of the world.

St. John of the Cross also does not state categorically that souls in the mystical marriage are free of all trials and inner turmoil. For instance, in the *Living Flame of Love*, describing the soul in transforming union, the Saint notes: "A man should hold in esteem the interior and exterior trials God sends him, realizing that there are few who merit to be brought to perfection through suffering and to undergo trials for the sake of so high a state."[147]

The third objection noted above states that Thérèse's "trial of faith" was an instance of passive purgation which terminated in the mystical marriage at the moment of her death. As noted already, a certain superficial reading of the account of her death provided by Mother Agnes of Jesus might lead to this hasty conclusion. It must be recalled though, that before and throughout the last eighteen months of her life, that is, during her "trial of faith," Thérèse was convinced that she could die at any moment as a direct result of her consuming love of God.

Having St. John of the Cross' *Spiritual Canticle* and *Living Flame of Love* always at her disposal during her terminal illness,

---

[146] *Interior Castle*, p. 445.
[147] *Living Flame of Love*, p. 669.

Thérèse was well aware of the fact, and articulated this frequently, that the death of love is not caused by the termination of passive purgation but rather by an intense encounter with God by a soul already enjoying the transforming union. Thérèse's certainty that she was being consumed by love and would indeed die of love rather than as a result of her pulmonary tuberculosis, is perhaps the clearest indication that she had attained to the transforming union. As I have already amply noted, Thérèse's growth in virtue and especially in charity solidly confirms the conviction that she had entered the mystical marriage at least by the time of her "Oblation to the Merciful Love of God."

In answering the major objections to the thesis that Thérèse had entered the mystical marriage before the initiation of her "trial of faith" three conclusions may be drawn:

1. Although Thérèse did indeed experience mystical phenomena on her journey of faith, she minimized their importance in behalf of a life of union with God through naked faith and sacrificial charity;

2. While both St. John of the Cross and St. Teresa of Jesus teach that the soul in the transforming union is perfectly governed by the Holy Spirit in peace, neither holds that interior trials and turmoil of a serious nature are incompatible with the mystical marriage;

3. Thérèse re-articulated and, in a sense, purified St. John of the Cross' teaching on the "death of love" by explaining it exclusively in terms of a participatory sharing in Christ's redemptive death. Her certainty that she would die of love reveals both the degree of her mystical union with the Crucified as well as her conviction that her death would be the result of the intensity of this union.

These facts each lead to one conclusion: that since Thérèse had attained to the mystical marriage before her entry into the "trial of faith," the trial may not be understood in the category of passive purgation. In the concluding chapter of this book, I shall offer an interpretation of Thérèse's "trial of faith."

Chapter V

THE TRIAL OF FAITH:
AN INTERPRETATION

Discussing a malady particularly virulent in the twentieth century, namely, the Christian's temptation to abandon faith as an illusion of the unenlightened past, Dom John Chapman, O.S.B., in one of his letters, has noted:

> In the seventeenth and eighteenth centuries most pious souls seem to have gone through a period in which they felt sure that God had reprobated them. This doesn't seem to happen nowadays.
>
> But the *corresponding trial* of our contemporaries seems to be the *feeling of not having any faith*: not temptations against any particular article (usually), but a mere feeling that religion is not true. The only remedy is to despise the whole thing and pay no attention to it — except, of course, to assure our Lord that one is ready to suffer from it as long as He wishes, which seems an absurd paradox to say to a person one doesn't believe in! But then, that is the trial. Faith is really particularly strong all the time.[1]

While not having his vision focused on Thérèse in this letter, Dom Chapman, nonetheless, aptly describes both her "trial of faith" and her method of dealing effectively with it.

---

[1] Dom John Chapman, OSB, *Spiritual Letters* (London: Sheed and Ward, 1959), pp. 47-48.

As I noted earlier in this book,[2] less than a year after she had offered herself as a victim to the merciful love of God, as Thérèse experienced profound peace and growth in virtue — especially in charity — as a result of her vivid life of faith, she suddenly, and without any previous warning, began to doubt the existence of eternal life. She continued in this state of spiritual agony for a year and a half — up to and including the day of her death — September 30, 1897.

Analyzing Thérèse's description of her "trial of faith," five characteristics are readily discernible.

First of all, the "trial of faith" was accepted by Thérèse herself as a deep mystery willed or at least permitted by God in order to accomplish His inscrutable designs in her life. She accepted the trial as a specific component of her unique vocation. It is certain, that she, a faithful disciple of St. John of the Cross, never explained the "trial of faith" in terms of either the passive purification of the senses or of the spirit.[3]

Second, Thérèse insisted that the trial centered exclusively on the existence of heaven. She continued to believe firmly in all of the mysteries of the Catholic Faith. She notes explicitly the Trinity, the Incarnate Word, the Redemption, the sacramental means of grace. Thérèse observes that she had made more conscious acts of faith during the months of her trial than throughout all the previous years of her life. She wrote out the Creed in her own blood, carried it on her person — over her heart — and prayed continually: "My God, with the help of Your grace, I am ready to pour out all my blood in order to prove my faith."[4] Interestingly, Thérèse during the "trial of faith," maintained a vivid awareness of Jesus' presence in her life as the "Thief" Who would come suddenly to take her to Himself, and Mary as her spiritual mother. Obviously, Thérèse had clearly understood faith's essential relationship to the

---

[2] See Chapter I, p. 47.

[3] See Simon Tugwell, OP, *op. cit.*, p. 343.

[4] Thérèse de L'Enfant-Jésus et de la Sainte-Face, *Prières* (Paris: Desclée de Brouwer, 1988), p. 53.

Church's Creed as well as its intellectual and volitional nature. Her specific temptation was not to doubt or deny the Creed *in toto*, but rather the existence of heaven for herself.

Third, Thérèse acknowledged with lucidity that the trial united her with all those who had sinned deliberately against the Catholic Faith. The trial also offered her an opportunity to make reparation for that apostasy through acts of charity animated by faith. Before her trial, Thérèse prayed and offered sacrifices for "poor sinners." Throughout her trial, she offered everything for her "brothers and sisters" struggling with faith, thus indicating that her spiritual agony was vicarious in nature.

Fourth, as she progressed deeper into the "dark tunnel" of her trial, Thérèse discerned in herself a mysterious identification with Christ in His Passion and death — a union that was consuming her human existence in the fire of love. In July of 1897, Thérèse, intimating the experience of mystical union with Jesus in His dereliction, explained her "trial of faith" by drawing an analogy with Christ's suffering in the garden of Gethsemane. Although He possessed the beatific vision, Our Lord still endured indescribable mental agony as a result of His victimhood. With due respect for the proper proportionality, Thérèse acknowledged that this "mystery" had helped her to deal with her own mental agony which coexisted along with the vivid sense of Christ's mystical presence in her soul. She said: "Our Lord enjoyed all of the delights of the Trinity when He was in the Garden of Olives, and still His agony was nonetheless cruel. It is a mystery, but I assure you that I understand something about it by what I am experiencing myself."[5]

She also indicated on several occasions that her "passion"[6] (which included physical, mental, and spiritual agony) was a "miniature" or, to be more precise, a deep participation in Christ's death on the Cross: "Our Lord died on the Cross in agony, and yet this

---

[5] *L.C.*, p. 75.

[6] See Guy Gaucher, OCD, *The Passion of Thérèse of Lisieux*, trans. Sr. Anne Marie Brennan, OCD (New York: The Crossroads Publishing Co., 1990), for a splendid exposition of Thérèse's suffering during her last eighteen months.

is the most beautiful death of love. This is the only one that was seen; no one saw that of the Blessed Virgin. To die of love is not to die in transports. I tell you frankly, it seems to me that this is what I am experiencing."[7]

Fifth, Thérèse in *Her Last Conversations*, indicated subtly that her trial was an infused, mystical state related to her posthumous mission of making God known and loved. Throughout the duration of her trial, Thérèse came to the conviction that people must know the "story" of her soul and also be aware of her temptations against faith.

As I have demonstrated in Chapter IV of this book, since Thérèse had indeed attained to the mystical marriage before her "Oblation to Merciful Love," the trial must be understood, not in the context of the purification of her soul, but rather as an expression of transforming union oriented toward apostolic fecundity.

The trial was, in a definite sense, the logical conclusion of her life of sacrifice. As a child, Thérèse had asked God for a life devoid of all consolation: "O Jesus, unspeakable sweetness, change all the consolation of this earth into bitterness for me."[8] She had sensed in her reception of the sacrament of Confirmation that her special vocation was to suffer for the sake of others: "On that day I received the strength to *suffer*, for soon afterwards the martyrdom of my soul was about to commence."[9]

Thérèse had offered herself to God as a victim for priests on the occasion of her profession and in her Oblation, as a living sacrifice for all those who rejected God's love through sins against the Catholic Faith. Although it is difficult and perhaps even impossible to prove textually, one is tempted to assert that Thérèse has offered herself as a victim to the merciful love of God specifically for priests who had lost the faith. As we have noted, until her

---

[7] *L.C.*, p. 73.

[8] *S.*, p. 79.

[9] *S.*, p. 80.

death, the apostate priest, Hyacinthe Loyson, was the special object of her prayers and sacrifices.

In the discovery that people actually existed who did not believe in God or His Church, Thérèse fell headlong into her "trial of faith." Since she was expert in using every cross as a means of "giving God pleasure," Thérèse accepted the "trial of faith" as a gift which offered her an opportunity to make expiation and reparation for sins committed against the Faith. Also, instinctively celebrating the strength of Jesus in the experience of her personal powerlessness, Thérèse accepted the trial as a means of participating in Jesus' mysterious cry from the Cross: "My God, my God, why have you abandoned me?" (Matthew 27:46).

Thérèse had been exquisitely prepared for her trial by God's grace. As in every other difficult situation in her life, she used the trial as a means of showing her love for God and others. She found in it deep mystical union with Christ in the mystery of His redemptive love. Discussing Thérèse's ability to find Christ and to unite herself joyfully to Him in her suffering, Susan Leslie has remarked:

> Thérèse personified suffering. It was never a mere phenomenon but always one of the faces of God. When she entered Carmel, she tells us that she threw herself lovingly into the arms of suffering. This was not a natural reaction for Thérèse any more than it is for the rest of us. It was a learned response arising out of faith and love. Thus suffering became for Thérèse — as it can become for us — an encounter with the Person of Christ who calls us to resurrection by way of the Cross. Whenever Thérèse met with a cross, great or small she rushed eagerly to meet it, as a woman flies to meet her lover.[10]

In the "trial of faith" her mystical penetration of Isaiah's Song of the Servant of Yahweh attained fullness. The words of the prophet: "He was pierced for our offenses, crushed for our sins,

---

[10] Susan Leslie, *The Happiness of God: Holiness in Thérèse of Lisieux* (New York: Alba House, 1988), pp. 64-65.

upon him was the chastisement that makes us whole.... The Lord laid upon him the guilt of us all" (Isaiah 53:4, 6) were fulfilled in Jesus' victimhood as He took upon Himself the guilt of every human sin in His Passion. Likewise, in her union with her Bridegroom, Thérèse, innocent and undefiled by grievous sin, had offered herself to God as a victim of His merciful love for the salvation of her brothers and sisters who had lost the faith. In this act of Oblation she identified herself with the "Suffering Servant," lovingly bearing the guilt of the sins of the world.

The Church's spiritual tradition, founded solidly on Sacred Scripture, discerns three levels of suffering in Christ crucified: (1) the physical suffering endured in His Passion;[11] (2) the mental and affective agony of His Victimhood; that is, the objective knowledge and the subjective guilt of every human sin and weakness;[12] (3) the consuming love for the human race that led Him to the acceptance of physical and mental agony on the Cross, and ultimately to His "death of love."[13]

As we again keep in mind the proper proportionality demanded in any comparison of the divine Person of Christ and any human person, it is clear that Thérèse had been graced with what might be an unparalleled participation in Christ's Passion and death. For eighteen months as she suffered the ravages of terminal pulmonary tuberculosis, she experienced a mental agony that gave her not a moment's respite:

> If you only knew what frightful thoughts obsess me! Pray very much for me in order that I do not listen to the devil who wants to persuade me about so many lies. It's the

---

[11] See William D. Edwards, M.D., Wesley J. Gable, M.Div., Floyd E. Hosmer, M.S., A.M.I., "The Physical Death of Jesus," *Journal of the American Medical Association* (March 21, 1986).

[12] See John Henry Cardinal Newman, "The Mental Sufferings of Our Lord in His Passion," *Discourses Addressed to Mixed Congregations* (London: Longmans, Green and Co., 1902), pp. 303-341.

[13] Cf. St. Francis de Sales, *Sermons on Our Lady*, trans. by Nuns of the Visitation (Rockford, IL.: TAN Books & Publishers, Inc., 1985); see especially Sermons I & V.

reasoning of the worst materialists which is imposed upon my mind: later, unceasingly making new advances, science will explain everything naturally; we shall have the absolute reason for everything that exists and that still remains a problem, because there remain very many things to be discovered, etc., etc., O little mother, must one have such thoughts like this when one loves God so much! Finally, I offer up these very great pains to obtain the light of faith for poor unbelievers, for all those who separate themselves from the Church's beliefs.[14]

However, in spite of these physical and mental sufferings, one aggravating the other, Thérèse was on fire with the love of God and neighbor which, as she had foretold frequently and with certainty, would consume her earthly existence and cause her death. In fact, it was love alone that gave meaning and direction to her suffering. Commenting upon Jesus' farewell discourse (John 17) in manuscript "C" of the *Story of a Soul*, Thérèse clearly revealed the mystery of love that had become the sole motivating force of her life:

Your love has gone before me, and it has grown with me, and now it is an abyss whose depths I cannot fathom. Love attracts love, and, my Jesus, my love leaps towards Yours; it would like to fill the abyss which attracts it, but alas! it is not even like a drop of dew lost in the ocean! For me to love You as You love me, I would have to borrow Your own Love, and then only would I be at rest. O my Jesus, it is perhaps an illusion, but it seems to me that You cannot fill a soul with more love than the love with which You have filled mine.[15]

Interestingly, Thérèse abruptly concludes the *Story of a Soul* reflecting upon her immense love, which, as she acknowledges again and again, is absolutely the result of God's grace:

---

[14] *L.C.*, pp. 257-258.
[15] *S.*, p. 256.

I do not hasten to the first place but to the last; rather than advance like the Pharisee, I repeat, filled with confidence, the publican's humble prayer. Most of all I imitate the conduct of Magdalene; her astonishing or rather her loving audacity which charms the heart of Jesus also attracts my own. Yes, I feel it; even though I had on my conscience all the sins that can be committed, I would go, my heart broken with sorrow and throw myself into Jesus' arms, for I know how much He loves the prodigal child who returns to Him. It is not because God, in His anticipating mercy, has preserved my soul from mortal sin that I go to Him with confidence and love.[16]

A number of ascetico-mystical theologians have seen in Thérèse's "trial of faith" a mystical identification with Christ in His work of salvation and a prime example of the Pauline doctrine that the suffering of a Christian is not only a participation in Christ's Passion, but also a divinely ordained means of communicating the efficacy of Christ's salvific death to others. In fact, her last months were a commentary upon the text: "Now I rejoice in my sufferings for your sake, and in my flesh I complete what is lacking in Christ's suffering for the sake of his body; that is, the Church" (Colossians 1:24).

For instance, Simon Tugwell, O.P., notes:

Thérèse's way is almost a "descent from Mt. Carmel." The intimacy of her love of God, which characterized her childhood, made way for aridity when she became a nun, and then finally she fell into this total darkness. Yet it was precisely in this way that she came to know the reality of love, and to enter into her apostolate of love. All that is left, finally, after the consolations have gone, is the desperate cry, "*J'ai soif!*" "I thirst!"[17]

Father Marie-Eugène, O.C.D., observes that Thérèse's trial

---

[16] *S.*, pp. 258-259.
[17] Simon Tugwell, OP, *op. cit.*, p. 344.

"supplies the redemptive suffering that merits for others the light to walk in the way of salvation."[18]

M.V. Bernadot, O.P., likewise, has noted:

> The trial undoubtedly belonged to the unitive life, for it was rather a consequence of transforming love than a preparation for it. Thérèse suffered because she was transformed into Jesus crucified, and with Him and in Him was redeeming her brethren. The sufferings of the perfect differ from those of souls who are in the state of spiritual espousals. In those who have not yet attained to the mystical marriage, darkness alternates with light, sorrows with joy; but in the perfect, the extremes of anguish and of bliss harmonize continually in the heights of a "peace which surpasses all understanding" (Philippians 4).[19]

In her article "Thérèse and John of the Cross" Margaret Drogan notes:

> Thérèse's trial of faith must be seen as a response to her longing to serve the Church. Her last suffering, in this interpretation, enters into the redemptive agony of Christ, the innocent Victim. The anguish of her night of faith is not based on what (St.) John says are the two determinants of the second night: the first being the person's need for purgation, and the second being the degree of sanctity to which God intends to raise that person. Thérèse's pain was an overflow beyond those conditions. She seems to have reached this judgment herself when on the day she died, she said to her sisters, "Never would I have believed it was possible to suffer so much! Never! Never! I can't explain this except by the ardent desires I have had to save souls."[20]

---

[18] Fr. Marie-Eugène, OCD, *I Want to See God: A Practical Synthesis of Carmelite Spirituality*, trans by Sr. M. Veronica Clare, CSC (Chicago: Fides Publishers, 1953), p. 542.

[19] M.V. Bernadot, OP, *op. cit.*, p. 60.

[20] *Carmelite Studies: Experiencing St. Thérèse Today*, ed. John Sullivan, OCD (Washington, DC: ICS Publications, 1990), p. 115.

In *The Three Ages of the Interior Life*, R. Garrigou-Lagrange, O.P., discusses a "night of the spirit" suffered by certain servants of God who have already experienced the passive nights and the mystical marriage. This night, he asserts, is not chiefly purificatory, but rather reparative. This trial, he notes, is endured by those "especially dedicated to reparation, to immolation for the salvation of souls or to the apostolate by interior suffering."[21]

Garrigou-Lagrange observes brilliantly that the many trials of Christ and His Mother, as well as their self-offerings on Calvary, were obviously not for their purification but rather for the salvation of the human race. Similarly, "the more souls advance in the spiritual life, the more their interior sufferings resemble those of Jesus and Mary."[22] Hence, the suffering of the perfect is of the nature of reparation for the sins of others.

Illustrating the trials of the reparatory night of the spirit, Garrigou-Lagrange says:

> When this trial is chiefly reparatory, when it has principally for its end to make the already purified soul work for the salvation of its neighbor, then it takes on an additional character more reminiscent of the intimate sufferings of Jesus and Mary, who did not need to be purified. In this case, the suffering makes one think of that of a lifesaver who, in a storm, struggles heroically to save from death those who are on the point of drowning. In a way, these reparative souls must resist the temptations of the souls they seek to save that they may come efficaciously to their assistance. Reparative souls are intimately associated with our Savior's sorrowful life; in them St. Paul's words are fully realized: "Heirs indeed of God, and joint heirs with Christ; yet so, if we suffer with Him, that we may also be glorified with Him."[23]

---

[21] See Reginald Garrigou-Lagrange, OP, *op. cit.*, p. 503. For a complete treatment of this phenomenon, see pp. 497-510.

[22] *Ibid.*, p. 504.

[23] *Ibid.*, pp. 509-510.

Although Garrigou-Lagrange cogently demonstrates the existence of this so-called "reparatory night of the spirit" in the lives of saints who possess an expiatory mission (for example, St. Paul of the Cross, the Curé of Ars and St. Thérèse of Lisieux), I would question the necessity of positing this special category, except perhaps as a didactic means used by God to recall to the minds of believers the truth of the Church's mission to share in the paschal mystery of Christ. Might it not be more accurate and consistent with the Second Vatican Council's teaching on the "Universal Call to Holiness" to assert that in every instance, as it is purified in its sensory and spiritual components, the soul is mystically transformed in Christ and comes to share ever more deeply in His redemptive work for the sake of the world?

Pope John Paul II has eloquently described this essential dimension of the Christian life in his apostolic letter, *On the Meaning of Human Suffering (Salvifici Doloris)*. First of all, exalting Christ as the Redeemer of man *precisely through His sufferings*, the Holy Father underscores Jesus' unique capacity to suffer as a Victim for the entire human race:

> Christ's sufferings have — unique in the history of humanity — a depth and intensity which, while being human, can also be an incomparable depth and intensity of suffering, insofar as the man who suffers is in person the only begotten Son Himself: "God from God." Therefore, only He — the only begotten Son — is capable of embracing the measure of evil contained in the sins of man: in every sin and in "total sin," according to the dimensions of the historical existence of humanity on earth.[24]

In this apostolic letter, John Paul II also discusses Christ's dereliction on the Cross which was, it seems, the source of Thérèse's mystical union with the Lord in her "trial of faith":

---

[24] Pope John Paul II, *On the Meaning of Human Suffering (Salvifici Doloris)* (Boston: St. Paul Editions, 1984), No. 17.

When Christ says: "My God, my God, why have you abandoned me?" one can say that these words on abandonment are borne at the level of that unspeakable union of the Son with the Father, and are borne because the Father laid on him "the iniquity of us all" (Isaiah 53:6). They also foreshadow the words of St. Paul: "For our sake he made him to be sin who knew no sin" (2 Corinthians 5:21). Together with this horrible weight, encompassing the entire evil of turning away from God which is contained in sin, Christ, through the divine depth of His filial union with the Father, perceives in a humanly inexpressible way, this suffering which is the separation, the rejection by the Father, the estrangement from God. But precisely through this suffering He accomplishes the Redemption and can say as He breathes his last: "It is finished" (John 19:30).[25]

The Holy Father also teaches in this letter that through Christ's Passion all human suffering possesses immense spiritual value and is rendered by grace the temporal "completion" of His redemptive work — a work, perfect in itself, yet seeking to be "re-enacted" in every human life for the salvation of all. In other words, Christ's redemptive death is the source of the forgiveness of every human sin and consequently the cause of our eternal life. However, the God-Man, in opening Himself to every human suffering, willed to suffer in His Mystical Body until the end of human history for the salvation of the whole world. In this sense, Christ continues to offer His sacrifice in the lives of those who are united to Him through sanctifying grace. The Holy Father observes: "Suffering seems in some way to share in the characteristics of the Church's divine and human nature. And for this reason suffering also has a special value in the eyes of the Church. It is something good, before which the Church bows down in reverence with all the depth of her faith in the redemption."[26]

---

[25] *Salvifici Doloris*, No. 18
[26] *Salvifici Doloris*, No. 24.

It is clear that Thérèse of Lisieux had been prepared by God from the first awakening of her consciousness for a life of vicarious suffering for others. Every grace she had received during her short life enabled her to comprehend more profoundly the mystery of Christ's redemptive love. As a result of her cooperation with "preservative grace," Thérèse was certain that she had never offended God in a grievous way. Consequently, she had been prepared to spend her life in reparation for the sins of others. It must be recalled that upon entering Carmel, she had offered her life for the formation and sanctification of priests. In the "Oblation to the Merciful Love of God," Thérèse fully accepted her "vocation" of victimhood — her mission to be the "Suffering Servant of Yahweh" for her "brothers and sisters" who had lost the faith.

Consequently, for eighteen months, Thérèse lived the crucifixion of Jesus Christ for the faithless. Like Him, she was racked by pain in all of her members. Because both Thérèse and her blood sisters recognized in her suffering the closest identification with Jesus in his crucifixion, I asked the eminent pathologist William V. Johnson, M.D., to comment upon the physical similarities of the death suffered by one crucified and by one suffering from pulmonary tuberculosis. The doctor explained:

> Death by crucifixion and death by tuberculosis have some similarities and some difference. Death by crucifixion is death by asphyxiation — not enough oxygen gets to the brain. Hanging by one's arms, the body is pulled down by gravity. The diaphragm, which is a thin muscle, has to work against this weight and move up and down to pump air into the lungs. Finally, this muscle gives out and the brain dies from lack of oxygen. Another factor is the heart having to pump blood to the brain against the force of gravity. Gravity tends to pool the blood in the lower extremities and there is less available to carry the oxygen. Also, with the violent scourging, the blood loss makes it less available so that death is hastened. By being able to stand, this support of the legs counteracts the pull of gravity on the rest of the body and makes it easier for the dia-

phragm muscle to pump air and the heart to pump blood. That is why, usually, the legs of the crucified would be broken in order to hasten death.

Basically all death occurs because the brain does not get oxygen in one way or another. In crucifixion this occurs slowly and with much agony and pain. It is inflicted by man against man in a humiliating and degrading manner. As a doctor, I cannot imagine a worse way to die.

In tuberculosis, a person also dies by asphyxiation, but in a slower, less traumatic way. Tuberculosis is caused by a bacteria (similar to that which causes leprosy). Until the 1950's there was no antibiotic to treat tuberculosis. Treatment was simply rest, good nutrition, fresh air. If the body was strong enough, it would overcome the infection; if not, the infection would slowly progress to death. Tuberculosis is primarily a pulmonary infection causing a slow and progressive pneumonia which crowds out the normal lungs. Tubercular bacteria can also go to other parts of the body, such as, kidneys, liver, general intestinal tract; tuberculosis in the bones causes an osteomyelitis that is very painful. It seems clear from the writings of Thérèse's sisters, that her pulmonary tuberculosis infected her intestinal tract and perhaps, as is evidenced by the intense pain she endured, even affected her bones near the end of her life.

It must be also noted that tuberculosis is contagious — like leprosy. Usually people would shun those who were infected with it so that they would not catch it. Thus, if a person had tuberculosis, he would become, by virtue of it, a "social outcast."

Thus, people would tend to turn away from the person dying from either crucifixion or tuberculosis and not want to get close or get involved. Dying from tuberculosis is like dying of cancer. The person gets very weak and slowly loses weight and strength. Near the end, the person might hemorrhage and die quickly, but usually the death process is slow in coming. The tuberculosis infiltrates and pus fills the lungs so that the person cannot get enough air.

Usually the person suffering from tuberculosis becomes too weak to struggle and usually is unconscious for a while, and expires.

It is evident to me that there are clear similarities in the agony of one crucified and in the agony of one who dies of pulmonary tuberculosis. It would seem from her own writings and from those who wrote about her, that Thérèse had understood her physical suffering in terms of Christ's agony on the Cross.[27]

In union with Christ, Thérèse recognized and personally experienced, although innocent, the malice of sin. In particular, she experienced the sin peculiar to the century that lay before her, apostasy from the Catholic Faith. She mysteriously assimilated the guilt of those who deliberately abandoned the Faith. Like her divine Bridegroom, Thérèse, in her passion, was unable to draw consolation from her intimate knowledge of the Father. She felt, in every sense, abandoned by God for eighteen months. During this period she experienced an indescribable dereliction — as if she herself were guilty of revolt against God, apostasy and atheism.

In spite of these sufferings and, in fact, precisely through them, Thérèse knew that she, in union with her Crucified Lord, was being consumed by love in order to bring many people to eternal salvation. Significantly, in the thick of her "trial of faith," Thérèse realized not only that she was saving souls from eternal death, but was also meriting a posthumous mission:

> I feel that I am about to enter into my rest. But I feel especially that my mission is about to begin, my mission of making God loved as I love Him, of giving my little way to souls. If God answers my desires, my heaven will be spent on earth until the end of the world. Yes, I want to spend my heaven in doing good on earth. I can't make heaven a feast of rejoicing; I can't rest as long as there are

---

[27] Personal letter from William V. Johnson, M.D., Lanesville, Indiana (March 15, 1991).

souls to be saved. But when the angel will have said: "Time is no more!" then I will take my rest; I'll be able to rejoice, because the number of the elect will be complete and because all will have entered into joy and repose. My heart beats with joy at this thought.[28]

Thérèse, called by God to a life of victimhood within a contemplative vocation, exemplifies for the believer, in every state of life, that Christian perfection is essentially comprised of the loving surrender to the specific "way" willed by God for the soul and a selfless availability to make God known and loved through the sufferings involved in that surrender. The various gradations of prayer as described by St. Teresa of Jesus and the mystical phenomena detailed in the writings of St. John of the Cross were understood by Thérèse as absolutely at the service of union with Christ in His redemptive love. On this point she was resolute: union with Christ in love is the essential component of the spiritual life.

The mystical phenomenon of Thérèse's "trial of faith" leads me to conclude that the Saint's precise doctrinal mission is to point to the often forgotten truth of the essential mission of the Christian and of the Church: to share in a personal way in Christ's redemptive love for a world estranged from God. Thérèse is, in a certain sense, the victim of this tragic amnesia. In her passion, she re-articulates for the contemporary Church, Christ's piercing cry from the Cross: "I thirst" (John 19:28). Thérèse experienced immolation in union with Christ for the sake of His Body, the Church (Colossians 1:24).

In summary, Thérèse's "trial of faith" should not be understood as passive purification but rather as a very high manifestation of the unitive way — a way open to every believer who sincerely seeks the perfection of Christian charity. The trial is mystical on at least two counts:

First, Thérèse, experiencing a staggering identification with

---

[28] *L.C.*, p. 102.

Christ in her physical, mental and spiritual sufferings during her passion, savored not only the divine presence of the Crucified pervading her entire being, but also was perfectly one with Him in His redemptive love for all — especially for those who refuse to believe in His word.

Second, since she understood her mission as a summons to teach, or to be more precise, to re-teach modern man the "Little Way" of evangelical holiness, it was fitting that she be a living model of transformation in Christ — specifically in His mission as Redeemer of the fallen human race.

Thérèse's mystical state in her "trial of faith" was the direct result of the intense operation of all of the gifts of the Holy Spirit. In particular, through the gift of understanding, she came to comprehend, to the degree that is humanly possible, the agony endured by the Crucified as a result of sins committed against the Faith. In this "understanding," she participated mystically in Christ's inexplicable experience of abandonment by His Father in the Passion.

Furthermore, through the operation of the gift of wisdom, Thérèse intellectually and volitionally experienced the presence of Christ Crucified offering His suffering and death again in her for the salvation of the world. In this passive state, Thérèse was not only possessed by the Crucified but also, reposing in His saving work being accomplished through her, was consumed by love.

It is difficult to enlarge upon Thérèse's mystical union with Christ in His redemptive sacrifice. One stands stunned before the silent transformation of lover into Beloved. On Thérèse's deathbed in the Lisieux Carmel, one is hard pressed to see a young, twenty-four year old religious dying of pulmonary tuberculosis. Rather, one stands face to face with the Suffering Servant of Yahweh, bearing with love the guilt of human revolt against God, and is forced to consider the price of redemption.

SELECTED BIBLIOGRAPHY

Primary Sources

Sainte Thérèse de L'Enfant Jésus. *Correspondance Générale*, Vol. I. Paris: Editions du Cerf-Desclee de Brouwer, 1972.

_____. *Correspondance Générale*, Vol. II. Paris: Editions du Cerf-Desclee de Brouwer, 1973.

_____. *Derniers Entretiens*. Paris: Editions du Cerf-Desclee de Brouwer, 1971.

_____. *Histoire D'une Ame; Manuscrits Autobiographiques*. Paris: Editions du Cerf-Desclee de Brouwer, 1972.

_____. *Poésies*. Paris: Editions du Cerf-Desclee de Brouwer, 1975.

_____. *Prières*. Paris: Editions du Cerf-Desclee de Brouwer, 1988.

_____. *Recréations Pieuses*. Paris: Editions du Cerf-Desclee de Brouwer, 1985.

Saint Thérèse of Lisieux. *General Correspondence*, Vol. I. Translated by John Clarke, OCD. Washington, DC: ICS Publications, 1982.

_____. *General Correspondence*, Vol. II. Translated by John Clarke, OCD. Washington, DC: ICS Publications, 1988.

_____. *Her Last Conversations*. Translated by John Clarke, OCD. Washington, DC.: ICS Publications, 1977.

_____. *Story of a Soul*. Translated by John Clarke, OCD. Washington, DC: ICS Publications, 1972.

_____. *Poetry*. Translated by Donald Kinney, OCD. Washington, DC: ICS Publications, 1996.

Books

Arintero, OP, Juan G. *The Mystical Evolution in the Development and Vitality of the Church* (2 Vols.). Translated by Jordan Aumann, OP. St. Louis: B. Herder Book Co., 1949.

_____. *The Mystical Life of St. Thérèse of the Child Jesus.* Translated by Jose L. Morales, PhD. Salamanca: Editorial Fides, 1926.

Arminjon, Charles. *The End of the Present World and the Mysteries of the Future Life.* Translated by Martin Research Associates. Illinois: Martin Books Edition, 1968.

Aumann, OP, Jordan. *Christian Spirituality in the Catholic Tradition.* San Francisco: Ignatius Press, 1985.

_____. *Spiritual Theology.* Huntington: Our Sunday Visitor, Inc., 1979.

Balthasar, Hans Urs von. *Thérèse of Lisieux: The Story of a Mission.* Translated by Donald Nicholl. New York: Sheed & Ward, 1954.

_____. *Unless You Become Like This Child.* Translated by Erasmo Leiva-Merikakis. San Francisco: Ignatius Press, 1991.

Baudouin-Croix, Marie. *Leonie Martin: A Difficult Life.* Translated by Mary Frances Mooney. Dublin: Veritas Press, 1993.

Bernadot, OP, M.V. *St. Teresa of the Child Jesus.* Translated by a Dominican of Headington. London: Burns, Oates and Washburn, Ltd., 1926.

Bouyer, Louis. *The Christian Mystery.* Edinburgh: T. & T. Clark, 1990.

_____. *Introduction to Spirituality.* Translated by Mary Perkins Ryan. Collegeville: Liturgical Press, 1961.

Bro, OP, Bernard. *The Little Way.* Translated by Alan Neame. London: Dalton, Longman & Todd, 1979.

Chanoine, Vidal F. *Aux Sources de la Joie avec Saint François de Sales.* Paris: Nouvelle Libraire de France, 1974.

Combes, André. *St. Thérèse and Suffering: The Spirituality of St.*

Thérèse in Essence. Translated by Msgr. Philip E. Hallett. New York: P.J. Kennedy & Sons, 1951.

_____. *The Spirituality of St. Thérèse*. Translated by Msgr. Philip E. Hallett. New York: P.J. Kennedy & Sons, 1950.

Curran, Thomas M., ed. *The Mind of St. Thérèse of Lisieux*. Dublin: Carmelite Center of Spirituality, 1977.

de Caussade, SJ, Jean-Pierre. *Abandonment to Divine Providence*. New York: Doubleday Books, 1968.

de Guibert, SJ, Joseph. *The Theology of the Spiritual Life*. Translated by Paul Barrett, OFM Cap. New York: Sheed & Ward, 1953.

de Meester, OCD, Conrad. *With Empty Hands: The Message of Thérèse of Lisieux*. Translated by Sr. Anne Marie, OCD. Sydney: St. Paul Publications, 1982.

_____, general editor. *St. Thérèse of Lisieux: Her Life, Times, and Teaching*. Washington, DC: ICS Publications, 1997.

Descouvemont, Pierre. *Sainte Thérèse de L'Enfant Jesus et son Prochain*. Paris: P. Lethielleux, 1959.

_____. *Thérèse and Lisieux*. Translated by Salvatore Sciurba OCD and Louise Pambrun. Toronto: Novalis Press, 1996.

_____. *Thérèse of Lisieux and Marie of the Trinity*. Translated by Alexandra Plettenberg-Serban. New York: Alba House, 1997.

Dubay, SM, Thomas. *Fire Within*. San Francisco: Ignatius Press, 1989.

Dupre, Louis & Wiseman, OSB, Janes A., ed. *Light from Light*. Mahwah: Paulist Press, 1988.

Flannery, OP, Austin, ed. *Vatican Council II: The Conciliar and Post Conciliar Documents*. New York: Costello Publishing Co., 1984.

Francis de Sales, St. *Introduction to the Devout Life*. Translated by John L. Reville, SJ, PhD. Philadelphia: The Peter Reilly Company, 1942.

_____. *Sermons on Our Lady*. Translated by the Nuns of the Visitation. Rockford: TAN Books & Publishers, Inc., 1985.

_____. *Treatise on the Love of God* (2 Vols.). Translated by John K. Ryan. New York: Doubleday & Co., Inc., 1963.

Garrigou-Lagrange, OP, Reginald. *The Three Ages of the Spiritual Life: Prelude to Eternal Life* (2 Vols.). Translated by Sr. M. Timothea Doyle, OP. St. Louis: B. Herder Books, 1947.

Gaucher, OCD, Guy. *The Passion of Thérèse of Lisieux*. Translated by Sr. Anne Marie Brennan, OCD. New York: The Crossroad Publishing Co., 1990.

_____. *The Story of a Life*. Translated by Sr. Anne Marie Brennan, OCD. San Francisco: Harper and Row Publishers, 1987.

Gautier, Jean, ed. *Some Schools of Catholic Spirituality*. Translated by Kathryn Sullivan, RSCJ. New York: Desclee Company, 1959.

Görres, Ida F. *The Hidden Face*. Translated by Richard and Clara Winston. New York: Pantheon Books, Inc., 1959.

Guitton, Jean. *The Spiritual Genius of St. Thérèse*. Translated by a Religious of the Sacred Heart. Westminster: The Newman Press, 1958.

Hoffman, OP, Dominic M. *Living Divine Love*. New York: Alba House, 1982.

Ignatius of Loyola, St. *The Spiritual Exercises*. Translated by Louis J. Puhl, SJ. Chicago: Loyola University Press, 1951.

Jamart, OCD, François. *The Complete Spiritual Doctrine of St. Thérèse of Lisieux*. Translated by Walter Van De Putte. New York: Alba House, 1961.

John of the Cross, St. *Collected Works*. Translated by Kieran Kavanaugh, OCD and Otilio Rodriguez, OCD. Washington, DC: ICS Publications, 1979.

John Paul II. *On Catechesis in Our Time (Catechesi Tradendae)*. Boston: St. Paul Editions, 1979.

_____. *On the Meaning of Human Suffering (Salvifici Doloris)*. Boston: St. Paul Editions, 1984.

Journet, Charles. *What is Dogma?* Translated by Mark Pontifex. New York: Hawthorne Books, 1964.

LaFrance, Jean. *My Vocation is Love.* Translated by Sr. Anne Marie Brennan, OCD. New York: Alba House, 1990.

Leslie, Susan. *The Happiness of God: Holiness in Thérèse of Lisieux.* New York: Alba House, 1988.

Marie-Eugene, OCD. *I Am a Daughter of the Church: A Practical Synthesis of Carmelite Spirituality.* Translated by Sr. M. Verna Clare, CSC. Chicago: Fides Publishers, 1955.

_____. *I Want to See God: A Practical Synthesis of Carmelite Spirituality.* Translated by Sr. M. Verna Clare, CSC. Chicago: Fides Publishers, 1955.

_____. *Under the Torrent of His Love: Thérèse of Lisieux, a Spiritual Genius.* Translated by Sr. Mary Thomas Noble, OP. New York: Alba House, 1995.

_____. *Where the Spirit Breathes: Action and Prayer.* Translated by Sr. Mary Thomas Noble, OP. New York: Alba House, 1998.

Martin, Céline (Sr. Genevieve of the Holy Face). *A Memoir of My Sister, St. Thérèse.* Translated by Carmelite Nuns of New York. New York: P.J. Kennedy & Sons, 1959.

Obbard, OCD, Elizabeth Ruth. *A Retreat With Thérèse of Lisieux: Loving Our Way Into Holiness.* Cincinnati: St. Anthony Messenger Press, 1996.

O'Connor, Patricia. *In Search of Thérèse.* London: Darton, Longman & Todd, 1987.

O'Mahony, OCD, Christopher, ed. *St. Thérèse of Lisieux by Those Who Knew Her: Testimonies from the Process of Beatification.* Dublin: Veritas Publications, 1973.

Petitot, OP, Henry. *Saint Teresa of Lisieux.* Translated by the Benedictines of Stanbrook. New York: Benzinger Brothers, 1927.

Pichon, SJ, Almire. *Seeds of the Kingdom.* Translated by Lyle Terhune TOCD. Westminster: The Newman Press, 1961.

Poulain, SJ, Augustin. *The Graces of Interior Prayer: A Treatise on Mystical Theology.* Translated by Leonora L. Yorke Smith. London: Kegan Paul, Trench, Trubner & Co., Ltd., 1912.

Redmond, Paulinus. *Louis and Zelie Martin: The Seed and the Root of the Little Flower*. London: Quiller Press, Ltd., 1995.

Regle Primitive et Constitutions des Religieuses de L'ordre de Notre-Dame du Mont Carmel. Selon La Reformation de Sainte Thérèse pour les Monasteres de Son Ordre en France. Poitiers: 1865.

Renault, OCD, Emmanuel. *L'Epreuve de la Foi: Le Combat de Thérèse de Lisieux*. Paris: Editions de Cerf-Desclee de Brouwer, 1974.

Royo-Marin, OP, Antonio and Aumann, OP, Jordan. *The Theology of Christian Perfection*. Translated by Jordan Aumann, OP. Dubuque: The Priory Press, 1962.

Sacred Congregation of the Clergy. *General Catechetical Directory (Directorium Catechisticum Generale)*. Vatican City State: Vatican Polyglot Press, 1971.

Six, Jean-François. *Light in the Night: The Last Eighteen Months in the Life of Thérèse of Lisieux*. Translated by John Bowden. London: SCM Press, Ltd., 1996.

Sullivan, OCD, John, ed. *Carmelite Studies: Experiencing Saint Thérèse Today*. Washington, DC: ICS Publications, 1990.

Teresa of Avila, Saint. *The Collected Works* (3 Vols). Translated by Kieran Kavanaugh, OCD and Otilio Rodriguez, OCD. Washington, DC: ICS Publications, 1976.

Thomas à Kempis. *The Imitation of Christ*. Translated by Clare L. Fitzpatrick. New York: Catholic Book Publishers, 1985.

Thomas Aquinas, Saint. *Summa Theologica*. Translated by Fathers of the English Dominican Province. New York: Benzinger Brothers, 1947.

Wojtyla, Karol. *Faith According to St. John of the Cross*. Translated by Jordan Aumann, OP. San Francisco: Ignatius Press, 1981.

GENERAL INDEX